SYNTACTIC VARIABLES

Studies in Natural Language and Linguistic Theory

VOLUME 24

Managing Editors

Joan Maling, *Brandeis University*
James McCloskey, *University of California, Santa Cruz*
Ian Roberts, *University of Wales, Bangor*

Editorial Board

Guglielmo Cinque, *University of Venice*
Jane Grimshaw, *Brandeis University*
Michael Kenstowicz, *M.I.T., Cambridge*
Hilda Koopman, *University of California, Los Angeles*
Howard Lasnik, *University of Connecticut at Storrs*
Alec Marantz, *M.I.T., Cambridge*
John J. McCarthy, *University of Massachusetts, Amherst*

The titles published in this series are listed at the end of this volume.

CAROL GEORGOPOULOS
Linguistics Program, University of Utah, Salt Lake City, Utah, U.S.A.

SYNTACTIC VARIABLES

Resumptive Pronouns and A' Binding in Palauan

SPRINGER-SCIENCE+BUSINESS MEDIA, B.V.

Library of Congress Cataloging-in-Publication Data

```
Georgopoulos, Carol Perkins.
    Syntactic variables : resumptive pronouns and A' binding in
  Palauan / Carol Georgopoulos.
       p.    cm. -- (Studies in natural language and linguistic theory
  ; v. 24)
    Revision of the author's thesis (Ph. D.--University of California
  at San Diego, 1985).
    ISBN 978-94-010-5412-6       ISBN 978-94-011-3202-2 (eBook)
    DOI 10.1007/978-94-011-3202-2
    1. Palauan language--Pronoun.  2. Palauan language--Grammar,
  Generative.  3. Government-binding theory (Linguistics)   I. Title.
  II. Series.
  PL5434.G46  1991
  499'.5--dc20                                              91-17384
```

Printed on acid-free paper

All Rights Reserved
© 1991 Springer Science+Business Media Dordrecht
Originally published by Kluwer Academic Publishers in 1991
Softcover reprint of the hardcover 1st edition 1991
No part of the material protected by this copyright notice
may be reproduced or utilized in any form or by any means, electronic
or mechanical, including photocopying, recording or by any information
storage and retrieval system, without written permission from
the copyright owner.

TABLE OF CONTENTS

Preface	ix

Chapter One: Introduction

0.	'Unbounded Dependencies'	1
1.	Outline of Government-Binding Theory	3
1.1.	The background	3
1.2.	Introduction to government-binding theory	6
1.3.	Bounding theory	14
1.4.	Resumptive pronouns	16

Chapter Two: Palauan — A Sketch of the Grammar

0.	Palauan; Earlier Grammars	21
1.	Overview	22
1.1.	The phonemes; the orthography	23
2.	Verb Morphology	24
2.1.	Morphological aspect marking	24
2.2.	Subject agreement	25
2.3.	Realis and irrealis mood morphology	26
3.	VP Structure	28
4.	NP Structure	31
4.1.	**a**	31
5.	Word Order	32
5.1.	Josephs' SVO analysis	32
5.2.	Josephs' passive	35
5.3.	Waters' analysis	38
5.4.	Other ordering considerations	40
6.	Complementation	42
7.	Null Arguments	43
7.1.	The structural existence of *pro*	48
8.	Affix or Clitic?	51
8.1.	Cooccurrence with full NPs	52
8.2.	Full pronouns	54
8.3.	Subject pronouns on non-V hosts	54
8.4.	Zwicky and Pullum's tests	56
9.	Summary	59

Chapter Three: The Variable Binding Structures

0.	Introduction	62

v

TABLE OF CONTENTS

1.	The Structures	62
1.1.	Relative clauses	63
1.1.1.	Free relatives	64
1.2.	Clefts and pseudoclefts	66
1.3.	WH questions	69
1.4.	Topicalizations	71
1.5.	Synthesis	72
1.6.	Clause structure in Austronesian studies	76
1.7.	The identification hypothesis	76
1.8.	Base generation, I: simplicity	79
2.	Islands	80
2.1.	No islands?	80
2.2.	Base generation, II: islands	82
3.	WH Agreement	84
3.1.	WH agreement in local dependencies	84
3.1.1.	Semantic mood and WH agreement	89
3.2.	WH agreement in long-distance dependencies	90
3.2.1.	The case of CP	94
3.2.2.	Relevance in other theories	95
3.3.	Multiple variables	96
4.	Summary: Chapter Three	97

Chapter Four: Variable Binding

0.	Introduction	100
1.	Properties of A' Binding	100
1.1.	Movement vs. base generation	101
2.	S-Structure Binding	102
2.1.	The 'resumptive pronoun strategy'	102
2.2.	WH agreement and S-structure binding	104
2.3.	Coordination	107
2.4.	Parasitic gaps	110
2.5.	The theory of resumptive pronouns	124
2.6.	Parallelism	126
2.7.	Subjects, adjuncts, and relative clauses	127
2.8.	Summary	130
3.	A' Chain Formation	130
3.1.	Chains and resumptive pronouns	133
3.2.	The chain and WH agreement	134
3.3.	A universal locality condition	135

Chapter Five: Embedded Questions and the Scope of WH Phrases

0.	Overview	140
1.	Embedded Questions: The Basics of the Analysis	141
1.1.	Embedded questions in nonmovement languages	144

TABLE OF CONTENTS

vii

2.	Embedded Questions: The Palauan Facts	145
2.1.	Free relatives vs. embedded questions	147
2.2.	The S-structure position of the WH phrase	149
2.3.	WH in situ	152
2.4.	Resolving ambiguity	155
2.4.1.	Agreement phenomena in yes/no questions	156
2.4.2.	Two kinds of topic?	158
2.4.3.	Yes/no questions vs. WH questions	159
2.4.4.	Agreement in embedded WH questions	159
3.	WH Movement in LF	162
3.1.	WH raising, WH filters, Spec-Head agreement	163
4.	Multiple-WH Questions	167
4.1.	[±WH] complements	168
4.2.	[+WH] complements	171
4.3.	ECP accounts	173
5.	On Scope Interpretation for WH Binders	175
5.1.	[±WH] and agreement within CP	176
5.2.	The status of Spec(C)	177
5.3.	The orientation of Spec(C)	178
6.	Summary	179

Chapter Six: Crossover Constructions		
0.	Overview	182
1.	Background	183
1.1.	Leftness	184
1.2.	C-command: strong crossover	185
1.3.	C-command: weak crossover	185
2.	Crossover in Government-Binding Theory	187
2.1.	Weak crossover	188
2.1.1.	Bijection	188
2.1.2.	Parallelism	190
2.1.3.	C-command accounts	191
3.	Strong Crossover in Palauan	191
3.1.	The definition of 'variable'	194
4.	Weak Crossover	197
4.1.	The structures	198
4.2.	Topicalizations	203
4.3.	Biclausal structures	204
4.4.	Impact; summary	205
4.4.1.	WCO as SCO?	207
4.5.	Parasitic gaps?	207
4.6.	The conditions on anaphora	210
4.7.	Anaphora between subject and object	214
5.	A Government-Theoretic Account of Weak Crossover	216

5.1.	Resumptive pronouns subject to the ECP	217
5.1.1.	Resumptive pronouns as syntactic variables: theory	218
5.1.2.	Resumptive pronouns as syntactic variables: fact	220
5.2.	The specifier parameter	223
5.2.1.	The parameter	223
5.2.2.	Default values?	224
6.	Extensions; Conclusions	225
6.1.	Extraction site bound separately from other positions	225

References   230

Appendix   237

Index of Names   239

Index of Subjects   241

PREFACE

This book represents the culmination of an extended period of field work on the Palauan language, carried out while I was a graduate student at the University of California at San Diego. The book was born as a short term paper written in 1982; from a forgettable infancy, that paper grew and grew, reaching the age of majority in my dissertation at the end of 1985. Some of its offspring have gone off on their own, as independent papers, as course materials, or as thoughts that have not yet completely materialized. Some have been disowned.

The full adulthood of this study of Palauan is realized in the present book. Virtually every section of the dissertation has been rewritten, updated, or otherwise (I hope) improved. Where the dissertation was still struggling with various problems, the book has found solutions. The aim of the book remains, however, to give broad coverage of Palauan, with emphasis on A' binding, rather than to focus narrowly on a few highly specific theoretical issues. I hope to have achieved a balance between presenting the language clearly and nonprejudicially, and dealing with various of its properties in current theoretical terms. If I have, the book should prove to be a resource for further typological study of the phenomena it describes.

I have been extremely fortunate in the collaboration of several groups of people. One group is made up of teachers, colleagues, and friends in the community of linguists from whom I have learned much and with whom I have shared the joys of linguistic analysis. These include Adriana Belletti, Sandy Chung, Isidore Dyen, Elisabet Engdahl, Sam S. Epstein, Ray Freeze, Jeanne Gibson, Grant Goodall, Liliane Haegeman, Frank Heny, Robbie Ishihara, Ray Jackendoff, Ricky Jacobs, S.-Y. Kuroda, Beatrice Lamiroy, Diane Lillo-Martin, Jim McCloskey, Evan Norris, David Perlmutter, Luigi Rizzi, Ian Roberts, Ken Safir, Leslie Saxon, Bonnie Schwartz, Chilin Shih, Peter Sells, Lisa Travis, Sten Vikner and John Whitman.

Another group is made up of the Palauans with whom I worked in various capacities — most of them became informants of one kind or another, whether they knew it or not: Miriam Anastasio, Romana Anastasio, Merline Malsol, Isaias Ngirailemesang, Nina Ngirangol, Roy Ngirchechol, P. Kempis Mad, Ted Rengulbai, Sabeth, and Moses Uludong. Six other Palauan speakers in San Diego participated in questionnaire projects. Nearly all of these consultants are young adults who grew up in Palau after the end of the Japanese era. Though all of them are bilingual in English, Palauan is the primary language spoken in their daily lives.

The third group has one member — Costa, who supported, encouraged, aided and abetted me for so long. No one, not even the Red Sox, ever had a more loyal and long-suffering fan. His sacrifices mean more to me than I can say.

CHAPTER ONE

INTRODUCTION

0. 'UNBOUNDED DEPENDENCIES'

Much of the research in modern generative grammar concerns the dependencies found in the syntax of natural language sentences. These dependencies are of many different kinds: the coreference between pronouns and their antecedents, the thematic relations a set of arguments bears to a verb, and the sharing of features between agreeing elements (say, between subject and predicate) are just three examples. An important class of these dependencies comprises the structures currently known as A′ (read 'A-bar') binding; A′ binding is a relation between an antecedent in a non-argument (A′) position and a bound element in argument position. Some examples (all relative clauses) are seen in (1):

(1) a. Anne did not receive the perfect conviction **which** the Admiral meant to convey ____.

   b. It is a time of life **at which** scarcely any charm is lost ____.

   c. This was the principle **on which** Anne wanted her father to be proceeding ____.

   (Jane Austen, *Persuasion*)

Speakers of English interpret the WH phrase in each of the sentences in (1) as a 'filler' of the empty position to the right. The possibility of such an interpretation can be explained naturally in terms of a dependency (or binding relation) between the WH antecedent and the gap; this allows the antecedent to be interpreted as having syntactic properties that would naturally belong to an expression in the gap position.

Evidence that there actually is a gap is of several kinds. One indication is the ungrammaticality of the sentence when it does not contain this position (ungrammaticality is indicated by '*'):

(2) a. Anne did not receive the perfect conviction **which** [s the Admiral meant to convey ____]

   b. The Admiral meant to convey perfect conviction.

   c. *The Admiral meant to convey.

That is, the verb *convey* requires (at least) a direct object. The other

1

2   CHAPTER ONE

verbs in (1) impose similar requirements. And, of course, the 'missing' objects in (1) are interpreted ultimately as identical to the head of the relative clause, to which the WH pronoun corresponds.

For some time, these filler-gap dependencies were called UNBOUNDED DEPENDENCIES, 'unbounded' in that the antecedent may be indefinitely far from the gap:

> (3)   A jade chop is the kind of thing which I always think I'll have enough money some day to try to arrange to have someone make ____ for me.

Currently, such relations are conceived of as BOUNDED: syntactic principles and constraints dictate that they be analyzed into a series of local relations, or movements.

The source of a speaker's unconscious knowledge of the structure of and conditions on such dependencies has been the object of much research in syntactic theory over the last 25 years or so. This research reflects the linguist's view that a general theory of these dependencies will contribute crucial insight into the organization of the human language faculty. Examination of a sample of the data from Palauan, the language whose properties are explored in this book, reinforces this view. In Palauan, a Western Austronesian language superficially quite different from English, relative clauses appear to have properties similar to those in (1) (Palauan is VOS):

> (4) a.   a 'elde'edu' el   'elid el   kirel a re'ad
> *story*   *Ptc ghost that about   people*
>
> [el   mo er a buil   ____]
> *that go to   moon*
>
> The legend is about the people who went to the moon.
>
> b.   ng-soak el   omes er sei el   rael
> *I-want   that see   to that Ptc road*
>
> [el   bla rellii ____ a re'ad   er a Belau]
> *that PST build   people of   Palau*
>
> I want to see that road that the Palauans built.

A theory of sufficient generality will account simultaneously for the English structures in (1) and the Palauan structures in (4).

The class of A' binding structures encompasses WH questions, topicalizations, clefts, and certain other structures, as well as relative clauses. To say that they comprise a single class linguistically is to claim that they have the same properties at an abstract level of analysis, in all languages. In this book I will show how that claim is validated by Palauan, even though the Palauan structures, strictly speaking, fail to

INTRODUCTION   3

conform to the standard analysis: they are not generated by movement; the gaps are therefore not traces but rather (null) resumptive pronouns; standard locality conditions do not apply; and so on.

The picture that emerges is one of a language that, on the one hand, displays the entire range of well-formed A′ binding dependencies in surface structure, yet on the other hand cannot be analyzed in the usual terms of the movement theory. Palauan grammar is not a simple mix of properties of movement and non-movement languages, however. Resumptive pronouns play the central role, A′ chain formation applies, crucially, at the output of the syntax, and a unique locality constraint must be formulated.

Thus the topic of this book, SYNTACTIC VARIABLES, encompasses resumptive pronouns as well as traces. What is special about this case study is that resumptive pronouns are the *only* variables. Their resemblance to traces by all the critical syntactic criteria is what makes them both interesting in themselves and valuable to the study of syntactic variable binding in general. Ultimately, the terms in which Palauan is analyzed derive in a natural way from the general structure of the theory adopted. In this way, the type of study presented here supports the validity and generality of that theory.

In the next section I will outline the general theoretical framework within which the analysis will be worked out, Government-Binding Theory (GB). Following that I will review the standard GB analysis of A′ binding in particular, and give an overview of how the facts of Palauan will bear on the current conceptual network.

1. OUTLINE OF GOVERNMENT-BINDING THEORY

This section focusses on aspects of the theory that are relevant to A′ binding and attempts to make clear the set of assumptions that will be explored in the body of the book. I begin with a brief look at the historical background.

1.1. *The Background*

The formative work is Ross (1967), the source of many of the concepts central to the later development of the theory. Indeed it is difficult to imagine what the theory would be like today, were it not for Ross's contributions.

Ross distinguished 'unbounded dependencies' from other 'extraction' transformations (either movement or deletion) in that unbounded dependencies involve movement of a noun phrase leftward over an ESSENTIAL VARIABLE, that is, over an arbitrary syntactic distance. The role of the essential variable is maintained in current approaches in the

CHAPTER ONE

important distinction (mediated by the distinction between WH-trace and NP-trace that led to binding theory) between A' binding and A binding, the latter characterized by local dependencies like passive, reflexivization, and raising.

Ross also showed that these 'unbounded' movements all obey his ISLAND CONSTRAINTS, a formulation of general conditions on rules that blocks extraction of constituents from certain syntactic configurations, such as relative clauses, coordinate structures, and sentential subjects. The following examples are from Ross:

(5) a. The man [who I read a statement about ____] is sick.

 b. *The man [who I read a statement [which was about ____]] is sick.

(6) a. [That I brought this hat] seemed strange to the nurse.

 b. *The hat which [that I brought ____] seemed strange to the nurse was a fedora.

Remarking on the similarities among rules that reorder an element over a variable, Ross suggests that the class of structures generated by these rules may "all derive from the same deep structure source" (p. 215).

A third important contribution in Ross's analysis was the distinction between COPYING RULES and CHOPPING RULES. Chopping rules are those reordering rules that create a gap, whereas copying rules are those that leave behind a pronominal trace, in Ross's terms, of the reordered phrase. Ross presents evidence that chopping rules are sensitive to all of the island constraints, while copying rules freely violate the constraints. English appears to use a copying rule in occasionally allowing a 'pronoun copy' — a resumptive pronoun — inside an island, expressly to save a sentence from violating one of the constraints:

(7) a. This is the elevator that its doors are always flying open.

 b. There were all these kids around our house that nobody knew where they came from.

As the Standard Theory developed, it was argued that the almost unlimited power of transformational rules must be restricted radically. Only a theory limited to generating all and only the sentences that occur in natural language would potentially be able to explain a child's mastery of a language on the basis of the limited data of early experience. Constraints on rules other than Ross's structural constraints were therefore explored. One development with far-reaching consequences was the pro-

INTRODUCTION 5

posal that there are no transformations that introduce meaning-bearing lexical items (see n. 12, Chomsky 1977; Jackendoff 1972). One consequence of this approach to transformations is that all cases of resumptive pronouns (such as those in (7)) are base generated rather than transformationally inserted.

In the Extended Standard Theory (EST) the focus shifts away from the description of particular rules and toward the contraints on classes of rules (e.g. the class of movement rules in general, or the class of rules of semantic interpretation). One constraint, the SUBJACENCY CONDITION (Chomsky 1973), is central to all subsequent versions of the theory of movement. Subjacency, in its original formulation, prevents extraction across more than one CYCLIC NODE (NP or S).

(8)   SUBJACENCY: No rule can involve X, Y, X superior to Y, if Y is separated from X by more than one cyclic node.

Subjacency, combined with the theory of ITERATED CYCLIC (COMP-to-COMP) MOVEMENT, is taken as the explanatory condition underlying several of Ross's constraints (on movement to COMP, see Bresnan 1970). That is, subjacency has the effect of barring cycle movement out of some of the configurations defined by Ross as islands, namely complex NPs and sentential subjects.

In Chomsky (1973) it is proposed for the first time that movement rules leave a TRACE. Trace is described as a phonologically null element which is introduced as a by-product of movement, and plays a role in the subsequent derivation of a sentence. The theory of traces is not pursued further there, but is fleshed out in Chomsky (1977). Here trace is described as an empty category dominated by a (maximal) phrasal node remaining at an origin site after movement; trace and the moved category are coindexed, allowing (in the case of WH movement) a quantifier-variable interpretation of their relation. The later articulation of trace theory becomes central to the development of generative grammar.

What has been referred to as *surface structure* is now more abstract: it is a level 'enriched' by the coindexed traces of movement. Since this enrichment encodes the derivational history of a sentence, semantic interpretation can be read off of surface structure alone, without reference to deep structure. Deep structure configurations are therefore much less important at this stage than in the earlier Standard Theory, and the interpretive properties of surface structure now allow strictly representational accounts of transformational sentences.

Finally, in Chomsky (1977) it is hypothesized that a large class of rules can be reduced to a single rule, WH MOVEMENT. Chomsky begins by listing the characteristics of WH movement: it leaves a trace; it

6   CHAPTER ONE

observes the island constraints and subjacency; and it is permitted to operate from COMP to COMP. Assuming that this set of properties is a 'diagnostic' for WH movement, he argues that WH movement is in fact the rule responsible for a large number of constructions that had been considered to involve distinct transformations: restrictive and nonrestrictive relative clauses, direct questions, indirect questions, comparatives, topicalizations, clefts, *tough* constructions, and others. All these separate transformations are now eliminated from the grammar, which is thereby greatly simplified. This paper represents an important step in the reduction of the transformational component to a single rule, as found in the GB model.

1.2. *Introduction to Government-Binding Theory*

Government-Binding Theory (GB) began as the *Pisa Lectures*, delivered by Chomsky in the spring of 1979. It has been expanded and modified in a number of books, both by Chomsky (Chomsky 1981, 1982, 1986a, 1986b) and by many others, as well as in hundreds of papers, dissertations, and published articles. GB is both a continuation of and a departure from the Extended Standard Theory of the late 1970s; it carries over many important currents from EST, but also embodies important innovations and improvements. The theory is now expanding so quickly and on so many fronts that the following short overview is necessarily sketchy and eclectic.

The object of study in GB is a hypothesized UNIVERSAL GRAMMAR (UG), an abstract cognitive system which corresponds to the innate human language faculty.[1] The structure of UG includes both universal PRINCIPLES, which account for what is common (and necessary) to all languages, and adjustable PARAMETERS, which are set on the basis of learning and experience, and which determine typological differences among languages. Once its parameters have been fixed, UG constitutes the CORE GRAMMAR of a language. Among many proposed parameters are those fixing word order (distinguishing head-initial from head-final languages: Huang 1982); presence or absence of the rule Move Alpha, and/or in what components this rule applies; licensing of empty categories (the '*pro*-drop parameter'); and the choice of bounding nodes for subjacency (e.g. Rizzi 1982a). Core grammar (UG) accounts for most of a speaker/hearer's knowledge of language, which is seen to be otherwise greatly underdetermined by the available data.

In the typical GB analysis of any given set of facts, properties of Universal Grammar are integrated with language-particular properties. The latter participate in the analysis only to the extent that no concept of

Universal Grammar accounts for them. That is, the general principles of UG are made to account for the greatest range of facts possible, while language-particular facts are appealed to only as a last resort. This approach reflects the major role played by innateness in the generative analysis of language. Language-particular facts constitute what is called the 'marked periphery' and must be learned, along with parameter settings, through exposure to a particular language. The example of a peripheral construction most frequently cited is preposition stranding in English.

Phenomenologically, the theory's main interest is in the various syntactic dependencies found in language and the principles constraining them. The fundamental notion underlying the analysis of these dependencies is GOVERNMENT. Government in GB is a structural relation between a governor and a governed element. It is assumed to underlie the *Aspects*-type subcategorization of lexical items, and the prototypical government relation is that holding between a lexical head (the governor) and its complement(s). However, the search for the definitive formulation of government is an ongoing one and the topic of much discussion. One current definition of government is given below:

(9)   GOVERNMENT (after Aoun and Sportiche 1983; Chomsky 1986b):

A governs B iff

(i)   A is X^0

(ii)   every maximal projection that dominates B dominates A and vice versa, and

(iii)   A $\neq$ B.

In other words, A is a head and A and B share all maximal projections; these terms are taken from X' theory (see below). This particular formulation of government incorporates what is called M-COMMAND: command of all positions within a maximal projection.

The terminology used in defining government and all other structural concepts of GB come from X' THEORY (Jackendoff 1977; Chomsky 1986b). X' categories standardly have three levels: the X^0 level ('X-zero' or LEXICAL level) and two projections of X^0, X' and X'' (the latter also written XP). X^0 is the HEAD and X'' is the MAXIMAL PROJECTION (of the head). There are two functional X^0 categories: C (complementizer) and I (inflection);[2] and four lexical X^0 categories: N, A, V, and P. The functional categories extend V'' (VP) to a full clause (CP). The general scheme is sketched in (10); order irrelevant:

(10)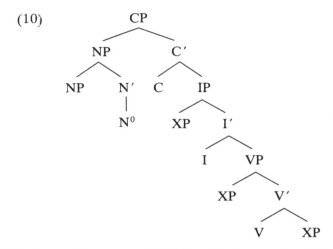

(The internal structure of NP is spelled out only within CP, for convenience.) In this sketch all categories conform to the same X' schemata, as suggested in Chomsky (1986b),

(11) a. XP = YP X'

b. X' = X ZP

where linear order is irrelevant and XP, YP, and ZP may be any category. The sister of the head (ZP in (11b)) is its COMPLEMENT. The maximal projection of C, CP, was formerly known as S'; IP is the former S. The other maximal projections are NP, AP, VP, and PP.[3] The XP daughter of CP is a landing site for A' movements, for example of WH phrases. The XP daughter of IP is the position of the syntactic subject. All [XP, XP] are informally referred to as the SPECIFIER of the respective head,[4] often written Spec(X). I assume that all XP, including VP and NP, have specifier positions, contrary to Chomsky (1986b), who suggests that at least VP has no specifier.

Some important government relations in the tree above are the government by I of the subject (specifier of I) and the government by V of its complement. Many other government relations and refinements of the notion of government have been suggested recently; some of these will be mentioned at appropriate places below or in the chapters that follow. For some idea of the issues involved in defining government, see Chomsky (1981, Ch. 4); Aoun and Sportiche (1983); Saito (1984); Chomsky (1986b); Rizzi (1990).

As I have noted above, government is the fundamental relation in GB. This relation underlies the LICENSING of elements in a number of ways and at different stages of derivation. Via government, a head is able to express certain of its lexical properties on the arguments it selects. It

INTRODUCTION 9

assigns thematic ('theta') roles (such as AGENT, THEME, or GOAL) and ABSTRACT CASE (such as Nominative or Accusative) to NPs it governs. From the fundamental government relation, the subtheories and sub-systems of principles of GB arise. Among these are government theory, theta theory, and case theory.[5] Government also underlies binding theory, determining the domain within which anaphoric elements are associated with possible antecedents. These subsystems are, not surprisingly, highly interactive.

One of the subsystems important to our anaysis is bounding theory, which incorporates the Subjacency Condition and imposes distance constraints on movement. In recent theoretical work, the bounding nodes for subjacency are those which are not selected by a lexical head. This amounts to saying that adjunct nodes are barriers to extraction, while categories that are the complements of some lexical head are not (see Chomsky 1986b). The traces of movement themselves submit to a stronger licensing condition, proper government (see below). Bounding theory, therefore, also relies on government.

As did earlier versions of generative grammar, the GB model contains a number of components. One is the LEXICON, where lexical items are listed and their idiosyncratic properties specified. It is proposed that there is structure in lexical entries, to the effect that predicators are listed with the set of arguments they semantically select, and that those arguments are arranged hierarchically, perhaps even annotated with idiosyncratic Case and relational information (Williams 1984; Belletti & Rizzi 1988; Grimshaw & Mester 1988). The lexicon may also contain redundancy rules relating certain forms (like transitive and passive forms of verbs). Phrase structure rules (along the lines of X' theory) reside in the CATEGORIAL COMPONENT. In the view of many GB theorists, there are no phrase structure rules (see Stowell 1981, Chomsky 1986b); the configuration of constituents at various levels of representation is derivable from the schemata in (11) and such aspects of the theory as Case theory. For others, the categorial component must contain at least the traditional S-expansion rule, S → NP INFL VP (though if IP is a projection of Inflection as defined above, it partially replaces such a rule). The lexicon and the categorial component together constitute the BASE.

The base generates representations called D-STRUCTURES or DS (corresponding to what were formerly called 'deep structures'). D-structure is mapped onto an intermediate level of representation called S-STRUCTURE or SS by Move Alpha, the only transformational rule.[6] S-structure differs from D-structure primarily in containing the coindexed traces of movement. At the level of S-structure, representations feed separately into PHONETIC FORM (PF) and LOGICAL FORM (LF). The output of PF corresponds to what was formerly called 'surface structure'. Move Alpha also applies in PF (where it is responsible for 'minor movements' and stylistic movements) and in LF (where it raises quantified NPs to a structural position corresponding to their semantic scope). LF is a syntactic component in which rules of interpretation apply to S-structures and to representations at the various internal levels of LF. The output structures of LF have the scope properties of first order logic, including indication of such scope-taking elements as negation and modals, making LF the 'interface' between syntax and semantics (see also van Riemsdijk and Williams 1986, chapter 11).

The model is depicted in (12).

(12)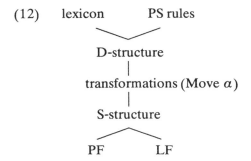

Various well-formedness conditions or principles apply in the various components or levels; some are specific to a level or to all levels, for others the level at which they apply is to be determined empirically.

The PROJECTION PRINCIPLE is a basic and a very general constraint on representations, stated informally as follows (from Chomsky 1982, p. 8):

(13) PROJECTION PRINCIPLE: The theta-marking properties of each lexical item must be represented categorially at each syntactic level: at LF, S-structure, and D-structure.

The Projection Principle expresses the relation between lexical structure (the function-argument complex described above) and syntactic structure, and constrains the structural configurations of each level of representation. Much of trace theory can be derived from the Projection Principle, since any selected NP position must be present at all levels of structure, whether or not it is lexically filled. In most formulations, the Projection Principle is construed as extending to subject position in clauses in which the verb assigns a theta role to its subject. Chomsky (1981) proposes the EXTENDED PROJECTION PRINCIPLE, which stipulates the existence of subject position. Ensuring the presence of subject position is currently a thorny problem, although the X' schemata in (11) suggest one solution: every projection has a specifier.

The Projection Principle works in concert with the THETA CRITERION. The Theta Criterion ensures that thematic relations are properly

INTRODUCTION 11

expressed in the arguments mapped onto D-structures by the Projection Principle (Chomsky 1981, p. 36):

(14)   THETA CRITERION: Each argument bears one and only one θ-role, and each θ-role is assigned to one and only one argument.

(Dummies like expletive *it* or *there* do not receive theta-roles, nor do the subject (positions) of verbs like *seem* and *appear*.) This principle ensures that all and only NP arguments selected by a head receive thematic roles, and, via the Projection Principle, it holds at all syntactic levels. That is, θ-roles are assigned to arguments mapped to D-structure positions, arguments maintain their thematic identity, and thematic information is not lost after D-structure.[7]

By the Theta Criterion (maintaining thematic roles) and the Projection Principle (maintaining structural positions), movement is limited to destinations that are non-thematic. This is illustrated below (where θ = position assigned a theta role, θ' = position not assigned a theta role):

(15)   (i) θ to θ' (e.g. subject raising, WH movement)

(ii)   *θ to θ (e.g. 'dative' movement, 'object raising')

(iii) *θ' to θ

(iv) θ' to θ'

Movement as in (i) observes the Projection Principle because thematic information is not interfered with. In (ii), theta roles would be doubly assigned, violating the Theta Criterion. (iii) violates the Projection Principle and the Theta Criterion, since θ-roles are assigned, and θ positions filled, at D-structure. (iv) is a thematically neutral case and could be instantiated by the raising of a derived subject of a passive. At the output of LF, each CHAIN (including as members any full NP and all of its coindexed traces including those in intermediate landing sites) is checked to ensure that it contains only one theta role (meaning that it contains only one true argument).

Empty categories play a major role in GB. So far I have mentioned only WH trace. There are actually four characterizations of empty categories: PRO, the null subject in control or equi analyses, occurs in ungoverned subject position in infinitival clauses; NP TRACE arises when an NP moves to an argument position; *pro* is a null pronoun which occurs in governed positions; and WH TRACE arises as a result of A' movement. Whether or not there is one EC, defined in different ways by the context in which it is found, or four ECs, each having an intrinsic definition, is a matter of debate, of which more below.

12 CHAPTER ONE

Traces are licensed by the EMPTY CATEGORY PRINCIPLE (ECP), a principle of government *theory* but a stronger relation than government, defined above:

(16) THE ECP: Trace must be properly governed.

PROPER GOVERNMENT: A properly governs B iff

(i) A lexically governs B or

(ii) A antecedent governs B. (Chomsky 1986b)

That is, a trace can appear only in those positions where it is governed by a lexical head or by a coindexed antecedent.[8] Thus I(nflection), for example, though a governor, is not a proper governor for the ECP in English.[9] The ECP is commonly understood to hold at LF (Chomsky 1981).

Though the intuition behind the ECP is generally held to be valid, i.e., traces must be "recoverable" through selection properties of a head or through the relation with the antecedent, the proper formulation of this intuition is a matter of ongoing debate and much intensive current research (see, e.g., Kayne 1981, 1983a; Jaeggli 1985; Stowell 1985; Rizzi 1987; Aoun et al. 1987; Georgopoulos 1991b; and others). One important proposal now developing is that the principle should be stated as a conjunction rather than a disjunction; that is, that trace must be *both* antecedent governed and lexically governed[10] (see the sources cited).

The ECP developed from the observation that, in many languages, long WH movement from subject position is more constrained than long movement from object position:

(17) a. The Captain thinks that the Admiral loves Anne.

b. *Who does the Captain think that ____ loves Anne?

c. Who does the Captain think that the Admiral loves ____ ?

The trace in (17c) is properly governed by *loves*, but the subject trace in (17b) is not properly governed, either lexically or by its antecedent (a trace in Spec(C) would not govern the subject, since C intervenes).

While WH trace and NP trace are subject to the ECP, the empty pronouns PRO and pro, mentioned above, are assumed not to be. The theory must therefore be able to distinguish traces from null pronominals. This can be done via the features [±anaphor, ±pronominal] (Chomsky 1981), which partition NPs, empty or lexical, into four classes. Chomsky (1982) proposes principles of contextual definition of ECs on the basis of these features. The following summary of contextual definition is taken from Chung (1982b):

INTRODUCTION   13

(18) a. If $[_{NP}$ e] is locally bound by an element in a non-θ-position, it is [-pronominal];

    i.   if [-pronominal] and A bound, it is [+anaphor]. (NP trace)

    ii. if [-pronominal] and A′ bound, it is [-anaphor]. (WH trace)

    b. If $[_{NP}$ e] is free, or locally bound by an element in a θ-position, it is [+pronominal].

    iii. If [+pronominal] and governed, it is [-anaphor]. (*pro*)

    iv. If [+pronominal] and ungoverned, it is [+anaphor]. (PRO)

CONTROL THEORY, which determines the reference of PRO, will concern us not at all here. The definitions of WH trace and of *pro* will concern us most. Note that (18) (a) (ii) makes available a representational rather than a derivational definition of WH trace, parallel to the definition of *pro*. This point will become important in following chapters, where I argue that all A′ bound variables, even resumptive pronouns, are [-pronominal, -anaphor].

The *PRO-DROP* parameter is one term applied to the theory of the distribution of *pro*. The essential question in this case is, what conditions license empty (referring) pronouns? The theory combines elements of government and of 'identification'; the following is adapted from Rizzi (1986):

(19)   *pro* is sanctioned by a formal condition and an interpretive condition.

    (i) *pro* is governed by X_y^0.

       (the set of governing heads determined by the language)

    (ii) *pro* has the features of X^0 coindexed with it.

That is, the language determines the set of heads that license *pro* and the features that 'identify' *pro* (in English both sets are null). We return to the subject of *pro* theory in later chapters.

The BINDING THEORY applies to lexical NPs, and to empty NPs as defined in (18), determining the contexts in which they are bound or in which they are free. The principles of the binding theory are in (19). Simplifying somewhat, we may think of 'governing category' as the minimal NP or IP containing both governee and governor; see also Chomsky (1982, 1986a).

14　　　　　　　　　　　CHAPTER ONE

(20)　　A. An anaphor is bound in its governing category.

　　　　B. A pronominal is free in its governing category.

　　　　C. An R-expression (name or WH trace) is free
　　　　　in all governing categories.

The binding theory refers to A binding only; therefore Principle C is not violated by the binding of a trace from Spec(C).

Finally, CASE THEORY (Rouveret & Vergnaud 1980) determines the assignment of abstract Case. As noted above, Case is assigned under government; [-N] heads (i.e. V or P) assign Case to their complements. I governs and assigns Nominative Case to the subject; V assigns Accusative Case to its direct object; and P assigns Oblique. Genitive Case is assigned (by means as yet undetermined) within NP; in Georgopoulos (1991a) I argue that N *assigns* Genitive in the standard way to its specifier, though Case *realization* may in some languages require overt markers. The core of Case Theory is the CASE FILTER, which requires that every overt NP receive Case. A derivation containing an NP that violates the Case Filter is terminated. By assumption, the Case Filter applies in PF.

1.3. *Bounding Theory*

In Government-Binding Theory, the essential distinction between long-distance and local binding is not based on their 'unbounded' or 'local' character per se, but rather derives from the position of the antecedent. 'Unbounded dependencies' involve an antecedent in the specifier of C, or in some other non-argument (A′) position, and so they are referred to as A′ binding, whereas passive and raising involve an antecedent in an argument (A) position, so they are known as A binding (Chomsky 1982).[11] This distinction is strongly motivated cross-linguistically, as binding from within CP (or from clitic position) has demonstrably different properties from binding from an argument position. One of the strongest arguments for this is 'WH agreement', to be described in Chapter Three. An A′-bound position is a VARIABLE (see below).

The distinction between A′ and A positions is not so clear-cut as in earlier stages of the theory, however, since there is no longer a necessary distinction between (former) COMP position and argument positions: there is only Spec(X) or Compl(X) (complement of X). Nor does the distinction derive from the difference between lexical and functional categories, as one might perhaps expect; Spec(I) is presumably an A position, Spec(C) is claimed to be A′. In addition, an A position may or may not be a θ position; by Theta theory landing sites are never θ positions, but a θ' position may be an A position. The designations A

INTRODUCTION 15

and A', then, are now purely stipulative. The problem seems to me to be a fairly serious one (cf. the impact on (18)). However, though one could think of a number of ways to derive the distinction,[12] my intention here is to pursue the ways that Palauan bears on the current set of assumptions that make up bounding theory, so I will assume the customary distinction.

A' binding is generated by application of Move α displacing some XP to Spec(C). A coindexed trace is left in the constituent's origin site. This coindexing relation is interpreted as operator-variable binding at the level of Logical Form, where traces are replaced by variables.[13] Since movement takes place 'in the syntax', however, this coindexing holds at S-structure; thus one can view A' binding as a property of S-structure representations. In addition, the Binding Theory holds at S-structure (Chomsky 1981);[14] WH traces must therefore be defined as variables and be A-free at that level. Note that although the dependency is analyzed in movement terms, the trace can be defined in terms of (18) (a) (ii) above, which is neutral between movement and base-generation origins of trace.

The A' relation is illustrated below:

(21) a. $[_{CP}$ **Who**$_i$ $[_{IP}$ t$_i$ is hiding behind the sofa]]?

b. Emma is the person $[_{CP}$ **Who**$_i$ $[_{IP}$ t$_i$ is hiding behind the sofa]]

c. $[_{CP}$ **What**$_i$ is $[_{IP}$ Emma hiding behind t$_i$]]?

Another important property of A' dependencies generated by movement is that they observe subjacency.[15] Subjacency prohibits movement across more than one bounding node — NP, IP, or CP for English — in a single move. The examples in (21) observe subjacency; that in (22) does not:

(22) *$[_{CP}$ **What**$_i$ $[_{IP1}$ did you believe $[_{NP}$ the report
$[_{CP}$ t$_i$ $[_C$ that] $[_{IP2}$ Emma was hiding behind t$_i$]]]]]?

Even if WHAT in IP$_2$ moves into Spec(C), it cannot then cross all of CP, NP, and IP$_1$ to get to the matrix Spec(C). Thus Bounding Theory accounts for the ungrammaticality of (22).

Finally, the trace must be properly governed ((16) above).

To sum up, the properties of A' binding include these: there is an A' binder, there is a coindexed bindee (the trace), the binding relation between the two obeys subjacency, and the trace is properly governed.

A non-movement alternative to this analysis is sometimes considered, in which the relation is base-generated and binding between antecedent and trace is determined by interpretive rules (= construal rules) in Logical Form (Chomsky 1981, 90 ff.; Chomsky 1982, 33 ff.). The form of 'base-generated' structures in GB is determined by X' theory, the Extended Projection Principle, and Case theory (Chomsky 1982). As in EST, a base-generated trace represents an XP that is (optionally) un-expanded by lexical material. The antecedent is generated in Spec(C), and both trace and antecedent have an index (not necessarily the same index) by the level of S-structure.

In this alternative theory, the binding in LF must satisfy the *same* conditions as those summarized above for the movement analysis. In other words, A' binding always has the same properties, whether gener-ated by movement or by interpretive rules. We may therefore speak of a particular 'Move α Relation' in which the antecedent is in an A' position, the coindexed trace is properly governed, and subjacency is observed. The core cases of A' binding have these three necessary properties.

The notion of a Move α Relation legitimizes an analysis of A' bind-ing that does not refer to movement, and, in fact, movement rules are no longer important to the theory of traces. An empty category may be base-generated; the binding principles, plus the definitions in (18), distinguish A binding from A' binding, and the bounding constraints are well-formedness conditions that fall out from operation of the LF inter-pretive rule. The question then arises whether the coindexing relation between a trace and its antecedent can be defined on *S-structure*, without the device of the movement rule.

The notion of the CHAIN is an alternative to the movement analysis and a means by which coindexing is determined. Chains are developed by Chomsky (esp. 1981, Ch. 6) as devices which encode the derivational history of S-structures: the head of a chain is the antecedent in its surface position, and the tail is the antecedent's (coindexed) origin site; there may be intermediate traces as well, as in (23):

(23)   Who$_i$ [$_{IP}$ do you believe [$_{CP}$ t$_i$ [$_{IP}$ t$_i$ will be found t$_i$ guilty]]]?

In (23), all the elements indexed i belong to the same chain. Case and θ-role are assigned to the chain; a chain may bear only one Case and one θ-role (see also Safir 1982; Kayne 1983b; Brody 1984). In the view of Rizzi (1982b), chains have a representational rather than a deriva-tional character: they can be read off of S-structures and are independent of Move α (see Chapter Four).

1.4. *Resumptive Pronouns*

The final issue to be introduced here is the treatment of RESUMPTIVE PRONOUNS, elements which are central to the analysis of Palauan, though they only appear marginally, in relative clauses, in English. Examples are in (24):

INTRODUCTION   17

(24) a. There's the guy who you always want to stop and talk to **him**.

   b. This is related to the functional definition of empty categories which I can't remember if I talked about **it** the first time.

Today, the question of the proper theoretical account of resumptive pronouns goes to the heart of generative theory, as it involves the central problem of reducing the power and number of available grammars.

The A′ dependency formed with a resumptive pronoun is *not* an instance of the Move α relation, primarily because it does not observe subjacency. Resumptive pronouns are in fact regarded in the theory as devices for 'circumventing' subjacency; thus, for example, one does not find 'local' A′ binding using pronouns, as in ***The woman who I saw her was blond*. They are not created by movement in the syntax, and are therefore not interpreted as variables at S-structure. In GB it is assumed that resumptive pronouns arise only in what are called 'structures of predication', a class that includes relative clauses but does not include interrogatives.[16] Chomsky (1977, 1982) proposes that a RULE OF PRE-DICATION applies in relative clauses, to coindex a resumptive pronoun and its binder (the head). The workings of predication are described as follows (1982, note 11):

... the general principle of relative clause interpretation applies to (not prior to) LF [and] determines that the relative clause, taken as an open sentence, is predicated of the head. For example, suppose that the LF representation of [his] (8a) is (i):

   (i)   [the man]$_i$ [who$_k$ John saw t$_k$]

The rule of Predication ... identifies i and k, yielding the representation (ii):

   (ii)   [the man$_i$] [who$_i$ John saw t$_i$]

The predication rule, in other words, translates an 'aboutness' relation somewhat like λ abstraction. It ensures that coreferential phrases which are not related by movement have the same index. Subjacency does not apply to the output of this rule.

By way of contrast, consider the various Palauan A′ dependencies illustrated in (25), containing resumptive pronouns:

(25) a. ngte'a a 'omulme'ar tiang el   mo er **ngii**
        who   *2-buy*   *this* *Comp* *go* *P* *him/her*
        Who did you buy this for?

   b. ngngera el rum   a lulngetmokl er **ngii** a Willy
       what   *L* *room*   *3-clean*   *P* *it*
       Which room did Willy clean up?

This pronoun is locally A′ bound, and has a number of S-structure

18   CHAPTER ONE

binding properties. Later chapters will argue for the existence in the language of null resumptive pronouns as well, with the same properties as those in (25). It is these structures, and others like them, that concern us in this book.

The goal of this book is to describe variable binding in Palauan and to bring this description to bear on central claims and issues within Government-Binding Theory. Chapters Two and Three provide the descriptive background to the more theoretical chapters that follow them. Chapter Two contains much of the detail of verb morphology which, though complex, crucially underlies the later analyses. This chapter also discusses the phrase structure and the basic constituent order of Palauan sentences. It considers the evidence that Palauan is a *pro*-drop language, and here I describe the difficulty of attempting to attribute *pro*-drop to 'identification' in terms of overt morphology. I conclude that a more abstract and possibly compositional theory of *pro* is needed. The chapter ends with arguments supporting a distinction between inflectional morphology and clitics.

In Chapter Three each type of variable binding structure is illustrated and described, and the class as a whole is argued to be based on relativization. Chapter Three also describes the productivity of structures containing resumptive pronouns, and demonstrates that Palauan does not observe the island constraints. The facts of relativization, resumptive pronouns, and the island violations lead to the conclusion in Chapter Three that the entire class of Palauan A' binding is base-generated. This chapter closes with a description of WH agreement, a special agreement system that applies in dependencies involving S-structure variables.

The fourth chapter attempts to deal with the problems raised by base-generation and the lack of coindexing that comes from movement. Here I argue, on the basis of the WH agreement rule and the facts of coordination and other multiple variable binding structures, that the antecedent and variable in Palauan are coindexed at S-structure, and that Palauan A' binding is thereby equivalent to A' binding arising from syntactic movement in languages like English. This is further supported by evidence that there *is* a locality condition in Palauan, of which WH agreement is a morphological effect. Chapter Four closes with a description of the chain formation algorithm on S-structures, which ensures the well-formedness of the syntactic A' binding relation, and on which the locality effect can be based.

Chapter Five deals with the problems for scope interpretation of embedded WH phrases raised by the fact that WH phrases may optionally take in situ positions or A' positions which do not correspond to their syntactic scope. Similar facts have been described in other languages, but the Palauan case is distinguished by the complexity of options available, as well as by unexpected scope behavior. The chapter reviews current approaches to [±WH] selection and to problems of multiple WH interrogation in embedded questions, and shows that the variety of positions that Palauan grammar makes available to WH phrases leads to some underdetermination of scope in the syntax. I argue here that, since the position of Spec(C) is crucial to WH scope interpretation, WH phrases in all other positions (in situ, adjoined to IP, clefted, etc.) are effectively in situ. This is supported by the failure of WH phrases in Palauan (never in Spec(C) at S-structure) to conform to predicted scope interpretations.

Crossover phenomena, and especially weak crossover, are addressed in Chapter Six. Here I demonstrate that Palauan resumptive pronouns have the expected properties of variables with respect to the strong crossover phenomenon, and argue on the basis of this for a featural rather than hierarchical definition of syntactic variable. I show that there is no weak crossover effect in Palauan, and relate this fact to the uniform direction of government in the language. That is, weak crossover is presented as an ECP effect: where canonical government holds (and modulo the possible effect of other systems), there is no weak crossover. The findings of this chapter also strongly support an absolute distinction between strong and weak crossover phenomena.

To sum up, the book is a case study in the interaction between theory and 'new' language facts. While GB theory is shown to be an efficient and natural tool for exploring the properties of a particular grammar, those properties themselves may require shifts of emphasis, fine tuning in new areas, and rethinking of given analyses within the overall theory. I will attempt to demonstrate that, while Palauan A' binding is in important respects like A' binding in Move α languages, adjustments within the conceptual network of GB will be necessary. For example, it seems to me that the best way to approach Palauan A' binding, and especially the facts of resumptive pronouns, is to maintain the conceptual connection between subjacency and movement. The lack of subjacency effects in Palauan can then be ascribed to the lack of movement. In Chomsky (1986b) and in other recent work, it is suggested that subjacency may be viewed as a condition on representations, stated in terms of the number of barriers between antecedent and variable. If this view is taken, then we have no explanation for the fact that Palauan does not have subjacency effects. That is, I have chosen to retain the distinction between movement and nonmovement structures as a basis for analyzing Palauan, rather than adopt the hypothesis that subjacency is not a universal condition.

In showing the ways in which the Palauan language can be analyzed in standard theoretical terms, the initial exoticism of the language is reduced to more general principles. This is precisely the result predicted by a theory of universal grammar.

20   CHAPTER ONE

NOTES

[1] This concept has been in view since the earliest stages of the Standard Theory (see, e.g., Chomsky 1965). However, GB is characterized by its exclusive focus on UG.

[2] There are currently proposals suggesting further functional categories: for example, D (determiner) (Kuroda 1988; Abney 1986) and W (WH quantifier) (S.-Y. Kuroda, personal communication).

[3] See Pollock (1987) and subsequent literature for an enriched theory of the set of heads and projections. I do not consider that system here.

[4] Thus a WH phrase may become the specifier of C, the subject is specifier of I, etc.

[5] Theta theory incorporates the insights of Fillmore, Gruber, and Jackendoff, in that theta roles are modelled on semantic case roles and reflect the semantic properties of verbs. The theory of abstract Case (with a 'C') emphasizes abstract Case assignment over morphological case (but see Williams (1983)).

[6] In recent work, Chomsky hypothesizes that the movement rule is subject to a 'least effort' constraint, and applies only to satisfy some other principle or condition (see Chomsky 1986a, 3.3.3; 1986b). For example, an NP object of a passive verb may move to subject position in order to get Case, or a WH phrase may move to Spec(C) in order to satisfy a [+WH] feature requirement and/or to take scope over a sentence.

[7] The Theta Criterion also applies to chains at the output of LF. (Chains are discussed in detail in Chapter Four. See also 1.3 below.)

[8] A coindexed antecedent is in a position that c-commands the trace.

[9] It has been suggested that N and P are never proper governors (e.g. Aoun 1985, Ch. 2). Since it is clear that in some languages either N or P may be proper governors (for N, see Chapter Three below, and Georgopoulos 1991a; for P see McCloskey and Hale 1984), the issue may depend on parametric typology rather than any universal principle.

[10] In Chapter Six I propose that such a unified condition can account independently for weak crossover.

[11] Belletti and Rizzi (1981, p. 11) attribute the notion 'argument position' used in GB to a 1977 paper of G. Cinque.

[12] A fruitful direction might be to assume, following Kuroda (1988) and others, that subjects originate under VP universally, arriving in Spec(I) by NP movement. Georgopoulos (1991a) shows that the same analysis can be applied to predicative NPs. That is, A positions could be defined as theta positions, those occupied by arguments of a lexical head in D-structure. Then Spec(I) and Spec(C) are A′ positions. The distinction between Spec(I) and Spec(C) would then have to be clarified (pursuing Chomsky's intuition (1986b) that IP is 'defective'). See Chapter 5 on the unique properties of Spec(C).

[13] See, e.g., Chomsky (1977, p. 83); issues of reconstruction and the proper treatment of pied-piped elements are irrelevant here, so I do not discuss them.

[14] Arguments to this effect contrast the c-command relations of pronouns and referring expressions (names and variables) between D-structure and S-structure, and those at S-structure with their reversed relations at LF, after such rules as Quantifier Raising (May 1977) have applied. That is, it is argued that the Binding Theory applies after WH movement but before LF movement. See Chomsky (1981, p. 197), Belletti & Rizzi (1988).

[15] *Barriers* theory (Chomsky 1986b) derives the equivalent analysis. I assume VP is not a bounding node/barrier, either intrinsically or because of the possibility of adjunction. The definition of bounding node/barrier is not at issue here, as will become evident in Chapter Three.

[16] Chomsky (1982) suggests that such a rule also applies to topicalization structures, in which the clause is "an open proposition taken to be satisfied by the referent of the focused NP." See Huang (1984) for comments on a typology of predication structures.

CHAPTER TWO

PALAUAN: A SKETCH OF THE GRAMMAR

This chapter constitutes a short introduction to Palauan grammar, including an overview of the complex morphosyntax of the language. Some grasp of these details is necessary to following later discussions that involve noun and verb morphology. The chapter also covers more general aspects of syntactic analysis as they are reflected in Palauan, including underlying constituent order and issues concerning null arguments.

0. PALAUAN; EARLIER GRAMMARS

Palauan is spoken in the Republic of Palau, a cluster of 200 beautiful islands in the Western Carolines of the Pacific. Palau is located about 800 miles southwest of Guam, 600 miles east of the Philippines, 1890 miles south of Tokyo, and 4500 miles west-southwest of Honolulu.

Palauan is a member of the Western Austronesian language family (Bender 1971). Although Palau is geographically within Micronesia, Palauan is not one of the nuclear Micronesian languages (Dempwolff 1934–38; Jackson 1984). The nuclear Micronesian languages include those of Truk, Ponape, Kosrae, the Marshalls, and Kiribati, while the nonnuclear (or western) Micronesian languages, including Palauan and Chamorro, are close to the languages of Indonesia and the Philippines.[1] Yapese is grouped with Palauan and Chamorro as one of the nonuclear languages, though the status of Yapese within Austronesian is "problematic" (Bender 1984; see also Voegelin and Voegelin 1964, p. 102). Palauan has no close relatives within the Western Austronesian family, however, and is best regarded as an isolate within this family.

Palauan has about 17,000 speakers, of whom about 80% live in the Republic of Palau.[2] There is very little dialectal variation from Kayangel atoll in the north to Angaur in the south. The languages spoken in the islands of Sonsorol and Tobi, south of Angaur, are nuclear Micronesian and therefore not closely related to Palauan.

The earliest grammar of Palauan appears to have been Bishop Walleser's (1911) *Grammatik der Palausprache*, written during the German administration of Palau; Walleser was evidently a member of the original Roman Catholic mission there. My only acquaintance with his work is the references made to it in Capell (1949) and McManus (1977). Both Capell and McManus acknowledge some reliance on Walleser, and note that he also produced a dictionary of Palauan.

22   CHAPTER TWO

Micronesia came under the jurisdiction of the United States at the
end of World War II, as one of the districts of the Trust Territory of the
Pacific Islands (TTPI) of the UN. Several different projects were then
organized to expand knowledge of the area. One such project, the Coordinated Investigation of Micronesian Anthropology (CIMA), produced Capell's *Grammar of the Language of Palau* (1949), among
other works. Capell's grammar describes the morphology and syntax of
Palauan in some detail and quite insightfully,[3] with a wealth of examples.

Patzold (1968) is based primarily on Walleser (1911) and Capell
(1949), and contains arguments for placing Palauan within the Indonesian subgroup of Austronesian. It is reviewed in Dyen (1971).

Josephs' *Palauan Reference Grammar* (1975) and McManus' *Palauan-
English Dictionary* (1977) are both products of the TTPI-sponsored
projects at the University of Hawaii of the late 1960s and early 1970s.
Josephs deals systematically with all aspects of the language, including
phonology, morphology, and syntax. It is the most complete work to
date, and is written more from a linguist's than a grammarian's point of
view. In covering such a breadth of topics, however, the book suffers
from lack of depth, especially where it deals with syntactic phenomena.
McManus' dictionary is the companion volume to Josephs'. It is based
on extensive word lists prepared by Fr. Edwin McManus, a Jesuit
missionary who lived and worked in Palau from 1948 until his death in
1969. The word lists were revised and expanded into the dictionary by
Josephs, assisted by Masa-aki Emesiochel.

Flora (1969) and Carlson (1968) are the basic sources on the taxo-
nomic phonemic analysis of Palauan. Wilson (1972) and Flora (1974)
are valuable analyses of the phonology and morphology of the Palauan
verb, written from within the generative phonology framework of *SPE*
(Chomsky and Halle 1968). Josephs relies substantially on Wilson's
work in his treatment of the morphology.

1. OVERVIEW

This grammatical sketch of Palauan draws on the sources described
above as well as my field notes, 1981 to 1985. There are two reasons for
including this extensive sketch, both important, I think. One is its
descriptive interest, independent of the theoretical analyses that may be
based upon it: the data, at a purely objective level, are fascinating. As a
description of the language the sketch should be useful to Palauans who
wish to study their own language, as well as to scholars in the field of
Austronesian studies and to general linguists seeking to extend the
coverage of linguistic theory to a wider variety of languages and language
types. The second reason the sketch is included is its indispensability

PALAUAN GRAMMAR

(along with Chapter Three) to a theoretical understanding of the language, especially the analyses that begin in Chapter Four.

The sketch has essentially three parts. The first part deals with the phrasal and sub-phrasal units of the language. It begins with phonological and orthographical observations, then works through the verb morphology and the structure of noun phrases and verb phrases. The second part of the sketch deals with the important issue of underlying word order. The third part is at a rather more theoretical level than the rest of the chapter; it is concerned with evidence for the existence of null arguments. Section 7 addresses the *pro*-drop question directly, while section 8 contains arguments distinguishing agreement morphology from clitics.

1.1. *The Phonemes; the Orthography*

The phonological system of Palauan has 16 phonemes: ten consonants and six vowels. These are charted in (1).[4]

(1) a. *Palauan consonants*

	bilabial	dental	alveolar	velar	glottal
stop: voiced	b				
voiceless				k	ʔ
fricative: voiced		d			
voiceless		t	s		
nasal	m			ŋ	
liquid			r, l		

b. *Palauan vowels*

	front	central	back
high	i		u
mid	e	ə	o
low		a	

There are some interesting synchronic oddities in the consonant inventory. Though Palauan has the voiced bilabial stop *b*, it does not have the less marked voiceless bilabial stop *p*. Historically, this is explained by the evolution of Proto-Austronesian (PAN) *p into Palauan *u* (*w* in Wilson (1972) and Flora (1974)). Similarly, Palauan has the nasals *m* and *ŋ* but not the less marked *n*; here, PAN *n > Palauan *l*.

The Palauan orthography employs letters corresponding to phonetic symbols in most cases. The inter-dental consonants are represented by **d** and **t**, the velar nasal by **ng**, and the glottal stop by **ch**. /ə/ and /e/ are not distinguished orthographically. On various decisions regarding the

24   CHAPTER TWO

orthography, see the Report of the Palau Orthography Committee (1972).

2. VERB MORPHOLOGY

Palauan verb morphology is extremely complex.[5] However, a proper understanding of certain aspects of this morphology is absolutely indispensable to understanding the description of Palauan syntax. In order to simplify this section, I will describe only transitive verbs, which participate in much of what is central to the later analysis; the transitive-intransitive distinction itself does not figure in the discussion (but see the discussion of passive in section 5). Tense is also largely ignored. The distinctions that we are interested in encode aspect, mood, and agreement with various arguments. (This description of verb morphology relies largely on Wilson 1972.)

2.1. *Morphological Aspect Marking*

Transitive verbs in Palauan occur in one of two morphological aspects, perfective or imperfective. An imperfective verb[6] contains a morpheme called the *imperfective marker* (IM), whose surface forms are -l-, -m-, or -ng-. The IM is derived historically from a single nasal (recall that Palauan *l* < Proto-Austronesian *n). The assimilation of this nasal to the initial consonant of the following root can still be observed in the surface forms of the IM.[7] Root-initial consonants delete following the IM, and are therefore not observed in imperfective verbs. Derivations of some imperfective forms are given in (3) below.

The great majority of imperfective verbs have a corresponding morphological perfective.[8] The perfective stem lacks the imperfective marker described in the last paragraph (the IM), but contains an object agreement suffix. This suffix may be considered the marker of perfective aspect. The object suffixes are given in (2).[9]

(2)   *Object agreement (perfective verbs)*

	Singular	Plural	
		Exclusive	Inclusive
1	-ak	-emam	-id
2	-au	-emiu	
3	-ii	-terir	

Object agreement is registered overtly when the referent of the object is, very loosely speaking, definite. *All* NPs referring to humans, even to indefinite and plural groups, and all NPs referring to a singular, definite non-human object are treated as a class by the syntax of object agree-

PALAUAN GRAMMAR

ment. Excluded from this class are indefinite and/or plural nonhuman objects. Thus any [+human] NP and any [+singular, +definite] NP triggers overt object agreement. Assuming that in Palauan all expressions referring to humans are presupposed to be definite, I will simply refer to the class of NPs corresponding to overt object agreement as 'definite', although this notion of definiteness departs from the notion of definite descriptions in logic (see, e.g., Russell 1905; Strawson 1950). Indefinite objects trigger zero agreement.

Both imperfective and perfective stems may contain another morpheme, called the *verb marker* (VM). The VM appears only in realis forms. In imperfectives the VM is a prefix whose surface form is **me-** ([mə]) or **o-**. In perfectives it metathesizes with the initial consonant, yielding an infixed **-m-** or **-o-** which usually undergoes further assimilation.[10]

Some derivations of imperfective and perfective verbs are given in (3) and (4).[11] On imperfective objects, see section 3 below. The perfective forms are given with both third singular and third plural object agreement.

(3) *Imperfective verb formation*

VM		IM		abstract or nominal root		
me	+	l	+	dang'	⇒	melang' 'find out'
me	+	l	+	tolketek	⇒	meleketek 'construct'
me	+	ng	+	'itakl	⇒	mengitakl 'sing'
me	+	ng	+	kang	⇒	mengang 'eat'
o	+	m	+	boes 'gun'	⇒	omoes 'shoot (at)'
o	+	m	+	bart	⇒	omart 'hide'

(4) *Perfect verb formation*

C_1...		VM		...root	Agr		
d-	+	o	+	-ang'	+ -ii (3sg)	⇒	dong'ii 'find (it) out'
d-	+	m	+	-ang'	+ -ø (3 pl)	⇒	dmang 'find (them) out'
k-	+	o	+	-al	+ -ii (3sg)	⇒	kolii 'eat (it)'
k-	+	m	+	-al	+ -ø (3 pl)	⇒	kma 'eat (them)'

Summing up to here, the marker of imperfectives is the IM, the marker of perfectives is object agreement, and both types contain the VM. The significance of these three morphemes to the syntactic analysis will soon become apparent.

2.2. *Subject Agreement*

Verbs of all types (including intransitives) carry an agreement prefix which registers the person and number features of the subject. (5) con-

26 CHAPTER TWO

tains the paradigm of realis subject agreement markers. The surface realization of these markers varies somewhat, due to phonological assimilation processes.

(5)   *Subject agreement (realis)*

	Singular	Plural	
		Excl	Incl
1	ak-	aki-	kede-
2	ke-	kom-	
3	ng-	te-	

The examples in (6) display realis subject agreement (glossed R):[12,13]

(6) a. ak-mo   er a katsudo
        R-1s-go P   movies

        I am going to the movies.

    b. ng-kiltmeklii a ulaol a Peter
        R-3s-clean-3s   floor

        Peter cleaned the floor.

    c. te-dilu   el kmo ng-ngera a retonari
        R-3p-said that   what   neighbors

        What did the neighbors say?

Subject agreement ((5) above) cooccurs with full NP subjects; when the subject is a pronoun, however, subject position is empty and only the agreement form surfaces. The examples in (7) illustrate these facts.

(7) a. ak-remurt (*ngak)   b. te-remurt a reme'as
        1s-run   I   *3p-run   women*

        I am running.   The women are running.

    c. ng-'illebed-ii a bilis (*ngii) d. ng-'illebed-ii a bilis a buik
        3s-hit-3s   dog   s/he   *3s-hit-3s   dog   boy*

        S/he hit the dog.   The boy hit the dog.

The significance of the complementarity of subject agreement and overt pronoun subjects is explored in section 7 below.

2.3. *Realis and Irrealis Mood Morphology*

The verb marker described above is most accurately characterized as a marker of realis mood. A verb that lacks this marker is irrealis.[14] Thus Palauan verbs register a distinction between realis and irrealis mood via

PALAUAN GRAMMAR

the presence or absence of the verb marker, henceforth referred to as the realis morpheme.[15] Realis morphology characterizes statements about realis events, as well as yes/no questions and some WH questions. See (6) above and the following; note that future tense is also marked realis.

(8) a. ng-ome'ar er a mlai a Willy?
   R-3s-buy   P   car

   Is Willy buying the car?

  b. ke-mle   er tia   er oingerang?
     R-2s-came P here P when

     When did you come here?

  c. ng-mo   er a ngebard er a klukuk
     R-3s-go P   west   P   tomorrow

     She's going to America tomorrow.

Among the factors that require *irrealis* verb morphology are negation, conditional (*if*-clause) statements, commands, and adverbials. Irrealis subject agreement morphemes are displayed in (9); grammatical number is not distinguished for second and third person:

(9)   *Subject agreement (irrealis)*

	Singular	Plural	
		Excl	Incl
1	ku-	kimo-	do-
2	('o)m(o)-		
3	l(e)-		

Examples of irrealis verbs (glossed IR) are in (10):

(10) a. ng-diak ku-nguiu   er a hong
      Neg   IR-1s-read P   book

      I am not reading the book.

   b. a lo-me'ar er a mlai, e   ng-omekall er ngii e oltak er kid
      IR-3-buy P   car   Ptc R-3s-drive P it   take P us

      If he buys a car, he'll take us for a ride.

   c. u'ei   er 'om-'iuii til'a el buk, e   beskak
      before P IR-2-read this L book Ptc IR-2-give-1s

      Before you read this book, give (it) to me.

28 CHAPTER TWO

(10) d. m-kimdeterir   a rengalek
      IR-2-cut.hair-3p   children

      Cut the children's hair!

The mood of the verb, based on the distribution of the realis morpheme, determines the form of subject agreement. In certain syntactic contexts, however, a realis verb carries no subject agreement. In contrast, an irrealis verb obligatorily takes one of the subject agreement affixes in (9). As a result, any one of four verb forms is possible in a transitive sentence: the perfective or imperfective realis form, possibly lacking subject agreement, or the perfective or imperfective irrealis form, on which subject agreement is always marked.[16] For example, from the abstract root **'uiu** 'read', the following (first-person) forms are derived:[17]

(11) a. (ak)menguiu   '(I'm) reading' (realis)
      /(ak) me- ng- 'uiu/
      Agr   VM   IM   read

     b. kunguiu   'I'm reading' (irrealis)
      /ku- ng- 'uiu/
      Agr   IM   read

     c. (ak) 'iuii   '(I) read' (realis)
      /(ak) 'uiu +o   -ii/
      Agr   read+VM Agr

     d. ku'iuii   'I read' (irrealis)
      /ku- 'uiu- ii/
      Agr   read Agr

The crucial fact about mood morphology is that it is used not only to encode semantically motivated mood distinctions, but also to reflect purely formal properties of the syntactic structures in which the verb occurs. This is discussed in Chapter Three.

3. VP STRUCTURE

There is little question that Palauan has a VP; given basic VOS order, the null hypothesis is that there is a VP. Further, the usual binding phenomena are observed:

(12)   ng-milamk er ngii$_i$ a Droteo$_i$
        3s-shave   P   3s

        Droteo shaved himself.

Such binding would be ungrammatical if there were not asymmetrical

PALAUAN GRAMMAR   29

c-command between the name and the pronoun. (See more on this in Chapters Five and Six.)

The VP, along with all other phrasal categories in Palauan, is head-initial. All subcategorized phrases follow the verb. Obliques and adverbial phrases either precede or follow the subject.

Object marking depends on the aspect of the verb. We have already seen that object suffixes appear on perfective verbs. In imperfective clauses, the verb stem registers no object agreement morphology; rather, the (notional) object of an imperfective verb may be realized as the object of the preposition **er** ([ər] or [r]). Direct objects occur as objects of a preposition in imperfective clauses under the same conditions that trigger object agreement in the perfective: when the objects are definite (in the sense described in section 2.1). Other objects are unmarked.

Er is Palauan's only preposition. It also appears in various oblique phrases. As an oblique marker, however, it is not sensitive to the definiteness of its object. That is, **er** in nonsubcategorized phrases never deletes.[18]

The examples in (13) through (15) illustrate the interaction of aspect and object marking within the verb phrase. First, compare object marking in the two types of clause:

(13) a. ak-uleldanges er a resensei er ngak
       1s-Im-honor   *P*   *teachers* *P* *me*

     I respected my teachers.

   b. ak-uldenges-terir a resensei er ngak
       1s-Pf-honor-3p   *teachers* *P* *me*

     I respected my teachers.

In the imperfective (13a), no object morphology is contained in the verb, and the logical object **a resensei er ngak** 'my teachers' is structurally the object of the preposition **er**. In the perfective (13b), in contrast, the verb bears the object agreement morpheme **-terir** 'third plural', and the object NP itself has no other marker.

Next, observe in (14) the effect of the definiteness of the object on the verb phrase morphology:

(14) a. ng-milengelebed er a bilis
       3s-Im-hit   *P*   *dog*

     S/he hit the dog.

   b. ng-milengelebed a bilis
       3s-Im-hit   *dog*

     S/he hit a dog/the dogs/some dog(s).

30   CHAPTER TWO

The object in (14a) is a definite NP, which is realized as object of the preposition; in (14b) the object is indefinite, nonhuman, so it has no grammatical marker. Finally, observe the definiteness effect in perfective clauses:

(15) a. te-'illebed-ii a bilis a rengalek
       3p-Pf-hit-3s   dog   children
       The kids hit the dog.

     b. te-'illebed a bilis a rengalek
        3p-Pf-hit-ø   dog   children
        The kids hit a dog/the dogs/some dog(s).

Third person singular object agreement on the verb in (15a) tells us that the object is definite, while lack of that agreement in (15b) marks the fact that the object is indefinite.

Pronominal objects may occur in clauses of either aspect. The definite pronominal objects of imperfective verbs are marked with **er**, as expected, and must be overt; the pronominal objects of perfective verbs trigger verb agreement, and must be silent:

(16) a. te-milengede'edu' er ngak a rrubak
        3p-Im-talked   P me   old.men
        The old men were talking to me.

     b. te-rirell-ii ø er a oingerang
        3p-Pf-made-3s P   when
        When did they build it?

The paradigm of full pronouns in Palauan is given in (17):

(17)   *Independent pronouns*

                Singular   Plural

                             Excl   Incl
        1   ngak   kemam   kid
        2   kau   kemiu
        3   ngii   tir

These pronouns occur not only as objects of the preposition but also in topic position.

The complementarity of overt and null pronouns extends to other NP positions; in section 7 I present a unified treatment of the conditions regulating the distribution of null and overt arguments.

PALAUAN GRAMMAR

4. NP STRUCTURE

Like VP and PP, NP is head-initial; both complement and specifier follow N, and relative clauses follow the head NP. Adjectives and other modifiers precede N, and are joined to the head by the connecting morpheme **el**.[19] Some examples of adjective-noun structures are in (18):

(18) a. bekeu el 'ad
brave L man

   b. ungil el 'elitakl
good L song

   c. obereberk el kai
flat   L shell

Either the head registers agreement with its specifier, or else the 'possessor' surfaces as the object of the preposition **er**. This is seen in (19):

(19) a. [$_{NP}$ a 'im-al   a Dan]
hand-3s

   Dan's hand

   b. [$_{NP}$ a 'im-al]

   his hand

   c. [$_{NP}$ a buk   er a 'ekabil]
book P   girl

   the girl's book

   d. [$_{NP}$ a buk er ngii]
her

   her book

   e. [$_{NP}$ a telemall]
PPrt-destroy

   the destruction

   f. [$_{NP}$ a telemall er a Oreor]
P   Koror

   the destruction of Koror

As the examples in (19b) and (19d) show, a pronoun possessor is silent in case the head agrees with it, and overt when it is object of the preposition.

A relative clause contains no relative pronoun; it immediately follows the head, and is introduced by **el**:

(20) [$_{NP}$ a 'ad [el   mil'er-ar tia   el buk]]
man Comp Pf-buy-3s Dem L book

   the man who bought this book

4.1. a

It will have been observed that the morpheme **a** has a rather complicated distribution. In the examples immediately above it precedes NPs but not pronouns, and in (10) it precedes NPs and the conditional clause

32   CHAPTER TWO

((10b)) but not a NP with a demonstrative specifier (**til'a el buk** 'this
book' in (10c)). Leaving aside (10b) for the moment, **a** seems never to
mark verbs. The correct generalization appears to be, then, that **a** marks
full NPs, including NPs with lexical subjects (e.g. (19a)), but not pronouns, and does not cooccur with demonstratives.

Let us assume for now that **a** is a marker of full NPs (in complementary distribution with demonstratives), though it is not a marker of
definiteness. This provisional account hardly captures the full distribution of **a** or its real significance in the grammar, however. In Chapter
Three I will propose that the distribution of **a** extends to nominalized
clauses (of which the conditional in (10b) is one), and show that the
nominalization analysis is central to the analysis of a wide range of
syntactic phenomena.

Finally, note that **a** marks *all* NP positions; it cannot, therefore, be
construed as a case marker or a preposition.

With the details of verb morphology, VP structure, and NP structure
in these sections as background, we are now ready to examine the
important question of the order of constituents in the clause.

5. WORD ORDER

In Josephs' *Grammar* (Josephs 1975), the underlying order of constituents in Palauan sentences is described as subject-verb-object. The
SVO analysis of this language, however, fails to account for a number of
important phenomena. This section will explore the question of order in
some depth, for two reasons. First, the issue of word order involves the
analysis of a broad range of contructions. And second, the analysis of
variable binding, which is our main focus, depends upon the resolution
of the word order issue. The arguments in this section may also provide
a model for arguing for a particular basic constituent order in languages
that present heterogeneous surface configurations. The section concludes
that the simplest and most revealing analysis of Palauan word order is
that it is VOS.

5.1. *Josephs' SVO Analysis*

First, let us briefly review how the SVO analysis is constructed (Josephs
1975, Ch. 17, relying on Wilson 1972). There are two aspects of
Josephs' account of Palauan word order to be considered here: order-
changing rules per se, and the analysis of the so-called passive. The
discussion below is essentially pretheoretical.

Josephs observes that the structures paired in (21) and (22) are
equally productive:

PALAUAN GRAMMAR

33

(21) a. a Droteo a mla mei   'Droteo has come'

     b. ng mla mei a Droteo

(22) a. a ralm a mekelekolt   'The water is cold'

     b. ng mekelekolt a ralm

He analyzes them as follows: The (a) sentences, with subject-first order, are basic. The (b) sentences, with verb-first order, are derived from the (a) sentences by a proposed rule of *subject shifting*, which moves the subject rightward and leaves behind a "pronominal trace" (**ng** here).[20] The morpheme **a**, which (for Josephs) normally marks NPs and VPs, exceptionally does not appear when there is a pronominal trace before the VP. In this respect, the trace patterns like other non-emphatic pronoun subjects (the forms in (5)), which also suppress the appearance of **a**.

Subject shifting is only one of the reordering processes that must be posited in the SVO analysis. Another is *preposing of possessor* (Josephs 17.3), which operates on the output of subject shifting if the subject is a possessed NP. This rule moves the possessor of the (shifted) subject back to pre-verbal position, where it replaces the pronominal trace. The examples in (23) are from Josephs:

(23) a. [a 'imal   a Droteo] a meringel   (SS) ⇒
        hand-3s   *hurt*

     b. ng meringel [a 'imal   a Droteo]   (PP) ⇒
        hurt   *hand-3s*

     c. a Droteo a meringel [a 'imal   ____]
               hurt   *hand-3s*

     Droteo's hand hurts.

Josephs claims that subject shifting and possessor preposing are widespread in Palauan grammar, and that subject shifting is obligatory with certain predicates (17.4). The (a) sentences and the (b) sentences of (21) and (22) are synonymous for most speakers, according to Josephs, but speakers who detect a meaning difference are reported to use the "normal" word order ((a) sentences) "to express new or unexpected information" (p. 337) and the (b) sentences to "merely confirm that something expected has happened" (p. 89).

The analysis so far is odd in certain respects. First, the distribution of the morpheme **a** is not accounted for. In Josephs' account, **a** occurs as a marker of NPs and VPs (p. 46). But in (21) through (23), it does not occur before the predicate in the (b) sentences. Rather, the "pronominal trace" occurs where **a** would be expected. If **a** marks VPs, however, the

34   CHAPTER TWO

fact that it does not appear before the "trace" should be explained. Though small, this morpheme is ubiquitous; its function and importance will become clear in Chapter Three.

A second problem is that, although Josephs claims that any transitive or intransitive sentence can undergo subject shifting (p. 337), all of the examples adduced are intransitive (including numerous examples with obligatorily possessed NP predicates like **soal** 'his liking' and **'etil** 'his disliking'). Depending on the way in which Josephs' rule is formulated, subjects could shift to a position between the verb and the object in a transitive sentence. VOS clauses are possible in Palauan, however, but VSO clauses are not.[21] Josephs' analysis thus predicts both VOS and VSO structure-types, though the latter occurs only marginally. In fact, there is no account here at all of the possibility of VOS sentences (transitive sentences derived by subject shifting), which are common surface structures.

Third, subject shifting is "obligatory" in many of Josephs' examples, but not in others; no account of the obligatory cases is given (see Josephs 1984). If SVO order is basic, however, then certain subject NPs must be attributed a special feature which requires them to shift rightward. In the VOS hypothesis, subjects are expected to be final, so the "obligatory" cases themselves would not be a problem. The VOS hypothesis then has to explain why these subjects do not topicalize. In fact, though, all these cases involve obligatorily possessed **reng-** idioms expressing psychological states; order (and meaning) in these expressions is frozen:

(24) a. ng-ungil a renguk   b. ng-klou a rengul
        3s-good   heart-1s   *3s-big   heart-3s*

        I'm happy.   He's calm.

     c. ng-sme'er a rengud
        3s-sick   heart-1p

        We're lonely.

Analogous sentences in reverse order are interpreted literally, and are rejected:

(25) a. *a renguk a ungil (My heart is good)

     b. *a rengul a klou (His heart is big)

     c. *a rengud a sme'er (Our heart is sick)

The fact that the grammatical expressions are subject-final is, of course, damaging to the SVO analysis.

Finally, and perhaps most tellingly, all the examples of possessor

PALAUAN GRAMMAR

preposing move an NP out of a (shifted) subject. Implicit in Josephs' analysis is the claim that, since only subjects shift, only possessors of subjects may 'return' to sentence-initial position. Possessors of direct objects or other nonsubjects are not mentioned. The problem here is that Josephs' presentation makes predictions which are not borne out by further investigation. In fact, the grammaticality of preposing of possessors of nonsubjects (illustrated below) represents a problem for this analysis, and shows that an important generalization has been missed.

I will return to these observations below, and demonstrate their significance to the VOS hypothesis. First, we must look at another construction involving word order in Josephs' analysis, the passive.

5.2. *Josephs' Passive*

Josephs identifies as passive the sentence types in (26b) and (27b). These sentences are derived from "actives" in his SVO analysis (19.7), in the following way: The underlying object is preposed to sentence-initial position, leaving a "pronominal trace" if it is marked with the preposition **er**. The underlying subject shifts to sentence-final position, and triggers irrealis agreement on the verb. (This is essentially the analysis of Wilson (1972, pp. 144—8)). Note that this is a different type of subject shifting from that described above, which has different properties (the earlier rule does not trigger irrealis agreement, etc.). Some putative active-passive pairs are seen below (= Josephs' (32), (33)):

(26) a. a ngalek a menga er a ngikel   ⇒
      child   R-eat P   fish
      The child is eating the fish.

    b. a ngikel a lo-nga   er ngii a ngalek
       fish   IR-3-eat P it   child
       The fish is being eaten by the child

(27) a. a sensei a mengelebed er a rengalek ⇒
      teacher   R-hit   P   children
      The teacher is hitting the children.

    b. a rengalek a lo-ngelebed er tir   a sensei
       children   IR-3-hit   P them   teacher
       The children are being hit by the teacher.

In the (b) sentences, the subject is shifted rightward (but does not otherwise receive any special marker) and the object is preposed. A

36   CHAPTER TWO

pronominal trace fills the original position of the object (**ngii** in (25b)
and **tir** in (26b)), and the irrealis verb agrees with the shifted NP (the
subject). The (b) sentences are glossed in terms of passive meaning.

Again, this analysis leaves quite a bit unexplained. The fact that the
passive verb takes irrealis form is unusual, but perfectly possible. Its
agreement with the 'old' subject, now the postposed agent, is more
unusual, if the preverbal NP is really the surface subject. Oddest of all is
the fact that the verb is morphologically transitive. The sentences in
(26b) and (27b) contain imperfective transitive verbs (recall the discussion of verb morphology at 2). In (28) below are sentences (also taken
from Josephs) containing perfective transitive verbs that register agreement with the (deep) direct object:

(28) a. a tole'oi a l-ulekerng-ii   a 'errode'   (=Josephs (39))
        baby   *IR-3-wake-3s*   *noise*

      The baby was awakened by the noise.

      b. a hong a k-bils-**terir**   a rese'elik
         book   *IR-1s-give-3p*   *friends-1s*

      The book was given by me to my friends.

Object agreement on perfective verbs indicates that these verbs assign
accusative case, i.e., they are transitive.

Josephs observes further that not only objects, but locatives and other
oblique NPs can be passivized (=Josephs (44), (45)):

(29) a. a tereter a l-se'er   er ngii a ngelekek
        cold   *IR-3-sick P it*   *child-1s*

      It's a cold that my child is sick with.

      (A cold is being sick by my child. (?))

      b. a kerrekar a le-silebek er ngii a belo'el
         tree   *IR-3-fly   P it*   *pigeon*

      The tree was flown out of by the pigeon.

These two examples, and others like them, Josephs considers unusual for
passives because they are intransitive, and because the "trace" **ngii**
follows the *oblique* preposition **er** rather than the *object* preposition **er**
(cf. note 18).

Finally, the broad range of grammatical relations that can be passivized (for Josephs) includes NPs originating in embedded complements. The examples in (30) occur in my field notes, and are similar to
those analyzed by Josephs as passive (I gloss these examples with active
English sentences, and coindex the two related positions):

PALAUAN GRAMMAR
37

(30) a. a buk$_i$ a ldilu   a Rebes el kmo a Merii a
      book   *IR-3-said*   *Comp*

     milnguiu   er ngii$_i$
     R-IM-read   *P*   *it*

     Rebes said that Merii was reading the book.

   b. a skuul$_i$ a ldilu   a Nina el kmo ngmilngiil er a
      school   *IR-3-said*   *Comp*   *R-3s-wait*   *P*

     ngelkel el   mo er ngii$_i$
     child-3s Comp go   *to*   *it*

     Nina said she was waiting for her son to go to school.

   c. kid$_i$ a lullasem el   lomekdakt er kid$_i$
     us   *IR-3-try Comp IR-3-scare P us*

     They're trying to scare US!

It is not necessary, or particularly relevant, to enter into a theoretically technical analysis of passive here, where pretheoretical comments on passive will suffice to show the shortcomings of Josephs' proposals. These comments and the following section will establish the VOS analysis beyond reasonable doubt.

The traditionally designated passive constructions in the world's languages are usually characterized as having some subset of the following properties: (a) they are superficially intransitive (or participial); (b) they are related to structures containing a (notional) direct object (or perhaps an indirect object, in the case of verbs that subcategorize two NP objects); (c) the (notional) object takes on the subject relation; (d) passives are 'clausebound' constructions; (e) the agent, if expressed, is marked with oblique case; and (f) passive morphology is present. While none of these properties is *necessary* to the passive construction (except, perhaps, c), they are all nevertheless *compatible* with it and widely instantiated. The examples in (26), (27), and (28), however, have *none* of these properties. They are transitive; the derived subject may originate in any of a wide range of NP positions; the preposed NP does not have the properties expected of subjects (see the discussion of Waters 1979, immediately below); the dependency may extend over several clauses; the agent receives no oblique case marking, even though such marking is possible in Palauan; and there is no particularly passive morphology (nor are the verb forms participial). Thus, if the sentences in (26) through (30) are passive, they are, at the least, highly irregular typologically. In addition, Josephs' passive movement regularly leaves what appears to be a resumptive pronoun — otherwise an unattested effect (and in theory impossible) in passives. (These resumptive pronouns figure prominently in the A´ binding discussions in following chapters.)

38 CHAPTER TWO

Typological considerations, then, suggest that these sentences are not passive. How, then, should their word order be accounted for, and what is their relation to the structures represented by (26a) and (27a)? All the objections above are made in terms of Josephs' own analysis. Another sort of criticism of the SVO analysis is perhaps more important, the fact that there is a far more elegant and general account of Palauan surface phenomena, that based on underlying VOS order. Waters (1979) suggests an approach to this account, in a counteranalysis based on the recognized properties of subjects, to which I now turn. Waters' conclusion that Josephs' "passives" are topicalizations sets the stage for the analysis of A′ binding in the next chapter.

5.3. Waters' Analysis

Waters' (1979) rebuttal to Josephs begins with these assumptions: If the relevant structures in (26) through (30) are passives, then their subjects should participate in the syntactic phenomena that refer to *subjects*. On the other hand, if these structures are topicalizations, the preposed NPs should act like *topics* with respect to other syntactic phenomena. Waters first demonstrates that the proposed NP in (26b), (27b), (28) or (29) does not undergo Josephs' proposed subject shifting rule. He then shows that the pattern of agreement on perfective verbs (see, e.g., (28b)) "continues" to register the features of the postposed NP as if it were the subject and the features of the preposed NP as if it were the direct object. (This last observation holds only for structures in which the preposed NP was a direct object underlyingly.) Finally, Waters establishes that a completely different construction, which Josephs calls the "ergative", has all the characteristics that are expected of true passives.[22] This "ergative" involves a verb form which contains the realis marker (the "verb marker") and the root, but none of the aspectual markers (or object agreement morphemes) found on transitive verbs. This construction is intransitive and may contain an agent marked with the preposition **er**.[23] "Ergative" subjects have the syntactic behavior characteristic of subjects (which Waters illustrates in control and causative constructions, for example), and feed other processes referring to subjects (including "subject shifting", and agreement in a wide range of clause types). Some examples of this form (glossed PASS) are in (31):

(31) a. a buk   er ngii a mil'uiu   er a rokui el ngalek er a skuul
       book P her   PASS-read P   all   L child P   school
       Her book was read by all the students.

   b. komlomedakt er a drumk
       2s-PASS-scare P   thunder
       Were you frightened by the thunder?

PALAUAN GRAMMAR

(31) c. a babier el lil'esii   a sensei a mildul   er a bulis
      letter   L   IR-wrote-it   teacher   PASS-burn P   police

The letter the teacher wrote was burned by the police.

     d. a Merii a mil'elebed er a redil   er a Kuam
              PASS-hit   P   woman   P

Merii got beat up by a woman from Guam.

     e. ngmla   mekang   a kall
        3s-PST PASS-eat   food

The food got eaten up.

Returning to (26b) and (27b), Waters concludes that these sentences are actually derived from (26a) and (27a) by a topicalization rule. In other words, he motivates a grammar of Palauan in which underlying word order is VOS and there is both a topicalization rule (= Josephs' passive) and a passive rule (= Josephs' ergative). Compare the sentences in (32) below. (32a) illustrates Waters' topicalization, while (32b) illustrates Waters' passive:

(32) a. a rengalek a lo-ngelebed er tir   a sensei
        children   IR-3-hit   P them   teacher

The children, the teacher is hitting them.

     b. a rengalek a mil'elebed er a sensei
        children   PASS-hit   P   teacher

The children were hit by the teacher.

Note also how Waters' analysis deals with the examples in (33), in which the preverbal NP is a possessor. The possibility of sentences like these calls into question the order-changing rule called possessor preposing ((23) above), because in both cases the possessor is extracted from a nonsubject. Being irrealis, the examples are more like Josephs' passive; but if they are passive, then all the objections made above apply to them. If they are viewed as topicalization structures in which a possessor has been topicalized, on the other hand, they raise no problems for either analysis (other properties of these structures are discussed in Chapter Three):

(33) a. a Naomi a le'ilitii   a 'ole'esel a John
             IR-3-throw-3s   pencil-3s

John threw away Naomi's pencil.

     b. a rubak   a k'iliuii   a buk er ngii
        old.man   IR-1s-read-3s   book P him

I read the old man's book.

40   CHAPTER TWO

To complete the contrast between the two analyses, I insert here the demonstration that VOS sentences, and topicalization based on a VOS structure, are grammatical, but VSO sentences are not (see also Chapter Six):

(34) a. ngulemekeroul a bung   a delak   er a sersel
     R-3s-grow   *flowers*   *mother-1s* P   *garden-3s*

   b. a delak a ulemekeroul a bung ____ er a sersel

   c. *ngulemekeroul a delak a bung er a sersel

   My mother was growing flowers in her garden.

To sum up, the topicalization process proposed by Waters does not alter grammatical relations, while the passive rule is relation-changing. Both rules behave as they are expected to from a cross-linguistic point of view. Waters' analysis thus allows a unified account of a range of sentence types, and I will assume in what follows that Waters' analysis is correct.

In the view of Palauan grammar developed by Waters, underlying word order is VOS. The structures that Josephs derives from underlying SVO sentences by subject shifting, possessor preposing, and a purported passive are instead accounted for by a single rule of topicalization operating on underlyingly VOS sentences. In addition to its greater simplicity, this analysis accounts for many of the properties of sentences left unexplained in Josephs' treatment. For example, the (b) sentences of (21) through (23) simply have basic verb-initial order. The verb in these sentences bears the usual subject agreement morphology. The particle **a** nominalizes a clause that is preceded by a topic (see Chapter Three), and topicalization may affect any NP, regardless of grammatical function. The pronominal "trace" is a resumptive pronoun.

Waters was primarily concerned to establish his passive hypothesis, however, and not to present arguments concerning word order in general. In Chapter Three I will flesh out the topicalization analysis begun by Waters, and extend this analysis to a description of all Palauan variable binding, viewed as a natural class. This extension to a large class of structures will considerably strengthen the VOS analysis introduced here.

5.4. *Other Ordering Considerations*

It has been observed, first by Ross (1967), that reordering of phrases most commonly takes place in main clauses, and that embedded clauses are better indicators of a language's basic word order. Certainly study of a variety of dependent clause types is necessary before arriving at

PALAUAN GRAMMAR 41

conclusions about basic word order (cf. word order studies in German). Although Palauan embedded clauses may contain a topic (subject or nonsubject) or a preposed WH phrase, they typically have VOS or verb-initial and subject-final order. Examples of this are seen in (35) (dependent clauses are bracketed):

(35) a. a babier [el   lil'esii   a sensei] a mildul   er a bulis
         letter   Comp IR-write   teacher   PASS-burn P   police

    The letter the teacher wrote was burned by the police.

   b. akulmes er a buk   [el   lulme'ar er ngii Donna er a Sie]
      R-1s-see P   book Comp IR-3-buy P it   P

    I was looking at the book that Donna bought from Sie.

   c. akmilnguiu er a buk   [er sei   er a lemei   a Moses]
      R-1s-3-read P   book P when P   IR-come

    I was reading a book when Moses came.

   d. 'omomdasu [e   ngmilskak   a ngera a Ioseb er a skuul]
      IR-2-think   Comp R-3s-give-me   what?   P   school

    What do you think Joseph gave me at school?

   e. ngte'a a lilsang   a Peter [el   lulengelebed er
      who   IR-3-see   Comp IR-3-hit   P

    ngii   a Mary]
    him/her

    Who did Peter see Mary hit?

   f. ngomdasu [el kmo ngmo me'ar er a bilas a ngelekel a
      R-3s-think Comp   R-go R-buy P   boat   child-3s

    se'elik]
    friend-1s

    He thinks that my friend's boy will buy the boat.

As an addendum to the language-specific or construction-specific considerations relating to word order above, some weight should be given to the fact that the linguistic subgroup to which Palauan belongs, Western Austronesian, is predominantly verb-initial. The Philippine languages and languages like Malagasy, Chamorro, and Toba Batak are all verb-initial. That is, the properties of Palauan syntax correlate to a very high degree with the observed properties of other languages in its linguistic phylum. (For further discussion of the properties that Palauan shares with its relatives and with other verb-initial languages, see Georgopoulos 1984.)

42 CHAPTER TWO

I do not include here, in this descriptive chapter, the strong theory-internal support for VOS order found in the lack of ECP asymmetries; for that evidence, see Chapter Six.

6. COMPLEMENTATION

Palauan has a number of complementizers, among which the most common are **el** and **el kmo**. The complementizer **el** introduces relative clauses, sentential subjects, control and raising complements, and various adjuncts, such as purpose clauses. The complementizer **el kmo** incorporates the quotative **kmo** (related to **dmu** 'say, tell'), and introduces the sentential objects of some "bridge verbs" (Erteschik-Shir 1973) like 'tell', 'hear', 'ask', 'think', and 'know'. However, many of the verbs allowing a sentential complement introduced by **el kmo** may take **el** instead, and it is not clear what considerations underlie the choice here. The complementizer **el ua sei** may appear in the place of **el kmo**; these two complementizers appear to be interchangeable. In addition to **el** and **el kmo**, complementizer-like roles are sometimes played by the conjunctions **e** and **me**. Some examples of clausal complementation are in (36).

(36) a. ng'emolt [el ngoltoir er a Tmerukl a Latii]
     3s-clear Comp R-3s-love P
     It's clear that Latii loves Tmerukl.

   b. akumdasu [el kmo te'illebedii a rubak a rebuik
     1s-think Comp R-3p-hit-3s old.man boys
     I think the boys hit the old man.

   c. akmedakt [el mo er a ngebard]
     1s-afraid Comp R-go P west
     I'm afraid to go to the States.

   d. akumdasu [e ngsoal ngak]
     1s-think Comp 3s-like me
     I think he likes me.

The NPs **a lsekum** 'if' and **a ulekum** 'if only' are employed as interrogative and conditional complementizers, respectively, although **el kmo** may also head interrogative complements (see also Chapter Five).

(37) a. nguleker [a lsekum a Yuki ngmla lu'esii a babier]
     3s-asked if 3s-Pst IR-3-wrote letter
     He asked if Yuki had written the letter.

PALAUAN GRAMMAR   43

(37) b. ngsebe'em   el   melang' [el kmo ngte'a a
      3s-ability-2s Comp guess   Comp who

      ngklel   a be'il   a Roy]
      name-3s spouse-3s

      Can you guess what Roy's wife's name is?

7. NULL ARGUMENTS

Let us review here what we have learned about the distribution of null
arguments in Palauan. By 'null arguments' I refer to pronouns that are
part of the semantic interpretation of a sentence but which have no
lexical or phonological content (below I consider their syntactic status).
First, we have seen (Section 2.2) that pronoun subjects trigger verb-
subject agreement but are themselves null:

(38) a. ng-remurt (*ngii)
      3s-run   he

      He is running.

   b. ak-umes er kau (*ngak)
      1s-see   P you   I

      I'm looking at you.

Within VP, we saw (Section 3) that overt object pronouns alternate
with agreement forms: when verb-object agreement is present object
position is empty, and when object position is marked by the preposition
er the object is overt:

(39) a. te-'illebed-ii (*ngii)
      3p-hit-3s   s/he

      They hit him/her/it.

   b. ak-ultir-au (*kau)
      1s-love-2s   you

      I love you.

   c. ak-umes er kau (*ak-umes er *pro*) (*akumes)
      1s-see   P you

      I'm looking at you.

Recall that these remarks hold for *pronominal* objects; object agreement cooccurs with full NPs (see Section 3).

In NPs the situation is like that in VPs: the pronoun argument that is
agreed with is null, while a pronoun that is the object of **er** is overt
(Section 4). (The examples in (40d, e) illustrate that obligatorily pos-

44 CHAPTER TWO

sessed nouns referring to body parts may function as prepositions in Palauan. This type of NP has the same properties as other NPs.)

(40) a. [NP a ngokel ____]
      flute-3s

   her flute

b. [NP a 'ermek ____ el bilis]
      pet-1s   *L dog*

   my dog

c. [NP a sensei er ngak]
      teacher P me

   my teacher

d. [NP a uriul   a Roy]
      back-3s

   behind Roy

e. [NP a uriul   ____]
      back-3s

   behind him

The generalization that immediately suggests itself is that agreement forms and overt pronouns are in complementary distribution in Palauan. Such a generalization depends on a distinction between agreement forms and pronouns, which will be motivated in the next section. Here I will assume that the distinction is valid, and confine this section to exploration of the hypothesis that the distribution of null pronouns varies with the distribution of agreement morphology. This hypothesis, in some form, is the focus of much current work. I will also establish, along the way, that Palauan is a *pro*-drop language. The interest of this fact will be seen in the next chapter, where I argue that what appear to be WH traces in Palauan A' binding are actually instances of the null pronoun *pro*.

As pointed out in Chapter One, formal variation among languages is attributed in generative grammar to variation in the settings of certain parameters of Universal Grammar. One suggested parameter is called the *pro*-drop parameter: the ability of some languages to have null subjects (*pro*) in finite clauses. This property has been linked to the ability of the I(nflection) node to 'identify' the empty category it governs in subject position. That is, I in some languages, via its overt agreement features or in some other way, licenses empty subjects (Taraldsen 1978b; Chomsky 1982; Jaeggli 1985; Rizzi 1986).

If sanctioning of empty categories somehow correlates with agreement inflection, then it is obvious that not only subject empty categories but

PALAUAN GRAMMAR

also empty categories in other positions are possible in many languages. McCloskey and Hale (1984), for example, describe the occurrence of *pro* in a variety of syntactic positions in Modern Irish; here, *pro* cooccurs with agreement. Morphology does not seem to be the whole story, however. Hoji (1985), for example, points out that *pro* can occur in Japanese in any position in which an overt pronoun can occur; Japanese has no agreement morphology, however. In the recent literature other languages and construction types have been described which allow *pro* in the absence of identifying morphology.

At first glance, Palauan seems to be the paradigm example of a language in which the identification hypothesis is instantiated. Person and number agreement allow identification of null pronouns in several positions: subject, perfective direct object, and subject of NP. There are, however, systematic cases in which the correlation of null pronouns and agreement breaks down, cases in which an empty pronoun cannot be related to any inflectional form. One such case is that of indefinite direct objects, discussed in Section 3 (examples (14) and (15), repeated below). In perfective clauses, agreement with these objects can be argued to be zero, since non-agreeing forms alternate with agreeing forms. But in imperfective clauses, neither agreement (since imperfective clauses *never* have object agreement) nor the prepositional marker **er** is present in such cases. Still, in both perfective and imperfective clauses, the object can be null:

(14) a. ng-milengelebed er a bilis
     3s-Im-hit   *P*   *dog*
     S/he hit the dog.

    b. ng-milengelebed a bilis
     3s-Im-hit   *dog*
     S/he hit a dog/the dogs/some dog(s).

(14)′ ng-milsa   ____ a Sabeth
     3s-Im-saw(gave)   (note homonymy of *milsa*)
     Sabeth saw (gave away) something.

(15) a. te-'illebed-ii a bilis a rengalek
     3p-Pf-hit-3s   *dog*   *children*
     The kids hit the dog.

    b. te-'illebed a bilis a rengalek
     3p-Pf-hit-ø   *dog*   *children*
     The kids hit a dog/the dogs/some dog(s).

46   CHAPTER TWO

(15)′   te-'illebed ____
         The kids hit them/something.

Another case where identification fails is in VPs headed by the
double object verb **msa** 'give'. This verb agrees with the *goal* argument
(the one to whom the transferred object is given) rather than the *theme*
(the transferred object).[24] Both theme and goal can be null, however,
even though no agreement is associated with the theme:

(41) a. ngmilskak   a ungil el kliou   a Cello
         3s-Pf-gave-1s   good L dessert

         Cello gave me the good pastry.

     b. akmilsa   a demal   a Miriam
         1s-Pf-gave-3s   father-3s

         I gave it to Miriam's father.

     c. akmilsang   ____ ____
         1s-Pf-gave-3s

         I gave it to her/him.

Finally, we should take into account the morphology of the irregular
perfective verbs like **nguu** 'take', **loia** 'put', and **muut** 'pile up' (see the
list in (54)), which have no overt object agreement forms for third
person singular but nevertheless allow null objects. None of these verbs
can be said to 'identify' their third person objects. In all these cases,
the possibility of zero agreement could not satisfy the identification
requirement.

In the terms of Huang (1984), an empty position with no agreement
to identify it is problematic. Huang suggests that this "zero form" is not
pro at all, but a variable bound by an empty topic. Variables are not
subject to identification in GB (pace Cinque 1984), since the features of
WH gaps are provided ultimately by the moved element, the A′ antecedent. But this zero form in Palauan (that claimed to be *pro*) does not
have the properties of a variable; in particular, it does not trigger WH
agreement, an agreement rule which applies in the A′ binding domain
only (described in the next chapter). WH agreement is only triggered by
variables bound by an A′ binder within the sentence.

Huang's project of accounting for some null arguments in terms of
coindexing with (i.e. licensing by) an empty operator has been questioned by a number of researchers, including Li (1985), Whitman
(1985), and Xu and Langendoen (1985). All of these authors argue that
the zero forms that Huang interprets as variables are actually null pronominals; they present convincing arguments that languages completely

PALAUAN GRAMMAR 47

lacking in agreement morphology, such as Chinese and Japanese (see Whitman), nevertheless exhibit *pro*. In sum, the correlation between agreement and *pro*-drop remains "imprecise" (Chomsky 1982, p. 86; see also Chomsky 1981, p. 241).

Despite the initial appearance of support for the identification approach to null pronouns, therefore, Palauan ultimately argues against the simplicity of this approach. Even if we were to refer to null agreement as satisfying identification, the hypothesis would thereby be trivialized.

A more elaborated theory has been described in Chapter One, that of Rizzi (1986). This theory requires parameterization of governing properties of heads; I assume a theory for *pro* along these lines. It seems obvious that government theory, and not surface morphology, is the appropriate basis for a theory of the distribution of null pronouns. Note that in a theory like Rizzi's the set of 'identification' features can be null, and the facts of surface morphology in a language are subsumed under the interpretive condition. The failure of identification over the range of cases described above supports an approach on which null pronouns are licensed not by agreement features but by the heads of the categories they appear in, like any other arguments, and subject to typological (parametric) variation.[25] Current research into the contexts allowing *pro* will eventually clarify the principles according to which languages choose the sets of heads that do and do not license null arguments.

It is probable, however, that other contextual features will figure in the ultimate theory of *pro*. That is, the referential features of *pro* can be built up compositionally. An example is the Palauan device of withdrawing object marking to indicate indefiniteness: the greater context indicates unambiguously that in these cases the *pro* object has the features [−human, −definite, +3]. This device does not depend on the choice of licensing head alone. Another source of information about *pro* is, of course, the *lexical* content of the head. See Jackendoff (1987, p. 385), where it is suggested that the verb adds its selectional features to the interpretation of *pro*. Similarly for the selectional information available for complements of verbs like 'give', independently of which argument triggers agreement.

In sum, Palauan does allow null pronouns and it does have rich agreement, but the occurrence of the former, surprisingly, does not depend on the latter.[26]

Another property hypothesized of *pro*-drop languages is "long" movement of the subject (see, e.g., Chomsky 1981; Pesetsky 1982a). The Palauan sentences in (42) exhibit this property. In (42a), the subject of the most embedded clause is WH extracted, in (42b) it is topicalized, and in (42c) it is relativized. Note that the extraction clause is introduced by an overt complementizer in each case:

48 CHAPTER TWO

(42) a. ngte'a$_i$ [ledilu a sensei [el kmo ngmilsa
who *3-Pf-say* *teacher* *Comp* *3s-Pf-saw*

[el meskak a buk ___$_i$]]]
Comp *Pf-give-1s* *book*

Who did the teacher say that he saw give me the book?

b. a John$_i$ [a ledilu a Ioseb$_j$ [el kmo ngmilngiil er a blai$_k$
3-say *Comp* *3s-Im-wait* *P* *house*

[el lebo loruul er ngii$_k$ ___$_i$]]]
Comp *3-Fut* *3-Im-do* *P* *it*

John$_i$, Joseph$_j$ said that he$_j$ was waiting for the house$_k$ that
(he$_i$) is going to build (it$_k$).

c. a Naomi a redil$_i$ [el Philip a mle medengelii
woman *Comp* *Pst* *Pf-know-3s*

[el kmo ngulsis'akl er a klas ___$_i$]]
Comp *3s-Im-teach* *P* *class*

Naomi is the woman who Philip knew that ____ was teaching
the class.

Whatever the analysis of the *Comp*-trace effect (e.g. failure of c-
command from Comp, à la Chomsky 1981, Kayne 1981; or failure of
government by minimality, à la Chomsky 1986b), the trace in subject
position in these examples is not properly governed from within the
projection of C. The sentences are grammatical, however, demonstrating
that the empty category in subject position is sanctioned somehow by the
grammar, that is, it is licensed independently (see the discussion in
Chapter Three).

7.1. *The Structural Existence of* pro

I have described *pro* as a null argument, semantically necessary but
phonologically empty. What, then, ensures the *syntactic*, structural existence of *pro*? There are several sorts of answer to this question. Some
depend on theory-internal considerations, such as the Projection Principle, and others on empirical considerations, such as the distributional
facts of NPs in Palauan.

First, the conditions governing the distribution of empty pronominals
can be stated syntactically (see above and Chapter One). Since their
presumed distribution corresponds to conditions statable naturally in
terms of the theory, the view is supported that they are structurally
represented.

More importantly, the Projection Principle requires that all positions

PALAUAN GRAMMAR

receiving a θ-role be present at every level of representation. Assuming extension of the Projection Principle to the subject, all θ-marked positions are syntactically present. By the principle of predication (Rothstein 1983; Chomsky 1986a), every VP has an external argument. Thus the syntactic presence of both referring (θ-marked) and pleonastic (θ') *pro* is guaranteed, in theory.

Beyond the Projection Principle, the following considerations argue that *pro* has a syntactic reality. First, pronominal interpretation alternates with overt, full NPs:

(43) a. a 'ole'es-em ＿＿＿＿   'your pencil'
   pencil-2s

    b. a 'ole'es-el a Marta   'Martha's pencil'
   pencil-3s

    c. ak-mil'er-ar ＿＿＿＿   'I bought it'
   1s-bought-3s

    d. ak-mil'er-ar a mlai   'I bought the car'
                 car

    e. ng-mil'er-ar a mlai ＿＿＿＿   'He bought the car'
   3s

    f. ng-mil'er-ar a mlai a Kasta   'Costa bought the car'

The full NPs in such expressions are interpreted as selected arguments, implying the same status for pronominals. In the cases in (43), both full NPs and null arguments are related to agreement forms; that is, there is no complementarity between overt NPs and inflection, as is found, for example, in Breton (Anderson 1982). If there were, it would be reasonable to argue that the agreement forms are in fact the arguments in question. But since the agreement morpheme is not the argument when a full NP is present,[27] there is no reason to expect it to be so elsewhere.

Another flaw in taking inflectional morphology to be sole representative of an argument in the syntax becomes apparent here: empty pronominal arguments often do *not* correspond to overt morphology (see above, as well as section 8).

A further argument is based on coordination: *pro* may be conjoined with a lexical NP:

(44) a. ak-milsa ＿＿＿＿ me a delal
       1s-saw-3s   *and*   *mother-3s*

    I saw her and her mother.

50   CHAPTER TWO

(44) b. ng-milsa   ____ me   a 'o'ollel
       3s-gave-3s   *and   younger.brother-3s*

       He gave it to her and her brother.

    c. ak-mla nguu el loia   ____ me   a olu'es
       1s-PST take L put-3   *and   pencil*

       I put them and the pencils (in there).

(The verb **msa** in (44b) is a double-object verb, both of whose arguments may be null.) Assuming that only like categories can be conjoined,[28] and especially that NP only conjoins with NP, the facts in (44) require that a null pronominal NP be a member of the conjunction.

It may be objected, however, that the verbs in (44) bear singular object agreement. This is actually consistent in terms of the grammar. Agreement with coordinate NPs in Palauan follows an unusual pattern: when a predicate precedes the coordinate structure, it agrees with the left conjunct only; when it follows, it agrees with the larger (plural) NP:

(45) a. ng-ngarngii a berrul a Sie me a Toki
       3s-have   raft-3s   and

       Sie and Toki have a raft.

    b. a Sie me a Toki a ngarngii a bererrir
                                   raft-3p

       Sie and Toki have a raft.

Thus agreement with coordinate NPs in Palauan, as in many languages, does not necessarily take the 'logical' course of registering plurality. (See McCloskey and Hale 1984 for discussion of similar conjunction facts in Modern Irish.)

Another class of argument for the existence of *pro* is based on the analysis of A′ binding structures. The following chapter establishes that all variables in Palauan A′ binding are pronominal, either null (*pro*) or overt. Chapter Four then presents a number of arguments that these resumptive pronouns are syntactically bound. Since both types of resumptive element trigger the same syntactic and morphological effects, they must in some syntactic sense be parallel elements. At the least, the structural status of *pro* must be the same as that of an overt pronoun.

As an alternative to the foregoing arguments for *pro*, we could assume that an NP node is present only when it contains lexical material, even though an argument selected by a head is not always lexical. This alternative entails that the structure of some categories is determined by the insertion of non-heads (a VP has a transitive structure when the object is lexical, but not when it is pronominal, and so on). Such a consequence is not only incompatible with X′ theory, theta theory, and theories of the

PALAUAN GRAMMAR 51

lexicon, but it requires parallel principles of structure where one (that the argument position is always present) will do. The alternative approach is therefore rejected.

We can assume, then, that the *pro* NP position is always present in the tree, whether or not it is phonologically filled. Such a hypothesis accords well with assumptions about the mapping of thematic positions onto syntactic trees.

In this section I have argued that Palauan grammar sanctions null pronouns, but by means of devices more abstract than the identification hypothesis. I have also shown that Palauan has other properties of *pro*-drop languages, including 'long movement' of subject. In arguing for the syntactic presence of *pro* and against identification of pronominal arguments with agreement morphemes, I have anticipated the final section of the chapter, which considers the issue of distinguishing inflectional morphology from pronouns.

8. AFFIX OR CLITIC?

Throughout the description of Palauan grammar presented in this chapter, I have assumed that various argument-related morphemes found on nouns and verbs arise via inflectional processes rather than cliticization (or incorporation). That is, I have assumed that these morphemes represent agreement forms and have no independent syntactic status as NPs at any level of representation. From this assumption has followed the analysis of noun and verb morphology and the resulting typological classification of Palauan as a *pro*-drop language. In the chapters that follow, the characterization of A′ binding in Palauan will depend crucially on this classification.

Another analysis is suggested by the incompatibility of agreement inflectional and overt pronouns, however: the agreement forms might be independent pronouns syntactically, and become phonologically part of an adjacent word in some other component. If this were the case, then Palauan would not be *pro*-drop, and pronominal arguments would be overt in all NP positions, not just those that follow a preposition.[29] A large part of the material in the following chapters would thereby be called into question. Aside from its value to the following discussion, however, a treatment of the morphology of inflection and clitics has intrinsic and current interest.

This section attempts to distinguish Palauan inflection from clitics in a principled way. In order not to prejudice the discussion, I will refer to the forms in question as 'pronouns', intending this term to be neutral between 'inflection' and 'clitic'. I will also refer to the alternative analyses as the 'inflection hypothesis' and the 'clitic hypothesis'.

The clitic hypothesis that I address here involves phonological clitics,

52   CHAPTER TWO

morphemes that are syntactically independent. Another view of clitics
has developed in recent years, in which clitics are features on lexical
heads, equivalent to person and number morphology. These syntactic
clitics are borne by the head throughout the syntax, and correspond to
an empty category analyzed as *pro* (see, e.g., Zubizarreta 1982; Borer
1984b). McCloskey and Hale (1984) analyze the inflectional morphology in Irish in this way. If this view of clitics is taken, there is no theoretical distinction between inflection and cliticization, as McCloskey and
Hale point out. I do not consider this analysis. The object of this section
is not to develop a theory of agreement as opposed to a theory of clitics-
as-features, but rather to argue that there are clear differences between
agreement and (phonological) clitics, that the difference concerns the
syntactic properties of arguments, and that theories of morphology
should recognize this difference and maintain the traditional distinction
between affix and clitic.

According to the 'inflection hypothesis', then, the pronouns found on
nouns and verbs in surface structure are affixes; they are part of the
word at the point of lexical insertion (see, e.g., Lieber 1980). At
D-structure, the phrase structure tree contains not only these fully
formed inflected words, but also NP nodes which do not contain any
lexical material at all. These NPs are specified for grammatical features
such as person and number, but have no phonological matrix. They are
analyzed as *pro*, a null pronominal argument. The person and number
features of *pro* match the features of the agreeing head (N or V).[30]
Finally, any structure in which *pro* is governed by **er** will be eliminated
(that is, P is not among the licensing heads for *pro*).

In the 'clitic hypothesis', Palauan has no null pronouns in governed
positions. Pronominal subjects, direct objects, and NP specifiers are all
overt, and are inserted under NP nodes in the base. They cooccur with
N or V heads which are uninflected in the syntax, but are phonologically
joined to those heads in the PF component. In the case of pronouns
governed by **er**, this cliticization exceptionally does not take place,
perhaps because **er** is not a suitable host for a clitic, or because **er** selects
pronoun forms that do not cliticize (see below).

The section considers various empirical bases supporting one or the
other hypothesis, in general terms. Then subject- and nonsubject-linked
morphology are treated independently. Finally, Zwicky and Pullum's criteria (1983) are brought to bear on the status of nonsubject morphology.

8.1. *Cooccurrence with Full NPs*

Perhaps the strongest argument in favor of the clitic hypothesis for
subjects is provided by the inability of full pronouns to cooccur with the
pronominal morphology on the head ((7a, c) repeated here):

PALAUAN GRAMMAR   53

(7) a. ak-remurt (*ngak)
        1s-run   I

    I am running.

    c. ng-'illebed-ii a bilis (*ngii)
        3s-hit-3s   dog   s/he

    S/he hit the dog.

This argues that the pronoun 'moves onto' the head, leaving an empty
category which it then governs. An immediate problem for this hypothesis arises, however, from the cooccurrence of these reduced pronouns with full, nonpronominal NPs, in all argument positions. We have
seen examples of this in (43) (repeated here as (46)):

(46) a. a 'ole'es-em   'your pencil'
         pencil-2s

     b. a 'ole'es-el a Marta   'Martha's pencil'
         pencil-3s

     c. ak-mil'er-ar   'I bought it'
         1s-bought-3s

     d. ak-mil'er-ar a mlai   'I bought the car'
                   3s   car

     e. ng-mil'er-ar a mlai   'He bought the car'
                   3s

     f. ng-mil'er-ar a mlai a Kasta 'Costa bought the car'
                   3s

In these examples, 'possessor agreement' cooccurs with a full NP possessor ((46b)), direct object agreement with an overt object NP ((46d)),
and subject agreement with an overt subject NP ((46f)). A single syntactic argument is not expected to occur as two lexical items, pronominal
and nominal. Every current theory of syntax has a way of ruling out such
cases; in GB, they are excluded by the Theta Criterion, since two positions would compete for the same θ-role, and by the Projection Principle, since one argument would be projected onto two positions.
Theories of clitic doubling, furthermore, have claimed that an NP can be
doubled by a clitic only when the NP is preceded by a preposition (see,
e.g., Kayne 1981). The cooccurrence of a pronoun with a full (non-
prepositional) NP suggests instead, rather strongly, that the pronoun is a
form of inflection rather than an argument. That is, the incompatibility
mentioned initially actually provides one of the best arguments for the
inflection hypothesis.[31]

54   CHAPTER TWO

This is not the place in which to develop a complete theory of object agreement. I will assume here, for simplicity, that any head can agree with an NP it governs. This should be the null hypothesis. Instantiations already seen include agreement of I with the subject and agreement of N with its specifier. Similarly, V agrees with its complement in Palauan, as in many other languages (though which argument V agrees with is probably determined by thematic role as much as position: cf. agreement of a verb like 'give' with the goal rather than the theme). In taking the basic assumption to be that a head can agree with an argument it governs, I am following Hale et al. (1991).

8.2. *Full Pronouns*

The section above showed that the independent pronouns (see (17)) do not represent pronominal arguments when affixed pronouns are present. The facts of the full distribution of independent pronouns provide further support for the inflection view. These forms occur as object of the preposition, as a conjunct, as the theme of a predicate NP (see Georgopoulos 1991a), and in topic position (cf. their distribution in French, for example). Presumably, the possibility of pronominal arguments becoming clitics is a property of the whole class, and (at least phonological) clitics are notoriously unselective as to their hosts. But in Palauan either pronouns exceptionally fail to cliticize to P or N or to a conjunction, or only the forms in paradigm (17) are syntactically independent pronouns. In topic position the full pronouns trigger pronoun affixes (i.e. agreement) like any other NP:

(47)   ngak$_i$ [a le-bilsk-ak ____$_i$ a buk a Harry]
        I   *IR-3-gave-is*   *book*

        Harry gave me the book.

8.3. *Subject Pronouns on Non-V Hosts*

Another potential problem for the inflection theory is the fact that subject pronouns occur not only on the verb, but also on certain adverbs:

(48) a. te-kmal el kltukl el kai-uetoir
        3p-very L clear L Recip-love

        They're obviously in love.

     b. ak-kmal el melemlim el kmo sei ngera el bung
        1s-very L curious   that Dem what L flower

        I really wonder what kind of flower that is.

PALAUAN GRAMMAR

(48) c. ak-ble'oel el menguiu aike el rokui el buk el lillu'es
   1s-always L read   Dem L all   L book L IR-3-wrote

   I used to read every book that he wrote.

These facts might seem to suggest that the subject pronoun is separable from the morphology of the verb, a suggestion consistent with the clitic hypothesis. However, there is another way of analyzing these examples: items such as **kmal** 'very' and **ble'oel** 'always' may be modal verbs. As such, they naturally take subject agreement, and subordinate the clause that follows. This analysis is supported empirically: the predicates in (48) are followed by the morpheme **el**, which functions as a complementizer (see section 6). Other adverbial predicates that can be analyzed in this way are **dmak** 'together'; **dirkak** 'not yet'; **mera** 'truly'; **lmuut** 'again'; **dikea** 'no more'; and **dirrek** 'also'. Note in (49) that they may also be inflected with the past tense infix **-il-**, like other predicates ((49c) and (49d) are from Capell 1949):

(49) a. ng-dmak   el oureor ngii me a 'o'ellel
   3s-together L work   him and   younger.brother-3s

   He's working with his brother.

   b. ng-dilak   el oureor ngii me a 'o'ellel
   3s-Pst-together

   He was working with his brother.

   c. ng-lmuut el mei
   3s-again L come

   He is coming back.

   d. ng-liluut   el mei   er a beluu
   3s-Pst-again L come P   village

   He came back to the village.

The fact that these adverbs take embedded complements and the fact that they can be inflected for tense suggest that they are raising predicates that take subject agreement in the normal way. The data in (48) are therefore no obstacle to the inflection theory.

Similarly, subject pronouns appear on the auxiliary, if there is one (the examples in (50) are from Josephs 1975, p. 124):

(50) a. aki-mle kaudenge   er a Kuam
   1p-Past Recip-know P

   We knew each other in Guam.

56   CHAPTER TWO

(50) b. ak-mle medengelii a Toki er se   er a lengalek
     1s-Pst   know   P when   IR-child

    I knew Toki when she was a child.

This again might seem to suggest that the subject pronoun is separable from the verb, and is a phonological clitic on the first member of the verbal complex. The inflection hypothesis can account for these facts, on the other hand, by analyzing the subject pronoun as a feature of Inflection that is spelled out on the first auxiliary instead of the main verb, in the context of the independent tense morpheme.[32] This is much like the case in English, in which tense is realized on the first auxiliary.

It is interesting to note that in the irrealis mood, the subject pronoun may appear on both auxiliary and verb (examples from Josephs, p. 109):

(51) a. a mubi el   **k**-bo   **ku**-mes er ngii a mubi er a Dois
     movie Comp IR-1s-Fut IR-1s-see P it   movie P   German

    The movie that I'm going to see is a German movie.

   b. a **le**-bo   **l**-se'er   a Droteo, e ngdiak lebo   er a skuul
      IR-2-Fut IR-3-sick   Neg   IR-3-go P   school

    If Droteo gets sick, he won't go to school.

This 'doubling' of pronouns suggests that the subject pronoun is a set of features that in some cases gets written onto both the auxiliary and the verb. Although these facts are awkward from the point of view of the inflection hypothesis, they constitute an even greater difficulty for the clitic hypothesis. A morphological rule that realizes person and number features on two separate words is complicated, but a syntactically independent pronoun ought to be incapable of appearing on two separate hosts. This intimate association of subject person and number marking with mood marking, furthermore, argues quite strongly that the former is an inflectional feature, i.e. 'real' agreement. Since the forms on irrealis verbs are quite clearly subject agreement, then it is reasonable to claim that Palauan has subject agreement in the realis mood too.

8.4. *Zwicky and Pullum's Tests*

Even if the clitic hypothesis could be maintained for subject pronouns, other problems are encountered when we submit the nonsubject pronouns to morphological tests for distinguishing inflection from clitics, such as those described by Zwicky and Pullum (1983).

Selectivity. For example, Zwicky and Pullum (henceforth Z & P) note that affixes are very selective of their hosts, while clitics are relatively indifferent in this regard. The selectivity criterion derives from the very different syntactic properties of affixes and clitics. Affixes depend on the

PALAUAN GRAMMAR

grammatical features of the items they combine with in the lexicon, and have a designated structural position within the word. Clitics, on the other hand, are not grammatically dependent on the item they are joined to, but simply combine with an item that is adjacent in the surface string.

The Palauan nonsubject pronouns are judged affixal by this test. Subject pronouns, of course, appear on all (and only) predicates. Object pronouns are more selective, appearing only on the subclass of regular perfective transitive verbs whose object is definite. There are no bare perfective verb stems. Genitive pronouns, too, are selective: they attach only to [+N] heads that are lexically capable of receiving the pronoun (i.e. they do not attach to nouns whose possessor must be marked with er). The selectivity of all these pronouns argues against the clitic theory and in favor of the inflection analysis.[33]

Irregularities. Another of Z & P's tests is based on paradigmatic irregularity. Inflectional systems are known to be prone to irregularity, while clitics, being syntactically independent, are not expected to participate in such irregularities. In subjecting the Palauan pronouns to this test, we ignore subject pronouns, which are quite regular. As for object pronouns, we observe irregularities of several types.

First, some paradigms contain object pronouns that differ systematically from the regular paradigm ((2) at section 2.1). The regular object forms have morphology that is clearly related to the morphology of full pronouns ((17) at section 3). But in the exceptional cases the pronoun contains a thematic vowel — a vowel which is not predictable phonologically — and **-r** as the final segment. Some examples are in (52). In these examples, the imperfective (citation) form of the verb is given first, then the perfective form in the third person singular; the object pronoun is underlined:

(52) | *Im* | *Pf* | *Gloss* |
|---|---|---|
| melau | to<u>ur</u> | 'heat (food)' |
| meluk | turk<u>ur</u> | 'cut' |
| melungel | turng<u>ur</u> | 'smell, kiss' |
| oldiu | odi<u>ur</u> | 'shout' |
| meleng | long<u>ir</u> | 'borrow, rent' |
| omed | bed<u>ir</u> | 'catch' |
| mele'el | do'el<u>ir</u> | 'increase (amount)' |
| meius | is<u>ar</u> | 'row, paddle' |
| ome'ar | me'er<u>ar</u> | 'buy' |

The facts of NPs illustrate the same point. In the inflection theory, NP may contain what we can call 'possessor agreement', which is linked to the empty specifier position. In the clitic theory, such an NP contains a genitive pronoun that cliticizes to the head. Morphologically, the pro-

58 CHAPTER TWO

nouns in question have a different shape from the pronouns linked to clausal object or subject position. One paradigm is found in (53):

(53)　*Genitive morphemes*

	Singular	Plural	
		Excl	Incl
1	-ek	-am	-ed
2	-em	-iu	
3	-el	-ir	

Genitive pronouns, like the irregular verbal paradigms mentioned above, are conjugated with a thematic vowel: u, a, i, or schwa (the thematic vowel in (53)). For the inflection hypothesis, this vowel is a fact of the morphology of the noun: it depends on the noun class. Thematic vowels are naturally accounted for as elements in lexical word formation, while it is difficult to imagine any theory of clitics that could account for their occurrence or distribution.

Arbitrary gaps. In a second type of irregularity involving object pronouns, the verb form may have the appearance of lacking the third person singular object pronoun altogether. These cases are what Z & P refer to as arbitrary gaps: cases in which the host unexpectedly fails to combine with some morpheme. Z & P suppose that this would never occur in the case of cliticization, since the pronoun should always be analyzable separately from the head in clitic-host structures. Some examples are seen in (54); again, the perfective forms listed are third person singular, which normally ends in -ii:

(54)

Im	*Pf*	*Gloss*
melai	nguu	'bring, take'
mele'a	loia	'put'
mengeterrerek	'oterrerek	'raise pitch of (voice)'
mengiues	kiues	'cross (one's legs)'
	oba (Pf only)	'carry, hold'
omes	mesa	'see'
omsa	msa	'give'
omuit	muit	'boil (starchy food)'
omuut	muut	'pile up'

The exceptions and gaps displayed in (52) and (54) (what Z & P refer to as *morphophonological idiosyncrasies*) are typical of affixal paradigms, but are not predicted of clitics. How can the clitic theory deal with the lack of the pronoun in the cases illustrated in (54), for example? For the inflection theory, such facts pose no serious problem, as idiosyncrasies in word formation are confined to the rules of the lexicon.

PALAUAN GRAMMAR 59

In conclusion, we have reviewed evidence based on the syntactic properties of these pronouns, as well as evidence by which agreement can be distinguished from clitics. The facts argue strongly for the inflection theory, at least for the Palauan cases described. There are of course phenomena which remain neutral between the two theories. The characterization of Palauan as a *pro*-drop language does not depend solely on the arguments of this section, however. The *pro*-drop issue depends on a number of other factors, including the properties of the larger construction in which null elements occur. It should be kept in mind that other aspects of Palauan grammar are typical of *pro*-drop languages, such as long movement of the subject of a tensed clause. In addition, as we noted in section 7, there are empty positions that are not linked to any pronoun (agreement) form. The existence of null arguments in these cases is independent of the considerations of the discussion immediately above, and shows that there is more to the *pro*-drop story than licensing by agreement.

9. SUMMARY

This chapter has provided a minimally technical sketch of the particular grammar of Palauan. As a descriptive piece of work, it should stand on its own. My primary intention in including this sketch, however, is that it should serve as a reference in reading the following chapters.

NOTES

[1] In the view of Dyen (1965), Palauan should not be included within the Indonesian (his "Hesperonesian") subgroup but is rather a separate branch of Austronesian.

[2] According to Schwalbenberg (1984), 22% of the Palauan population has emigrated to Guam, other Pacific Islands, or the United States. 38% of these emigrants live in Guam, 8%—9% in Saipan, 9.6% on Yap, and about 25% in the United States, including Hawaii.

[3] For example, Capell describes the distribution of the morpheme **a** (seen in examples below) as a marker of nouns, including "substantivalized verbs". The analysis of **a** bears on the ultimate analysis of word order (section 5 below). According to Capell, Palauan clauses are verb-initial, with transitive objects immediately following the verb. Capell further describes the Palauan passive as the (intransitive) participial form made up of the "verb marker" and the root. Compare Josephs' (1975) analyses of word order and of the passive, below. All of Capell's positions are supported in this book.

[4] In Bender (1971) and Wilson (1972), glides w and y are also listed as phonemes; Flora (1974) considers w phonemic but not y. I believe that a good case can be made that the Palauan glides derive from underlying vowels. Bender gives only five phonemic vowels, deriving schwa in every case; I adopt here the position of Flora (1984) that some cases of schwa are phonemic. The question of schwa is tantalizing, because much of its surface distribution can be attributed either to interconsonantal epenthesis or to reduction of some full vowel that surfaces under other stress patterns. Yet not all occurrences have so far been accounted for by rule, and it is these cases which force us to conclude that schwa is a phoneme. In Dahl (1976), schwa is presented as one of the four vocalic

60 CHAPTER TWO

phonemes of Proto-Austronesian. Some interesting work can be done here within modern phonological frameworks.

[5] As an example of this, observe the following forms containing the abstract root *kang 'eat', a regular verb (Bender 1971, taken from Carlson (1968)): k-l-ang 'things that have been eaten'; mengang 'eat' (Impf); m-l-engang 'ate' (Impf); ak-kol-ii 'I eat it'; ak-kil-ii 'I ate it'; kel-ii 'eat it' (non-indic.); okang 'food for animals'; omengang 'the eating'; omekang 'to feed' (caus.); mekang 'be eaten'; kall 'food'; kele-k 'my food'. This root also appears in kllel 'food already eaten'; ulengall 'garbage'; ongall 'large dish'; ongekall '(rice) cooking pot'; olekang 'cooking pot'; and so on.

[6] Wilson refers to this form as the "progressive". It is the citation form, and the form more commonly used in speech. Use of the perfective form (below) is more pragmatically restricted; for example, it is avoided in declaratives and in the present tense, being preferred in yes/no questions and in the past tense.

[7] The form of the IM cannot be accounted for by a synchronic rule. An assimilation process similar to that described in the text has been observed in Indonesian and Javanese (Wilson, p. 148). Nasal infixation as a general phenomenon is widespread in the Indonesian and Philippine languages (Dempwolff 1934–38). I have observed similar processes in Bahasa Malaysia and Tagalog.

[8] According to Capell (1949), use of the perfective is dying out; I do not find this to be so. See note 6.

[9] There are sets of irregular verbs whose third person singular form ends in -Vr, where V is a thematic vowel (see Wilson; see also section 8 below).

[10] The verb marker also derives verbal categories from nominal stems or from abstract roots that are not specified for category.

[11] The historical unity of the IM is suggested in (3): l occurs before dentals and alveolars (and also before ng, due to other historical factors), m occurs before bilabials, and ng before k and the glottal stop. The perfective examples in (4) show that the o and m forms of the VM are phonologically related (see the sources cited). Wilson (1972) derives the o form from mV in all cases.

[12] Since the realis morpheme is difficult to isolate segmentally, I will simply indicate its presence by 'R'.

[13] See the remarks on the orthography and the list of abbreviations used in the glosses in the Appendix.

[14] The form I refer to as 'irrealis' is called 'hypothetical' in Josephs (1975).

[15] According to Wilson (1972) and Josephs (1975), the verb marker has no semantic value. In Wilson (p. 131), the VM deletes when irrealis subject prefixes ((9)) are present.

[16] The second person form m(o)- deletes before homorganic root-initial b; beskak in (10)c is an example.

[17] Perfective forms occur in the present tense only to convey warnings about events immediately about to occur.

[18] Josephs (1975) analyzes these two cases of er as distinct morphemes, an approach that does not seem motivated. Dyen (1971) notes that Palauan shares with some Indonesian languages the property of having only one preposition.

[19] This is the morpheme called the 'ligature', or 'linker', which is found in most of the Philippine languages.

[20] Close inspection of the description of this rule (its "pronominal trace" and other properties discussed in the following paragraphs) shows that it has no kinship with subject inversion proposed, e.g. for pro-drop languages.

[21] It appears that sentences with VSO order are marginally acceptable, when no ambiguity of the grammatical role of the NPs is possible. Some speakers do not accept VSO sentences at all.

[22] The construction Josephs dubs "ergative" should not be confused with "ergative" constructions in modern GB analysis, i.e. unaccusatives. Whether or not unaccusatives

PALAUAN GRAMMAR

and passives belong to the same syntactic class, the unaccusative analysis does not play a part in Josephs' reasoning.

[23] As in passive in many languages, the agent is rarely expressed.

[24] This appears to be true of verbs like 'give' in most languages that have object agreement: the *goal* is the argument agreed with. Part of the same phenomenon, I think, are the facts of 'dative shift' structures in English. Note also that when one argument is incorporated by *away*, it is the goal: *He [gave away] the store.*

[25] See also Chung (1984, 1985) on the facts of a related language, Chamorro. In Chamorro, null subjects, passive agents, and possessors are identified by agreement, while null objects are not. As in Palauan, identification only partially accounts for null arguments in Chamorro. Chung (1985) also rules out government by agreement in Chamorro.

[26] In the next chapter I will discuss the ways in which the distribution of WH gaps parallels the distribution of null pronouns, and the observations in this section will be extended to cases of A'-bound empty categories.

[27] Pace Jelinek (1984), Bresnan & Mchombo (1987), and others, who argue to the contrary. For a critique of these arguments, see, e.g., Whitman (1991). In addition, Palauan cannot be considered a nonconfigurational language (cf. section 5).

[28] This assumption is a simplification; see, e.g., Sag et al. (1985). The assumption is valid for the cases discussed in the text, however.

[29] This is an alternative that is occasionally suggested to me. For an analysis of Palauan that assumes that certain argument-linked morphemes are clitics, see Clark (1983).

[30] We could assume that *pro*'s features are determined by the agreement on the head, or vice versa. Or we could assume that both *pro* and agreement are assigned features in D-structure, subject to a feature matching rule or filter applying later in the derivation. I take no position on this.

[31] Note that when one of the arguments in question is preposed, the pronoun remains affixed to the head. It is difficult to imagine how trace thory is to be reconciled with the clitic analysis for WH questions.

[32] Tense is often an infix between the verb marker and the stem, but is realized as a separate word (as in (49)) with the class of stative predicates like 'know'.

[33] More must be said about Romance clitics, since the selectivity test wrongly identifies them as affixes (L. Rizzi, personal communication).

CHAPTER THREE

THE VARIABLE BINDING STRUCTURES

0. INTRODUCTION

The grammar of Palauan A' binding poses many interesting problems of both descriptive and theoretical interest. In this chapter I will give a detailed description of the structures containing A' binding, while Chapters Four through Six deal with the associated theoretical problems, such as resumptive pronouns, locality, crossover, and scope. To recapitulate briefly from Chapter One, A' binding is found in those structures, such as WH questions, relativizations, and topicalizations, in which there is a dependency between an antecedent in A' position and a bound constituent in argument position.[1]

The structures under consideration are very productive in Palauan. In this chapter we will see that, as would be expected, they share a number of important properties, and on the basis of this sharing of properties they are treated as a natural class. However, they do not display the clustering of properties usually postulated of the class of WH-movement constructions (see, e.g. Chomsky 1977, 1981). One characteristic feature of these structures in Palauan is the regular occurrence of resumptive pronouns in *all* of them. Another is their lack of subjacency effects. In view of these and other facts, I will propose that the entire class is base-generated. Thus we have the very interesting case of a language presenting the entire range of A' binding constructions at S-structure yet lacking any signs of WH movement.

Among the structures described in this chapter, clefts and relative clauses will be analyzed as 'more basic', in the sense that the whole class can be described in terms of these two types.

1. THE STRUCTURES

In the subsections immediately below, I describe each structure type in turn. In the examples, the mood morphology of the verb (glossed *R* for realis or *IR* for irrealis) reflects a distinction between subjects and non-subjects. The importance of this morphology to the overall analysis will be made clear in section three, and in Chapter Four. At this point it should be noted simply that all of the examples are *semantically* realis (unless explicitly noted otherwise). Once again, I should stress the importance of referring to the grammatical sketch in Chapter Two in assimilating the facts laid out below.

62

VARIABLE BINDING STRUCTURES 63

1.1. *Relative Clauses*

A relative clause in Palauan follows the head NP and, in the most prevalent type of relative, is introduced by the complementizer **el**. Palauan has no relative pronouns. I assume the conventional analysis of relative NPs, as in (1):

(1)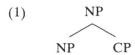

Unless topicalization has taken place in the relative clause,[2] the first constituent in the clause is the verb. The clause contains either a gap or a pronoun in the relativized position. Nonsubject gaps frequently occur in positions associated with agreement features, while the subject corresponds to a gap that is not linked to agreement. This is illustrated in the examples in (2). In (2a) the relativized NP is a subject, in (2b) it is a direct object, and in (2c) it is a possessor:[3]

(2) a. ak-medengel-ii a 'ad$_i$ [el   mil'er-ar   tia el buk ___$_i$]
       R-1s-Pf-know-3s man Comp R-Pf-buy-3s Dem L book

   I know the person who bought that book.

   b. ak-milsa a mlai$_i$ [el   ldilse'-ii   ___$_i$ tirkel el 'ad]
      R-1s-saw   canoe Comp IR-3-Pf-carved-3s   Dem L men

   I saw the canoe that those men carved.

   c. a buik$_i$ [el   k-'illebed-ii   [a 'obok-ul   ___$_i$]] a
      boy   Comp IR-1s-Pf-hit-3s   older.brother-3s
      se'el-ik
      friend-1s

   The boy whose brother I hit is my friend.

Note that subject position in (2a) is empty, but that the verb in the relative clause carries no subject agreement. The direct object ((2b)) and possessor position ((2c)) are also empty. The object position is governed by the verb **ldilse'ii** 'they carved', which bears person and number object agreement, and the possessor position is governed by the head **'obokul** 'older brother', which bears person and number morphology agreeing with the relativized possessor.

Relativized positions following the preposition **er**, in contrast, obligatorily contain an overt resumption pronoun. This is seen in (3): in (3a), the (prepositional) object of an imperfective verb (cf. the discussion in Chapter Two) is relativized, and in (3b), the relativized position is an oblique (note coindexing):

64 CHAPTER THREE

(3) a. ak-ulmes   er a buk$_i$ [el   l-uleme'ar   er ngii$_i$ a Helen]
R-1s-Im-see P   book   Comp IR-3-Im-buy P   it

I saw the book that Helen bought.

b. til'a el blai$_i$ [el   l-ulnga   er a ngikel er
Dem L house   Comp IR-3-Im-eat P   fish   P

ngii$_i$ a Robert]
it

That's the house that Robert was eating the fish in.

Where agreement is present, a resumptive pronoun may not appear:

(4)   ak-mla-mesa sei   el buk$_i$ [el
R-1s-Pf-saw   Dem L book   Comp

l-lil-es-ii   ___$_i$/ *(er) ngii$_i$]
IR-3-Pf-write-3s   P   it

I saw that book that they wrote.

The minimal pair in (5) contrasts only in the aspect of the verb **meruul**
'do', and demonstrates clearly how the appearance of a resumptive
pronoun depends on the distribution of the preposition **er**:

(5) a. ng-soak el   omes er sei el rael$_i$ [el   luruul
*R-1s-like Comp R-see P Dem L road   Comp IR-3-**Im**-did*

er ngii$_i$ a re'ad   er a Belau el   mo er a Babeldaob]
P   it   people P   Comp go P

b. ng-soak el omes er sei el rael$_i$ [el bla   rellii
*IR-Aux IR-**Pf**-did-3s*

___$_i$ a re'ad er a Belau el mo er a Babeldaob]
I'd like to see that road that the Palauans built to Babeldaob.

To sum up, relative heads correspond to gaps in subject position and
in positions governed by agreement, and to resumptive pronouns in
prepositional object position. Gaps and resumptive pronouns are in
complementary distribution in relative clauses.

1.1.1. *Free Relatives*

Another type of relative clause found in Palauan grammar is the free
relative. This type lacks not only an overt head, but also the complementizer **el**. As in all Palauan relative clauses, the examples in (6) and
(7) contain no relative pronoun (there is no word corresponding to the
WH word in the English gloss; none of these examples can be construed

VARIABLE BINDING STRUCTURES 65

as an embedded question (see Chapter Five on the latter)). I assume, though, that this construction is a complex NP that contains a null head; I indicate this by the symbol *e* in head position. The head and the gap or resumptive pronoun in relativized position are coindexed; (7b) contains a resumptive pronoun:

(6) a. ng-ngarngii a [e_i [melame' a dekool ___$_i$]] er kemiu
        R-3s-exist   R-chew   cigarette   P you(pl)

   Is there anyone among you who smokes cigarettes?

   b. ng-ulu-ais a delam   el   milsa   a [e_i [milskak a
       R-3s-said   mother-2s Comp R-Pf-saw   R-gave-1s

   'ema'el ___$_i$]]
   betel.nut

   Your mother said she saw who gave me the betel nuts.

   c. ke-medengel-ii a [e_i [mlo er a stoang ___$_i$]
       R-3s-know-3s   went P   store

   Do you know who went to the store?

(7) a. ak-umera a [e_i ['om-lekoi ___$_i$]]
        R-1s-believe   IR-2-tell

   I believe what you say.

   b. ak-medengel-ii a [e_i ['omo-ruul er ngii$_i$]
       R-1s-know   IR-2s-do   P it

   I know what you are doing.

Internally, these structures appear to contain IP rather than CP:

(8)

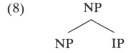

IP rather than CP is hypothesized in this structure for two reasons. First, the inability of a complementizer to appear in a free relative suggests that the clausal node involved is IP rather than CP.[4] Second, such a clause cannot have a topic:

(9) a. *ng-ngarngii a [e [a dekool$_i$ [$_{IP}$ a lolame' ___$_i$ er kemiu]]]
         3s-exist   cigarette   IR-3-chew   P you(pl)

   (Is there anyone who smokes cigarettes among you?)

   b. *ke-medengel-ii a [e [a stoang$_i$ [$_{IP}$ a blo er ngii$_i$]]]
       2s-know-3s   store   IR-go P there

   (Do you know who went to the store?)

66   CHAPTER THREE

Despite the fact that I analyze topicalizations below as pseudocleft structures rather than structures with an NP in Spec(C), the important point
here is that the occurrence of a cleft in an embedding appears to be
limited to CPs headed by a lexical complementizer. The failure of topics
and lexical complementizers to appear in free relatives is in contrast to
their appearance in other types of embedded clause in Palauan. Normally, complementizers do not delete and they cooccur with WH words
and topics. Since there is only a bare IP in the constructions above, there
is no possibility of movement of a null operator inside the relative.
Compare the standard analysis of relatives, as well as topicalizations and
clefts, in Chomsky (1977); see also Barss (1985).
    Note that the free relative construction is preceded by the NP speci-
fier **a**, indicating that it is in fact of the category NP. In the next section I
describe cleft structures, and analyze them as containing free relatives
like those described here.

1.2. *Clefts and Pseudoclefts*

In clefts (analogous to *it*-clefts in English), the clefted constituent
appears to the left of the matrix clause and is prefixed with the third
person singular morpheme **ng-**.[5] There is no overt copula in Palauan.
The rest of the sentence is preceded by the nominal marker **a**, and has
all the properties of the free relative described above.
    Clefted subjects correspond to a gap in the nominalized clause, as do
perfective objects, and subjects in NPs containing 'possessor agreement'.
That is, gaps appear in clefts in the same positions that support gaps in
relative clauses. When the clefted constituent is the object of **er**, a
resumptive pronoun appears in its argument position:

(10) a. ng- [Basilia]$_i$ a mengaus er tia   el tet   ___$_i$
         Cl-   *R-weave P   Dem   L   bag*

         It's Basilia who's weaving this bag.

    b. ng-[sualo]$_i$ a lo-ngaus   er ngii$_i$ a reme'as
        Cl-basket   *IR-3-weave P   it*   *women*

        It's the basket that the women are weaving.

In (10a) a subject is clefted, while in (10b) the object of **er** is clefted.
The examples in (11) are a minimal pair, contrasting a clefted subject
and a clefted nonsubject (the realis/irrealis feature is found on both the
auxiliary and the main verb):

(11) a. ng- ['obokuk]$_i$ a mla   merng-ii a se'elik   ___$_i$
         Cl- brother-1s   *R-Aux R-Pf-hit*   *friend-1s*
         (older)

         It's my brother who has hit my friend.

VARIABLE BINDING STRUCTURES

(11) b. ng-[se'elik]$_i$ a bla   le-berng-ii ____$_i$ a 'obokuk
       IR-Aux IR-3-Pf-hit

It's my friend who my brother has hit.

There is another type of cleft construction in Palauan, which corresponds to the pseudocleft or *what*-cleft in English. Some examples are in (12) and (13). The pseudoclefts in (12) contain subject gaps, and those in (13) object gaps.

(12) a. [a milruul er a malk   ____$_i$] [a Miriam$_i$]
      R-did   P   chicken

The one who cooked the chicken is Miriam.

   b. [a rirebet er a tebel ____$_i$] [a ngerang$_i$]
      R-fell   P   table   what

What fell off the table?

(13) a. [a lo-ruul ____$_i$ a rengalek er a skuul] [a mesuub]$_i$
      IR—do   children   P   school   R-study

What the schoolchildren do is study.

   b. [a l-omtanget er ngii$_i$ a rese'al] [a 'elibel   a uel]$_i$
      IR-polish   P   it   boys   shell-3s   turtle

What the boys are polishing is the turtle shell.

I will propose below that both clefts and pseudoclefts underlie other A′ binding types in Palauan grammar. Before moving on to the other types, however, it is important to be more precise about the structure of the examples in (10) through (13).

First, note the abstract structure of the cleft sentence:

(14)   *ng*-NP [$_{NP}$ *a* . . . variable . . .]

That is, abstracting away details, the sentence has essentially a NP-NP constituency. We may make two assumptions about this schematized structure, based on our earlier analyses (see also section 1.5): (a) it is only the predicate of a sentence that bears subject agreement in Palauan, and (b) the morpheme **a** is a specifier only of the category NP. If these assumptions are correct, then a cleft sentence can be analyzed like any other predicate-initial sentence in Palauan. The predicate (nominal) is presented first, and bears the third person singular agreement marker **ng-** (recall that there is no overt copula); the rest of the sentence bears the NP specifier **a**, and is plausibly analyzed as the subject. The nominalized clause, furthermore, contains a variable which takes its value from the NP in the predicate, just as the variable in a headed relative clause takes

68   CHAPTER THREE

the value of the head. In brief, the structure in (14) is analyzed here as a predicate-subject structure with a free relative as subject.[6] (This order of relations may be the reverse of what is expected; but see (29) below, and its associated discussion.)

Turning to the pseudoclefts in (12) and (13), we observe that in essence they have the NP-NP structure in (15):

(15)   [$_{NP}$ a ... variable ...] [$_{NP}$ a ...]

That is, these sentences have the usual *NP-NP* structure of pseudoclefts. Both predicate and subject are NPs, as shown by the fact that both are marked by **a**. In this case, the predicate, rather than the subject, is a free relative. The variable in the nominalized predicate is bound by the NP subject, to the right (see the coindexing indicated in (13)).

The structures corresponding to these two sentence types are sketched out in more detail in (16).

(16) a. *ng*-cleft (=*it*-cleft)   b. pseudocleft (= *what*-cleft)

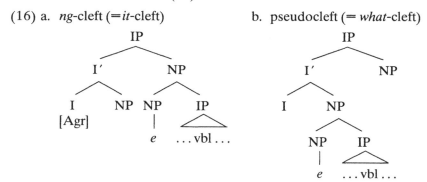

Compare the structures conventionally attributed to clefts and pseudoclefts (the following are taken from Barss 1985):

(17) a. cleft: b. pseudocleft:

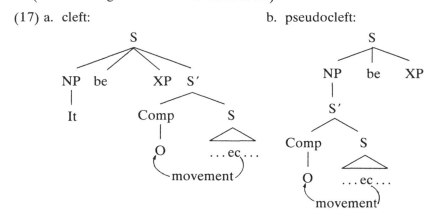

The Palauan structures always have an NP (the free relative clause)

VARIABLE BINDING STRUCTURES 69

where S′ occurs in the structures above. Furthermore, I have argued that the clause node dominated by this NP is IP (S) rather than CP (S′), barring the possibility of movement of a null operator in the Palauan structures. More superficial differences are the null copula, and lack of a pleonastic subject in (16a).

I turn now to the description of WH questions and topicalizations. Once these two types have been considered on their own, I will return to the structures analyzed in these two sections, and show how the analysis of the various structures can be integrated.

1.3. *WH Questions*

In a Palauan WH-question, a question phrase may be either in situ or in a non-argument position to the left of the clause. Some examples of simple questions with WH in situ are seen in (18):

(18) a. ke-lo'a   mo merek el   melu'es er a babilengem er **oingera**
       2s-maybe Fut finish   Comp write   P   paper-2s   P when?

   When will you finish your paper?

   b. ng-omele'a a **ngera** er a mlai a Sabeth
      3s-put   what? P   car

   What is Sabeth putting in the car?

   c. k-osiik   er a **te'ang**
      2s-look.for P   who?

   Who are you looking for?

   d. ng-osiik   er ngak a **te'ang**
      3s-look.for P   me   who?

   Who is looking for me?

   e. ko-me'ar er sei   el mlai le **ngngera a u'ul**
      2s-buy   P Dem L   car   what   reason

   Why are you buying that car?

Since I will be discussing WH in situ in detail in section 3 and in Chapter Five, I will describe here only the second type of question. In this type, the WH phrase is in cleft position, and is prefixed with the third person singular agreement marker **ng-**.[7] The clefted phrase is followed by a clausal structure that is marked by the NP specifier **a**, indicating that the clause is nominalized. When a subject is questioned, the extraction site is empty; this is also the case when the direct object of a perfective verb or the subject of NP is questioned:

CHAPTER THREE

(19) a. ng-te'a$_i$ [a kileld-ii   a sub   ___$_i$]
     Cl-who?   R-Pf-heat-3s   soup
     Who heated up the soup?

b. ng-te'a$_i$ [a dilu   er ngii ___$_i$ el kmo ng-mo   er a Belau]
     Cl-who?   R-said P   her   Comp R-3s-go P
     Who told her to go to Palau?

c. ng-te'a$_i$ [a l-ulekod-ir   ___$_i$ a rubak]
     Cl-who?   IR-3-Pf-kill-3s   old.man
     Who did the old man kill?

d. ng-ngera$_i$ [a le-silseb-ii   ___$_i$ a se'el-il]
     Cl-what?   IR-3-Pf-burn-3s   friend-3s
     What did his friend burn?

The verb carries no subject agreement when the subject precedes the verb, as in (19a, b). The gap in object position in these examples correlates with object agreement, as was the case in full relative clauses.

Also as in relativization, an extraction site that follows a preposition always contains an overt resumptive pronoun. This is illustrated in (20): in (20a), the (prepositional) object of an imperfective verb is questioned, and in (20b), the questioned phrase is an oblique:

(20) a. ng-ngera$_i$ [a l-uruul   er ngii$_i$ a rubak]
     Cl-what?   IR-3-Im-do P   it   old.man
     What did the old man do?

b. ng-ker$_i$ [a le-bilsk-au   a buk   er ngii$_i$ a Ruth]
     Cl-where?   IR-3-Pf-gave-2s   book P   it
     Where did Ruth give you the book?

It is also possible to question the specifier of NP. Recall that there are two types of 'possessed NP' in Palauan (section 4, Chapter Two): the type in which the head is inflected to agree with the specifier, and the type in which the specifier is object of **er**. If the generalizations made so far in this section are correct, then, all else being equal, the specifier should be accessible to question formation in either type; a gap should be allowed in the former case, and a resumptive pronoun in the latter. The result of questioning the specifier in each type is seen in (21a) and (21b):

(21) a. ng-te'a$_i$ [a 'o-mulsa   [a del-al   ___$_i$]]
     Cl-who?   IR-2-Pf-saw   mother-3s
     Whose mother did you see?

     (Lit. Who did you see 's mother?)

(21) b. ng-te'a$_i$ [a lo-nguiu   [a buk er ngii$_i$] tirkei el ngalek]
     Cl-who?   IR-3-Im-read   book P her   Dem-p L child
   Whose book are those kids reading?
   (Lit. Who$_i$ are those kids reading her$_i$ book?)

As predicted, extraction from NP is possible using either strategy.

In comparison, extraction from NP in English is ungrammatical; the entire NP must be pied-piped (see, e.g., Chomsky 1981):

(22) a. [whose mother]$_i$ [did John see ___$_i$]?

   b.*whose$_i$ [did John see [___$_i$ mother]]?

According to Chomsky, the extraction attempted in (22) is impossible because possessor position in English is not properly governed. The extraction possibilities in Palauan NPs and English NPs are in striking contrast, a contrast which, we will see, arises from the different governing properties of nouns in the two languages.

To close this section, we note that Palauan WH questions have the structure of clefts described earlier:

(23)

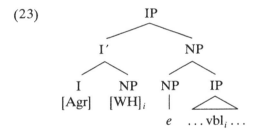

1.4. *Topicalizations*

We now turn to the structure of topicalizations. This section expands the initial description of topicalization in the section on word order in Chapter Two. There we saw that the Palauan topicalization strategy applies to NPs bearing a wide range of grammatical functions. As Waters (1979) has shown, this strategy accounts for observed SVO, OVS, and other surface word orders. Accessibility of NPs to topicalization is not constrained by their grammatical function, as it is in many languages. On the other hand, coindexing between a topic and its argument position in Palauan does obey the same constraints as does coindexing in WH questions and relative clauses.

In surface structure, a topicalized phrase is found in an A' position to the left of the clause. It is preceded (and followed) by **a**. The topic may be linked to either a gap or a resumptive pronoun, as can be observed in

72 CHAPTER THREE

the examples in (24). The topic in (24a) is subject; in (24b) it is an NP specifier; and in (24c) it is the complement of a perfective verb. An overt resumptive pronoun may not appear in any of these positions:

(24) a. a sensei$_i$ [a omes   er a rengalek ____$_i$ (*ngii$_i$)]
    teacher   R-Im-see P   children   she

    The teacher is looking at the children.

  b. a Naomi$_i$ [a le-'ilit-ii   [a 'ole'es-el ____$_i$ (*ngii$_i$)] a John]
      IR-3-Pf-throw-3s   pencil-3s   her

    John threw away Naomi's pencil.

  c. a blai$_i$ [a le-silseb-ii   ____$_i$ (*ngii$_i$) a se'el-ik]
    house   IR-3-Pf-burn-3s   it   friend-1s

    My friend burned down the house.

The topic in (25a) is the object of an imperfective verb, and the topic of (25b) is an NP specifier. Both extraction sites are structurally objects of a preposition, and a resumptive pronoun appears in both cases:

(25) a. a rengalek$_i$ [a l-omes   er tir$_i$ a sensei]
    children   IR-3-Im-see P them   teacher

    The teacher is looking at the children.

  b. a 'ekabil$_i$ [a k-'iliu-ii   [a buk er ngii$_i$]]
    girl   IR-1s-Pf-read-3s   book P her

    I read the girl's book.

Pronouns, as well as full NPs, may be topics, as seen in (26):

(26) a. kid$_i$ [a l-ullasem [el   l-omekdakt   er kid$_i$]]
    us   IR-3-try   Comp IR-3-Im-scare P us

    They're trying to scare us!

  b. ngak$_i$ [a le-bilsk-ak   ____$_i$ a buk a Harry]
    I   IR-3-gave-1s   book

    Harry gave me the book.

Note that the examples immediately above have the same properties as other topicalizations, showing that the resumptive pronominal forms following **er** are indeed independent pronouns, and not a form of agreement that attaches to prepositions.[8]

1.5. *Synthesis*

Let us return now to the structures posited for clefts and pseudoclefts in section 1.2 above; we return also to the claim that free relatives occur in both. By now it may already have been observed that the structure of WH questions and topicalizations can be reduced to the structures described earlier. Examples (19a) and (24c) are repeated in (27):

(27) a. ng-te'a$_i$ [a kileld-ii   a sub ___$_i$]
         Cl-who   R-Pf-heat-3s   soup

   Who heated up the soup?

   b. a blai$_i$ [a le-silseb-ii   ___$_i$ a se'el-ik]
      house   IR-3-Pf-burn-3s   friend-1s

   My friend burned down the house.

It is clear that the cleft analysis in (14) may be applied to WH questions and the pseudocleft analysis in (15) to topicalizations. The structures are repeated in (28):

(28) a. *ng*-cleft (=*it*-cleft)   b. pseudocleft (=*what*-cleft)

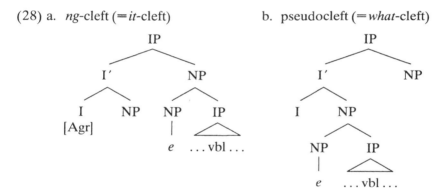

Note that in the case of WH questions the structure in (28a) fits perfectly (cf. (23)): the WH phrase is the predicate, and the free relative the subject. A more literal gloss for (27a), for example, would be *It is who that heated up the soup?*

In the case of the topicalization in (27b), however, the two NPs are in inverse order: in topicalization the free relative is contained in the *rightmost* NP, the subject, while in structure (28b) the free relative is the NP to the left, the predicate. That is, we have two structures, both of the form *NP-NP*, in which the two elements occur in opposite order. Such sentences can be analyzed along lines argued for in Williams (1983a).

Williams (following Higgins 1973) distinguishes *specificational* from *predicational* pseudoclefts. In a specificational pseudocleft the predicate is a free relative; in a predicational pseudocleft the subject is the relative. (29) is adapted from Williams' (11):

(29) *Pseudoclefts* (after Williams):

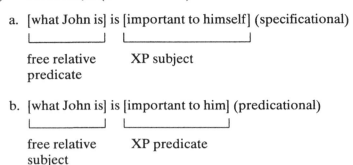

a. [what John is] is [important to himself] (specificational)
   free relative   XP subject
   predicate

b. [what John is] is [important to him] (predicational)
   free relative   XP predicate
   subject

A specificational pseudocleft is an equational sentence in which XP identifies the gap in the predicate, while in a predicational pseudocleft, the XP predicates some property of the subject. Williams incorporates the analysis of the two types of pseudoclefts into his overall argument that predicate NPs, though syntactically like referential NPs, are semantically of a different type.[9]

Williams' typology can be applied to the analysis of Palauan to account for the word order difference between what we refer to as topicalizations and pseudoclefts. In Williams' terms, the structure in (28a), which we refer to as a 'topicalization' structure, is a predicational pseudocleft, and the structure in (28b), which we will refer to simply as 'pseudocleft', is a specificational pseudocleft. This typology allows us to account for the difference between these structures: in topicalizations the subject is a relativized structure, and in pseudoclefts ((12) and (13)) it is the predicate that is relativized. The ability of Williams' analysis to account so neatly for the Palauan structures counts as strong support for that analysis. The language has also been pretty clever.

To sum up, clefts, topicalizations, pseudoclefts, and WH questions are all of the abstract form (I) NP-NP, and all contain a free relative as one of the two NP constituents. Headed relative clauses contain a full CP.

The structures can be compared in (30) through (32). (30) contains the basic structures; (31) the clefts; and (32) the pseudoclefts.

(30) a. Headed relative clause: b. Headless (free) relative clause:

(31) a. Cleft (*ng-*):   b. WH question:

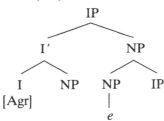
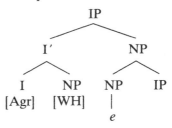

(32) a. Topicalization: b. Pseudocleft:

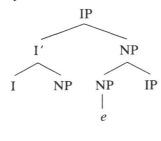
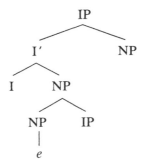

The fundamental characteristic of these formations is that they share a common syntactic structure, a relative clause. This finding is contrary to the standard analysis, in which these formations share a common transformation, WH movement. Later in the chapter it will be argued that all Palauan A' binding is base-generated. In light of those later arguments, it is perhaps not surprising that a relative clause structure underlies the whole class. Relative clauses are analyzed in GB as structures in which an interpretive rule of LF, rather than a movement rule, is responsible for the coindexing relation between an antecedent and a variable. (But see Chapter Four, on the level at which that coindexing holds.) The finding that the free relative structure is basic to all dependencies in this class (except for the headed relative) is also consistent with a non-movement analysis: the free relative contains IP but not CP, so there is no possibility of movement of a null operator.

Note that Josephs' (1975) problem of accounting for the distribution of the particle **a** (Chapter Two, section 4.1) disappears on this analysis. **a** marks only NPs, including complex NPs, but never VPs. Since the predicate in Palauan topicalizations is actually an NP, not a VP, it bears the **a** marker. A new problem now arises, however: why do pseudocleft predicates (including topics, cf. (32)) bear no agreement marker, while cleft NPs (31) do? At present I have no good answer to this question.

76   CHAPTER THREE

1.6. *Clause Structure in Austronesian Studies*

This analysis of the predicate-subject structure of Palauan sentences is consistent with the view of clause structure that is often taken in Austronesian studies. In many Austronesian languages, the relation of the predicate to its argument takes syntactic form in ways superficially quite different from the subject-predicate relation in Indo-European languages. This relation is commonly encoded in Indo-European languages via NP case marking and an agreement system in which (pretheoretically) the verb agrees with the nominative NP (= the subject). In Austronesian languages, the verb itself may encode the various grammatical functions of NPs, via a system of focus markers contained in the verb morphology.[10]

One consequence of the nature of clause structure in Western Austronesian (and probably in Proto-Austronesian: Dahl 1976) is what has been seen as a lack of the clear-cut distinction between the parts of the sentence traditionally called subject and predicate that is found in Indo-European languages. Dahl (1976), for example, analyzes both WH questions and certain NP-verb sentences in Malagasy as constructions in which an NP is the predicate and the verb (= the rest of the clause) is the 'topic' (= subject). The predicate contains the new information, or the questioned element, and the subject contains "what is present in the thoughts beforehand" (p. 120).

Although the foregoing analysis (section 1.2–1.5) is consistent with the traditional Austronesianist view, it is also consistent in Indo-European terms. Since 'subject' and 'predicate' are not primitives in the generative framework, the same structural apparatus used to analyze the syntax of English can be used to analyze Palauan. What is actually at issue is whether or not this framework is successful at analyzing any given language, and that cannot be decided on functional terms.

No new descriptive tools have been introduced (and none will be), and so far no violence has been done to the language. Thus at a (so far elementary) level of analytical abstraction the initial exoticism of Palauan is reduced to variation within universal themes. The theoretical devices involved in analysis of this variation are deployed in the next three chapters.

1.7. *The Identification Hypothesis*

The examples above have illustrated the fact that gaps and overt pronouns in Palauan A′ binding arise in different environments. We have so far seen that a gap is found in subject extraction sites, and also at any extraction site governed by a head carrying agreement. Overt pronouns do not appear in any of these positions, but appear obligatorily in an extraction site following the preposition **er**. One might see here evidence

VARIABLE BINDING STRUCTURES 77

of an "accessibility hierarchy" (Keenan & Comrie 1977; Comrie 1981), on which subjects and objects are accessible and objects of **er** are all oblique, or relatively inaccessible. Such hierarchies can easily be derived from government theory, however, in Palauan as in other languages.

What, then, does determine the distribution of WH gaps and pronouns? Note that the distribution of gaps resembles that of *pro* (Chapter Two); that is, it appears to depend on the distribution of agreement morphology, i.e. on identification. This is contrary to common assumptions (e.g. Chomsky 1982; Jaeggli 1982; Huang 1982), in which only *pro*, but not variables, must be identified.[11] Other principles, namely subjacency and the ECP, constrain the distribution of WH gaps. We extend the discussion of the identification issue to this chapter because it appears that *pro* and WH gaps are licensed by the same conditions in Palauan. This will figure in later arguments that WH gaps *are pro*'s, not movement traces. Therefore we may ask whether the gaps are subject to the ECP or to *pro* theory (or to both). When we arrive at those arguments, it will be important to have established the following points.

Since agreement appears to play an important role in licensing WH gaps, let us hypothesize that the proper government of extraction sites depends on the possibility of identification of the person and number features of the antecedent in some local and overt way. Pursuing this hypothesis, we note that the features necessary to identification in Palauan are usually available within some local domain. The features of an antecedent that is a subject are locally provided by the antecedent itself (the head of a relative or a clefted NP, or a WH phrase). The features of an antecedent that is a perfective object or a possessor (in some NPs) are provided by agreement. Elsewhere, the features of the antecedent must be recovered locally from an overt resumptive pronoun. Since resumptive pronouns can be *locally* A' bound, they do seem to play some such role. Just as pronouns cannot be null following a preposition, which carries no agreement features, a WH gap is impossible in that position.

Identification of WH-extraction sites further parallels the identification of *pro* in that there are systematic cases in which identification fails. One is the case of 'long' extraction of the subject: the antecedent is not local in this case, nor is subject agreement available (the following example is taken from the discussion of the *pro*-drop parameter in Chapter Two):

(33)   ng-te'a$_i$ [a ldilu   a sensei [el kmo ng-milsa
         Cl-who   *IR-3-said*   *teacher* *Comp* *R-3s-Pf-saw-3s*

        [el   meskak   a buk ____$_i$]]]
        Comp *R-Pf-give-1s* *book*

    Who did the teacher say that he saw give me the book?

78 CHAPTER THREE

In this question there is no subject agreement on the local verb **meskak**, and the antecedent is two clauses away. This example looks like WH extraction in more familiar languages.

Another case in which identification fails involves the verb **msa** 'give'; this verb agrees with the goal argument rather than with the theme. Extraction of *either* object of **msa** leaves a gap, even though the features of the theme are not supplied by any overt agreement. The following examples illustrate this:

(34) a. ak-milsterir a kall a rese'elik
     1s-gave-3p food friends-1s

    I gave the food to my friends.

  b. ak-milsterir a rese'elik a kall

    I gave my friends the food.

  c. a kall [el k-bilsterir a rese'elik ___]
    food Comp IR-1s-gave-3p friend-1s

    the food I gave my friends

  d. a redil [el k-bilsterir ___ a kall]
    women Comp IR-1s-gave-3p food

    the women I gave the food to

Again, the facts were parallel for *pro*: only the goal triggers agreement, yet the theme may also be realized by *pro*. Here, both may be extracted.

A third case is that of indefinite objects (see Chapter Two). These differ from other objects in that they correspond to no agreement form on perfective verbs, nor do they exhibit the preposition **er** when they are objects of imperfective verbs. When these objects are extracted, a gap rather than a resumptive pronoun appears:

(35) a. a blai [el dobil'ar ___] a bekerekard el rokui
    house Comp IR-1p-Pf-bought red L all

    The houses that we bought all were red.

  b. ak-mil'ar a bung [el lomekeroul ___ a Rosa]
    R-1s-Pf-buy flower Comp IR-3-Im-grow

    I bought the flowers that Rosa was growing.

Indefinite objects realized by *pro* also occur in this environment.

Finally, identification fails in free relatives in which a subject gap is coindexed with the (null) head (cf. the examples in (6)).

VARIABLE BINDING STRUCTURES

In sum, in the case of extraction as in the case of *pro*, the hypothesis of local identification works, and fails to work, in a regular set of cases. That set properly includes all the contexts in which *pro* occurs, with or without identification. As we did in accounting for *pro*, then, we must conclude that WH gaps are not licensed by morphology. In order to maintain the identification hypothesis, we would be forced to claim that some gaps, like some *pro*, can be identified even by null agreement, a position that vitiates the hypothesis. The same considerations apply if we were to posit intermediate traces in Comp to properly govern subject WH gaps: such traces would not provide identification in the intended sense.

Despite surface appearances, then, Palauan does not support a morphological approach to licensing of empty categories.[12] In Chapter Two we concluded that the distribution of *pro* depended on a mix of contextual and interpretive conditions. Here the conclusion is that WH gaps are licensed by properties of the binding construction independent of agreement morphology. For now I assume the licensing conditions involved are encoded in the ECP (see Chapter One). Positions that support gaps are properly governed, and overt resumptive pronouns arise as ECP effects: the preposition is not a proper governor. In Chapters Four and Six I will explore these questions in some detail; Chapter Six is especially concerned with how the ECP is formulated.

It is important to keep in mind that the conditions on the *path* between the extraction site and its antecedent are distinct from conditions applying to the extraction site itself. Path conditions in Palauan are unusual; they are discussed in section 3.

1.8. *Base Generation, I: Simplicity*

The data presented so far suggest a base-generation rather than a transformational analysis of Palauan A' binding dependencies, assuming that transformations do not insert lexical material (see, e.g., Jackendoff 1972, Chomsky 1977). A base-generation account is needed for the structures with resumptive pronouns, which, as we have seen, are very productive and include even local binding of arguments. If we extend this account to all A' binding, we can avoid postulating two distinct but similar analyses for each type of dependency, base-generation for the structures with resumptive pronouns and movement for the ones with gaps. Base-generation also allows us to account for the fact that resumptive pronouns and gaps in this language are equally productive in all structures. In the next section I will discuss island constraints, which are diagnostic of movement and in many languages condition the appearance of resumptive pronouns.

80   CHAPTER THREE

2. ISLANDS

The island constraints are an integral part of the generative analysis of
A′ binding. In this section we will consider the evidence of island
phenomena in Palauan, and we will see that it strongly supports the
tentative conclusion of the last section, that base generation is the
analysis of choice.

2.1. *No Islands?*

Consider the topicalization sentences below. In the first set, a topic is
bound to a position within a sentential subject; in (36a) the subject is
extracted, and in (36b) the object is extracted. (In the English gloss, I
insert a comma after the topic. This is simply to make the gloss more
coherent; in Palauan there is no pause after the topic.)

(36) a. a Mary$_i$ [a kltukl   [el kmo ng-oltoir   er a John ___$_i$]]
           R-clear Comp R-3s-Im-love P

      Mary, (it's) clear that ___ loves John.

   b. a John$_i$ [a kltukl   [el   l-oltoir   er ngii$_i$ a Mary]]
           R-clear Comp IR-3-Im-love P him

      John, (it's) clear that Mary loves (him).

In (37), topics are linked to object position within a relative clause:

(37) a. a buk$_i$ [a ku-dengel-ii   [a redil   [el
           book   IR-1s-Pf-know-3s   woman   Comp

      uldurukl-ii   ___$_i$ [el   mo er a delak]]]]
      R-Pf-send-3s   Comp go P   mother-1s

      The book, I know the woman who sent ___ to my mother.

   b. a buk$_i$ [a ku-dengel-ii   [a 'ad [el   uleme'ar er ngii$_i$]]]
           book   IR-1s-Pf-know-3s   man Comp R-Im-buy P it

      The book, I know the man who bought (it).

   c. [a 'elibel   a uel]$_i$ [a k-ulemes er [a rese'al
           shell-3s   turtle   IR-1-saw   P   boys

      [el   omtanget   er ngii$_i$]]]
      Comp R-Im-polish P   it

      The turtle shell, I was watching the boys
      who were polishing (it).

The next examples show that extraction is possible from embedded
questions. In (38a), the topic **delak** 'my mother' is extracted from a

VARIABLE BINDING STRUCTURES

clause headed by the WH phrase **ngera** 'what': and in (38b), the topic
'elibel a uel 'turtle shell' binds the object position within a clause headed
by the WH phrase **te'a** 'who':

(38) a. a del-ak$_i$ [a diak ku-dengei   [el kmo ng-ngera$_k$
        mother-1s   Neg IR-1s-Im-know   Comp   Cl-what

      [a bo   lo-ruul ___$_k$ ___$_i$ el mo belsoil]]]
      IR-Fut IR-do   L go   dinner

      My mother, I don't know what ___ will cook for supper.

  b. [a 'elibel   a uel]$_i$ [a diak ku-dengei [el kmo
       shell-3s   turtle   Neg IR-1-know   Comp

     [ng-te'a$_k$ [a ulemtanget er ngii$_i$ ___$_k$]]]]
     Cl-who   R-Im-polish P it

     The turtle shell, I don't know who was polishing it.

Each of the sentences in (36) through (38) violates one of the well-
known island constraints, but is grammatical in Palauan. (36) violates the
Sentential Subject Constraint, (37) the Complex NP Constraint, and
(38) the WH-Island Condition.

The island extractions illustrated in the examples above all involve
topicalization. WH questions and relativization violate island boundaries
with the same impunity. (39a) illustrates a WH question formed on a
constituent of a relative clause, and (39b) a relative embedded within a
relative:

(39) a. ng-ngera$_i$ [a 'om-omes er [a rese'al$_k$]
        Cl-what   IR-2-see   P   boys

      [el   omtanget er ngii$_i$ ___$_k$]]
      Comp R-polish P it

      What are you watching the boys who are polishing (it)?

  b. ng-te'a a milde'em-ii [a uel$_i$ [el   m-ulmes er [a rese'al$_k$]
       Cl-who R-caught-3s   turtle Comp IR-2-saw P   boys

     [el   omtanget er [a 'elibel ___$_i$] ___$_k$]]]
     Comp R-polish P   shell-3s

     Who caught the turtle that you saw the boys
     who were polishing its shell?

Two important points emerge from the examples in (36) through
(39): one is that Palauan grammar allows the full range of island violations, and the second is that it allows them using *either* a gap *or* a
resumptive pronoun. Examples (36a), (37a), (38a), and (39b) contain

82   CHAPTER THREE

gaps, while (36b), (37b), (38b), and (39a) contain resumptive pronouns, objects of **er**.

It should be kept in mind that an extraposition analysis of sentential subjects is not relevant (unless it applies vacuously). Subjects are already on a right branch, since the language is VOS. Therefore extraction out of subjects is expected to be grammatical. The grammaticality of sentences like (36) supports my analysis of Palauan word order in Chapter Two. The *reason* why extraction from a right branch is grammatical, however, is a matter for government theory, which also derives the other facts here. See Chapters Four and Six.

In sum, the island constraints appear not to apply, and the use of resumptive pronouns appears unrelated to this fact; even the structures with *gaps* cannot be reasonably characterized as movement structures, and resumptive pronouns appear even when the binder is local.

2.2. *Base Generation, II: Islands*

In EST, island phenomena are derived by the Subjacency Condition (Chomsky 1977, 1981, 1986b), a universal locality principle that prohibits movement across more than one bounding node. Since some of the island violations arise when more than one bounding node must be crossed in any one movement, these phenomena result from subjacency (see the discussion in Chapter One). It is evident that this analysis does not apply to the Palauan island facts.

A variation of this approach involves *parameterizing* the bounding nodes for subjacency. In the literature, island violations in various languages have been accounted for in this way. Rizzi (1982a), for example, shows that Italian disallows extraction from relative clauses but permits extraction from embedded questions, and proposes that S (IP) is not a bounding node for Italian. Similarly, it has been suggested (Huang 1982; Chomsky 1986b) that a node dominating an adjunct (such as an adverbial clause) is an absolute barrier to extraction, while a node subcategorized by some phrasal head may allow movement across it. The relativizing of bounding nodes to particular constructions, in the latter approach, restricts the generality of subjacency as an explanatory principle. However, the Palauan facts probably have nothing to tell us about (any formulation of) subjacency. Since Palauan ignores *all* the bounding constraints, there is no particular point to proposing an analysis that makes certain bounding nodes exceptional. The solution is rather to say that Palauan grammar simply has no WH movement.

The facts about island violations therefore support the analysis we reached above, in which all Palauan A' binding is analyzed in terms of base generation. There, we were motivated by the parallel occurrence of gaps and overt pronouns in all types of extraction. In this section, we

VARIABLE BINDING STRUCTURES 83

motivate the general base generation analysis by the lack of locality effects due to subjacency. As the Subjacency Condition constrains only movement rules, base-generated structures would not be expected to exhibit its effects.[13] And since islands are freely violated with either gap or resumptive pronoun, not even the structures containing *gaps* can be analyzed in terms of movement. I conclude, therefore, that all of the dependencies we have observed are base generated.

As noted above, the base generation account is the most simple and unified analysis, since it assumes only one strategy for both gap-containing and pronoun-containing structures. To posit two separate strategies, furthermore, would be to ignore one of the most important facts about Palauan grammar: that it treats gaps and overt resumptive pronouns as syntactically equivalent. Nothing in the theory predicts or requires, for example, that purely local binding of a direct object, as in (20a) or (25a), should involve a resumptive pronoun.

To assume base generation of the whole class of dependencies, however, removes the motivation for the separate LF analysis of (overt) resumptive pronouns in Chomsky (1982) (see Chapter One). Instead, Palauan motivates an analysis in which *all* extraction sites contain pronouns. What we have been referring to as 'gaps' and 'resumptive pronouns' are both pronominals in D-structure, and both become variables coindexed with their antecedents at the same level (see Chapter Four). Let us represent this analysis in a general descriptive statement about Palauan syntax:

(40)   Only pronominals can be variables.

This view of Palauan pronominal variables will be expanded in Chapters Four and Six.

Alternatively, since some positions always contain a gap, it may be suggested that these positions are accessible to movement while other positions are not. There is a serious problem with this alternative, which is that island violations can occur in extraction from all positions. Take subjects: if the subject extraction site contains a WH trace, its binding relation should observe subjacency. The failure of the island violations to distinguish subject gaps from other extraction sites argues that the element in subject position is the same category as the element in other NP positions.

To sum up to this point, the distribution of null and overt referring pronouns is practically identical to the distribution of null and overt resumptive pronouns.[14] This match suggests that these sets of free and bound elements are the *same* set in D-structure. For the gaps to be *pro* in the base, the distribution of gaps would have to be a subset of the distribution of *pro*. This is exactly what we find. If the gaps were *not pro* in an earlier life, on the other hand, then the correlation in the distribu-

84 CHAPTER THREE

tion of gaps and *pro* is fortuitous and unexplained.[15] As for the overt
forms, they are lexical and present at D-structure.

Many questions remain. What exactly does it mean, for example, to
base generate gaps? How, and at what level, is coindexing carried out?
Before these questions can be answered, another important aspect of
these structures remains to be described: the system of verb agreement
that is particular to A′ binding.

3. WH AGREEMENT

3.1. *WH Agreement in Local Dependencies*

Up to this point I have said nothing about the alternations in mood
morphology that I have noted in all Palauan variable binding structures.
This morphology is the overt effect of an agreement phenomenon that is
central to my overall analysis.

Consider the pairs of topicalization structures below. In the (a)
sentences the subject is topic, while in the (b) sentences a nonsubject is
topic:

(41) a. a rengalek$_i$ a rirell-ii   a bresent ___$_i$ el   mo
     children   *R-Pf-made-3s*   *present*   *Comp go*

     er a sensei
     P   teacher

     The children made a present for the teacher.

   b. a bresent$_i$ a l-lirell-ii   ___$_i$ a rengalek el   mo
     present   *IR-3-Pf-made-3s*   *children Comp go*

     er a sensei
     P   teacher

     The children made a present for the teacher.

The facts of (42) are similar; a resumptive pronoun is used in the object
case:

(42) a. a sensei$_i$ a omes   er a rengalek ___$_i$
     teacher   *R-Im-look P   children*

     The teacher is looking at the children.

   b. a rengalek$_i$ a lomes   er tir$_i$ a sensei
     children   *IR-3-Im-look P 3p   teacher*

     The teacher is looking at the children.

What interests us now is that these two sets of sentences differ in the
morphological *mood* that appears on the verb. In (41a) and (42a) the

VARIABLE BINDING STRUCTURES 85

verb has realis morphology and in (41b) and (42b) it has irrealis morphology.[16] The sentences differ in no other important respect, and have the same gloss.

The examples in (43) display a similar alternation in morphological mood in a minimal pair involving a WH question. In (43a) the WH word is in its argument position, and in (43b) it is at the head of the clause:

(43) a. ke-momerek el   melu'es er a babilengem er a oingerang
       R-2s-finish   Comp R-write P   paper-2s   P   when?

       When will you finish writing your paper?

   b. ng-oingerang$_i$ a 'o-bomerek el   melu'es er a babilengem
      Cl-when?   *IR-2-finish Comp R-write P   paper-2s*

      er ngii$_i$
      P   then

      When will you finish writing your paper?

There is no semantic factor present in the (b) sentences that is not present in the (a) sentences and that would require irrealis morphology. The real contrast is syntactic: the fronted NPs in (41) through (43) are linked to different structural positions. Looking back over all the examples presented so far, we see that when a subject is extracted the clause is realis, and when any nonsubject is extracted the clause is irrealis. Palauan grammar, in other words, distinguishes extraction of subjects from extraction of nonsubjects in an unusual way: via a distinction in morphological mood.

A secondary effect, but very important in distinguishing agreement in extraction sentences from agreement elsewhere, is that the subject agreement morpheme is lacking when the subject is extracted. The relevance of this fact will soon become apparent.

It is evident that the rule that determines the verb form in the sentences above is sensitive to the subject/nonsubject distinction. One means by which subjects and nonsubjects may be distinguished in Government-Binding theory is in terms of abstract Case. Recall that, according to Case Theory, subjects are assigned Nominative Case by Inflection, direct objects are assigned Accusative Case by the verb, and so on. Assuming Case Theory, then, we may say that verb forms in Palauan extraction are sensitive to the Case assigned to the extraction site.[17]

The most natural analysis of these facts is in terms of *agreement*. Though agreement rules most commonly involve personal features like number, person, and gender, those features are clearly not the only ones available to an agreement system. To 'agree with' is not necessarily to 'bear the person features of'. What *is* essential to agreement is that one

86   CHAPTER THREE

element trigger, or control, the form of another element within a certain (and usually local) domain. In Palauan, the controller is the variable, the target is Inflection (or the verb), and the form involved reflects Case. We can say that Inflection *agrees with* the variable *in Case*.

I will refer to the rule as *WH agreement*, adopting the term from Chung (1982a), where a similar rule in Chamorro is described. Let us provisionally state WH agreement in Palauan as in (44):

(44)   *WH agreement*: (preliminary version)

In the domain between an A′ binder and the variable it c-commands, Inflection agrees with the Case of the variable.

Certain terms of this rule, especially the reference to 'variable', anticipate developments in Chapter Four and remain to be justified; the rule will also be refined as more data are taken into account. Some of its properties are already apparent, however.

First, take the reference to c-command domain and to the A′ binder: the position of the binder (topic, WH phrase, and so on) takes syntactic scope over (c-commands) all argument positions that may contain an extraction site (the 'variable'), and takes scope over the verb as well. The position of the binder is an A′ position (a 'nonargument' position), as it is not assigned a θ-role or a grammatical relation (cf. Aoun 1985).[18]

Furthermore, in stating the rule in terms of the domain of the A′ binder, it is claimed that WH agreement applies only in variable binding; this is in fact the case. It is not triggered by null pronouns, nor by anaphoric relations between A positions. In (45) below, for example, there are several occurrences of *pro* but no A′ variables. In (45b), the passive construction is illustrated, and in (45c), a control construction. In none of these cases does WH agreement apply:

(45) a. ak-'illebed-au e le   u'ul   ke-kill-ii   a kel-ek
        R-1s-Pf-hit-2s because reason R-2s-Pf-eat-3s   food-1s

        I hit you because you ate my food.

     b. ng-mil'elebed a Merii er a redil   er a Kuam
        R-3s-PASS-hit   P   woman P

        Merii got beat up by a woman from Guam.

     c. ak-mellasm el   meruul er a life er ngak el   mo ungil
        R-1s-try   Comp make   P   P me Comp Fut good

        I'm trying to make my life better.

Third, the rule refers to 'variable', and therefore should apply indifferently to structures containing overt resumptive pronouns and those containing gaps. This aspect of WH agreement has already been amply

VARIABLE BINDING STRUCTURES

87

motivated. It will receive further support in the examples of long-distance dependencies below.

Let us assume for now that WH agreement copies the Case feature of the variable onto Inflection,[19] and is written out as part of the verb morphology in PF. The actual operation of passing on agreement features is described in Chapter Four, which introduces the necessary formal mechanisms.

As for the verb form itself, we recall from the discussion of verb morphology in Chapter Two that a realis verb contains the realis morpheme, while an irrealis verb lacks this morpheme. WH agreement therefore *directly* affects *only* the distribution of the realis marker, though it *indirectly* affects the form of subject agreement (see below).

Since the Case feature is copied from the variable, we may refer to the variable as a 'controller' of agreement. The morphological effects of WH agreement can then be summed up as in (46):

(46)   *Morphological effects of WH agreement*:

The verb is realis when the controller is Nominative, and irrealis otherwise.

Let us look again at examples of the various constructions, and verify that (44) and (46) in fact do what they claim to do.

In (24), for example (repeated below), we see that a topic associated with a subject variable ((47a)) triggers a realis verb form, while a topic associated with a nonsubject variable triggers an irrealis form ((47b, c)). Recall that a verb carries *no subject agreement* when the subject is the local A′ binder, though this verb *does* contain the realis morpheme.

(47) a. a sensei$_i$ [a omes   er a rengalek ____$_i$]
         teacher   ***R-Im-see*** *P* *children*
         The teacher is looking at the children.

b. a blai$_i$ [a le-silseb-ii   ____$_i$ a se'el-ik]
    house   ***IR-3-Pf-burn-3s***   *friend-1s*
    My friend burned down the house.

c. a Naomi$_i$ [a le-'ilit-ii   [a 'ole'es-el ____$_i$] a John]
    IR-3-Pf-throw-3s   *pencil-3s*
    John threw away Naomi's pencil.

A similar contrast obtains in all other A′ binding structures. Examples of WH questions were seen in (20) (repeated below). The Nominative variable in (48a) is accompanied by a realis verb form, and non-Nominative variables in (48b, c) by irrealis forms.

CHAPTER THREE

(48) a. ng-te'a*ᵢ* [a kileld-ii   a sub   ____*ᵢ*]
     Cl-who   ***R**-Pf-heat-3s*   *soup*
     Who heated up the soup?

   b. ng-te'a*ᵢ* [a l-ulekod-ir   ____*ᵢ* a rubak]
     Cl-who   ***IR**-3-Pf-kill-3s*   *old.man*
     Who did the old man kill?

   c. ng-ngera*ᵢ* [a le-silseb-ii   ____*ᵢ* a se'el-il]
     Cl-what   ***IR**-3-Pf-burn-3s*   *friend-3s*
     What did his friend burn?

Looking now at the relative clauses in (2) (repeated below), we see that relativized subjects trigger realis morphology ((49a)), and relativized nonsubjects trigger irrealis morphology ((49b, c)):

(49) a. ak-medengel-ii a 'ad*ᵢ* [el   mil'er-ar   tia   el buk ____*ᵢ*]
     R-1s-Pf-know-3s   *man Comp **R**-Pf-buy-3s Dem L book*
     I know the person who bought that book.

   b. ak-milsa a mlai*ᵢ* [el   l-dilse'ii   ____*ᵢ* tirkei el re'ad]
     R-1s-saw   *canoe Comp **IR**-3-carved-3s*   *Dem L men*
     I saw the canoe that those men carved.

   c. a buik*ᵢ* [el   k-'illebed-ii   [a 'obok-ul   ____*ᵢ*]] a se'el-ik
     boy   *Comp **IR**-1s-Pf-hit-3s*   *brother-3s*   *friend-1s*
     The boy whose older brother I hit is my friend.

Thus the alternations in mood morphology observed up to this point are accounted for by (44) and (46).

It has occasionally been suggested to me that only irrealis morphology needs to be mentioned in the statement of WH agreement, on the assumption that the realis morphology accompanying subject extraction need not be mentioned because the clause would be realis *anyway*, or the assumption that mentioning only nonsubjects would make the rule simpler. Such a view suggests that subject extraction does not really participate in WH agreement. In terms of the facts I have laid out here, the correct generalization is being missed.

For one thing, the suggested approach cannot explain why realis morphology in *non*-extraction cases occurs *with* subject agreement, while realis morphology in extraction is accompanied by *no* subject agreement (see, e.g., the difference between examples (18) and (19a, b); see also Chapter Two, section 2). Realis verb forms in subject extraction cases are *not* the same as they would be without extraction; the WH agreement analysis including reference to subjects accounts for this, an analysis failing to include subjects does not.

VARIABLE BINDING STRUCTURES   89

Second, as the discussion at the end of the section on multiple variables (section 3.3) will make clear, only such a formulation as is proposed here (i.e. with the coverage of (44) and (46)) can predict the morphology of *each clause* in cases of multiple, interacting dependencies.

3.1.1. *Semantic Mood and WH Agreement*

Finally, let us test the claim that the alternation in mood morphology induced by WH agreement is purely syntactic, and is not related to the *semantic* mood of a clause. The paired examples in (42) through (43) showed that syntactic factors could affect mood morphology. The examples in (50) show that WH agreement fails to affect irrealis morphology that is semantically conditioned. 'If' and 'when' clauses in Palauan can be expressed as a nominalized, irrealis clause, as seen in (50):

(50) a. a David a ldese'ii   a bilas, e   ngmou'ais er kid
          IR-3-build   boat Ptc R-3s-tell   P   us

   If David builds a boat, he will tell us.

   b. a bilas a ldese'ii a David, e ngmou'ais er kid
       If David builds a boat, he will tell us.

   c. a bo   lme'ellakl a skuul, e   ngungil   er a omesuub
       IR-Aux IR-3-calm   school Ptc R-3s-good P   R-study

   When school calms down, it's a good place to study.

   d. a skuul a bo lme'ellakl, e ngungil er a omesuub
       When school calms down, it's a good place to study.

The 'if'-clause in (50a) has a subject topic, and that in (50b) has a nonsubject topic. Neither subject nor object topicalization affects the form of the verb, which is semantically irrealis. Similarly in (50c, d), the adverbial 'when'-clause is semantically irrealis, and topicalization of a subject ((50d)) has no effect on the morphology of the verb.

The priority of semantic mood over the 'syntactic mood' induced by WH agreement is an example of what Anderson (1982) attributes to the Elsewhere Condition in inflectional morphology (see Chung & Georgopoulos 1988). Whenever the conditions for two morphological realizations are met simultaneously, the more restricted one takes precedence. In (50), realizations determined by true irrealis mood take precedence over realization of WH agreement, presumably because the former agreement system employs only the set of irrealis morphology while the latter employs both irrealis and realis markers. The ordering of morphosyntactic rules and rules controlled by lexical or semantic factors may also play a role: if WH agreement took precedence over semantic agree-

90   CHAPTER THREE

ment, semantic information (about mood) would be lost, but if WH agreement morphology is absent, no information is lost that is not available elsewhere.

The disjunction between the WH agreement system and a purely semantic agreement system, i.e. the fact that the latter blocks the former, is further proof that the two systems are distinct, and that WH agreement morphology, even when irrealis, is a strictly syntactic phenomenon. Of course, the point that WH agreement is syntactic is made another way by pairs like (41a, b): the mood alternation is induced by a *syntactic* alternation in word order. That is, the irrealis mood of (50) reflects the speaker's attitude toward the truth or factual status of the expression, while the irrealis mood of WH agreement does not.

Thus, given that an Elsewhere Condition or disjunctive principle like that described here is operative in the grammar, facts like those in (50) introduce no complications. WH agreement is realized only in semantically realis structures, but this fact need not be stated in the rule itself.

In Chapter Five (section 2.4.1) I describe another agreement phenomenon that can preempt WH agreement, one that applies in yes/no questions. Again, two agreement rules will be seen to be disjoint.

3.2. *WH Agreement in Long-Distance Dependencies*

When we extend the data base from monoclausal to multiclausal dependencies, several new and important properties of Palauan grammar are revealed to us. They all involve the phenomenon of WH agreement in some way. When the antecedent and its variable are separated by one or more clause boundaries, the agreement facts are not exactly as stated in (44). In these cases, inflection in higher clauses reflect the Case of the sentential argument that *contains* the variable, rather than the Case of the variable itself.

Consider the examples of topicalization of a constituent of a sentential subject; (36a, b) are repeated in (51):

(51) a. a Mary$_i$ [a kltukl   [el kmo ng-oltoir   er a John ____$_i$]]
             R-clear   Comp   R-3s-Im-love   P

   Mary, (it's) clear that ____ loves John.

   b. a John$_i$ [a kltukl   [el   l-oltoir   er ngii$_i$ a Mary]]
              R-clear   Comp   IR-3-Im-love   P   him

   John, (it's) clear that Mary loves (him).

In (51a), the embedded verb is realis, as expected: its subject, **Mary**, is the topic of the sentence. But the matrix verbal, **kltukl** 'clear', is also realis. In order to se which constituent of (51a) controls WH agreement

VARIABLE BINDING STRUCTURES

91

in the matrix, compare the morphology of (51b). Here, the variable bound by **John** is a nonsubject, inducing irrealis morphology on the lower verb. The matrix verbal in (51b) is realis, however. This indicates that a Nominative argument is the controller of WH agreement in the matrix. **John** is not Nominative, but the sentential (subject) argument containing the variable coindexed with **John** (the resumptive pronoun **ngii**) *is* Nominative. It is this subject argument that is controlling the mood morphology of **kltukl** 'clear' in the matrix, in both (51a) and (51b).

In (52), in contrast, we observe topicalization of a nonsubject phrase binding a position in a nonsubject clause; neither the variable nor the clause containing it is Nominative:

(52) a bung$_i$ [el   l-ulemdasu a del-ak   [el
         flower Comp IR-3-think   mother-1s Comp

       l-omekeroul ____$_i$ a Mary er a sersel]]   a mla   mad
       IR-3-Im-grow   P   garden-3s R-Pst R-die

The flowers my mother thought Mary was growing in her garden died.

The most embedded verb (**lomekeroul** 'grow') agrees with the Case of the direct object (non-Nominative) variable, and the intermediate verb (**lulemdasu** 'thought') is also irrealis, reflecting the Case of the object argument containing the variable.

Finally, we observe in (53) the extraction of a subject from a nonsubject argument:

(53) ng-te'a$_i$ [a l-ilsa   a Miriam [el   milnguiu er a
         Cl-who   IR-3-saw   Comp R-read   P

       buk   er ngii ____$_i$]]
       book P her

Who did Miriam see reading her book?

The lower clause, that containing the Nominative variable, is realis, while the matrix verb **lilsa** 'saw' agrees with the Case of its sentential object argument.

Summing up informally to here, the variable *locally* controls the mood of the verb, and non-locally it is the argument that *contains* the variable that is controller.

We observed earlier that WH agreement only applies inside the A binding domain. This fact can be dramatically illustrated by another unusual property of WH questions in Palauan, the possibility for a WH phrase to occupy, in S-structure, one of several positions. As we saw earlier, it may occupy its D-structure argument position. It may also be

92   CHAPTER THREE

found in cleft position in an embedded clause, or in cleft position in a
higher clause.[20] In all these positions it may take wide scope, so its
position at S-structure is unrelated to its semantic scope. In every case,
however, WH Agreement applies *up to* the S-structure position of the
WH phrase. These facts can be seen in the three forms of the question
'who do they believe that we think will go to Japan?' in (54):

(54) a. t-oumerang   [el   ked-omdasu [e   ng-mo   er a
       R-3p-believe Comp R-1p-think   Comp R-3s-go P

       siabal a **te'ang**]]
       Japan   who

   b. t-oumerang   [el   ked-omdasu [e   ng-**te'a**$_i$ a mo
      R-3p-believe Comp R-1p-think   Comp Cl-who   R-go

      er a siabal ____$_i$]]
      P   Japan

   c. ng-**te'a**$_i$ [a **l-oumerang** [el   d-omdasu   [e   ng-mo
      Cl-who   IR-3-believe Comp IR-1p-think Comp R-go

      er a siabal ____$_i$]]
      P   Japan

      (All three) Who do they believe that we think will go to
      Japan?

WH agreement is not triggered in (54a), where the subject WH phrase is
in situ. That no WH agreement effects are observed in (54a) is confirma-
tion of the prediction that structures not containing an A′ binding
dependency are not affected by the rule. In (54b), the WH phrase is in a
local A′ position, and the realis morphology of the lowest verb **mo** 'go'
(and the lack of subject agreement) indicates that the variable is a
subject. Both the higher verbs in (54b) are unaffected by the position of
the antecedent. In (54c), the WH phrase is in a matrix A′ position, and
the intermediate and matrix verbs have irrealis morphology, indicating
that the variable is not contained in a subject argument of either of these
verbs. The lowest clause contains a realis verb, however, since the
variable in this clause has Nominative Case.

   If, as has been concluded earlier, lexical pronouns and nonphono-
logical *pro* are resumptive pronouns in Palauan, overt pronouns and
gaps should pattern alike with respect to WH agreement. Observe, now,
the questions in (55), which are parallel to those in (54). Once again,
this time with respect to the S-structure position of the WH phrase and
the workings of WH agreement, we find that overt resumptive pronouns
participate in the *same* phenomena that gaps do. (55) displays four
versions of the constituent question corresponding to 'what did you say

VARIABLE BINDING STRUCTURES   93

that they're waiting for me to do?'. The questioned phrase **ngera** 'what',
is, consecutively, in situ ((55a)), clefted in the lowest clause ((55b)),
clefted in the intermediate clause ((55c)), and clefted in the matrix
((55d)). In these examples, the extraction site contains an overt resumptive pronoun:

(55) a. ke-dilu   [el   te-mengiil er ngak [el   mo   meruul
        R-2s-said Comp R-3p-wait P me   Comp R-Fut R-do

        er a **ngerang**]]
        P   what

     b. ke-dilu   [el   te-mengiil er ngak [el   ng-**ngera**$_i$ a
        R-2s-said Comp R-3p-wait P me   Comp Cl-what

        bo   kuruul er ngii$_i$]]
        IR-Fut IR-do P   it

     c. ke-dilu   [el   ng-**ngera**$_i$ a longiil   er ngak
        R-2s-said Comp Cl-what   IR-3-wait P me

        [el   bo   kuruul er ngii$_i$]]
        Comp IR-Fut IR-do P   it

     d. ng-**ngera**$_i$ [a 'om-dilu [el longiil   er ngak
        Cl-what   IR-2-said C IR-3-wait P me

        [el   bo   kuruul er ngii$_i$]]]
        Comp IR-Fut IR-do P   it

(All four) What did you say that they're waiting for me to do?

Neither the varaible itself nor any of the clauses containing it are
Nominative arguments, so that in every clause where the agreement rule
applies, the verb is irrealis. Again, the effects of the rule are observed
only up to the S-structure position of the WH-phrase.

Although the WH phrase in all of the examples in (54) and (55) has
semantic wide scope, and therefore is assumed to take structural wide
scope in LF (see May 1977), Palauan grammar obviously does not
require that this scope be expressed at S-structure. This fact and its
implications for the analysis of embedded questions are pursued in
Chapter Five. The examples in (56) demonstrate that WH agreement
does not affect the tree outside of the A′ binding domain described in
(44):

(56) a. a me'as$_i$ [el   k-ulnge'edu' er ngii$_i$ er a bilas] a ulu'ais
        woman   Comp IR-1s-Im-met P her P   boat   R-told

        er ngak el kmo ng-mei   er a Belau
        P me   Comp R-3s-come P

The woman I met on the boat told me that she was from Palau.

94 CHAPTER THREE

(56) b. ng-ngera$_i$ a l-rirellii   ____$_i$ el   mlo   mekngit
    Cl-what   *IR-3-Pf-did-3s*   *Comp R-Aux R-bad*

What did they do that was bad?

3.2.1. *The Case of CP*

The examples in (51) through (56) have also illustrated the fact that the subject/nonsubject status of *clauses*, in addition to NPs, is relevant to the workings of WH agreement. That is, CP as well as NP is a controller of agreement, and must thereby be assumed to bear a Case feature. There is some question in GB about clauses receiving Case, however. Stowell (1981) argues that a category that bears a Case-assigning feature cannot itself be assigned Case. This prohibition, called the Case Resistance Principle, extends to CP, since CP contains [+Tense], a Case assigner. Stowell proposes the CRP to unify facts about CP extraposition and certain assumptions about θ-role assignment (see pp. 146 ff.). However, the claim that CP is assigned Case seems well supported by WH agreement in Palauan long-distance dependencies (see also Chung, 1991; Levin & Massam 1985).

Aside from the requirements of WH agreement, there is morphological evidence in Palauan that CP is assigned Case by its governor. A subclass of the verbs taking sentential complements bear transitive morphology (the object agreement morpheme is bold in the examples below). The fact that these verbs are transitive implicates assignment of Accusative Case to their object complements. (When the complement of one of these verbs is an overt NP, of course, there is no question: the NP must be assigned Case.)

(57) a. ng-sebe'em [el   o'ot-ii   er ngak [el kmo
    3s-CAN-2s *Comp R-show-3s P me*   *Comp*

    ak-mekera   e   mo er a beluu]]
    R-1s-do.what? Comp go P   town

Can you show me how to get to town?

b. ke-medengel-ii [el kmo ng-te'a a mlo   er a stoang]
    R-2s-know-3s *Comp Cl-who   went P   store*

(Do) you know who went to the store (?)

Interestingly, (57a) shows that the object of 'show' is not the goal but the theme — the clause. (57b) is an embedded question.

To sum up, WH agreement is locally controlled, either by the variable or by the argument containing it, in the manner schematized in figure (58a) and *not* as schematized in figure (58b) (these figures are adapted from Chung and Georgopoulos 1988; 'WH' refers to any A′ binder):

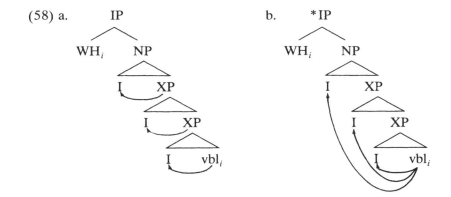

The provisional formulation of WH agreement, accordingly, is amended to take the extraclausal controller into account. At this point we may also incorporate into the statement of the rule the claim that it applies at S-structure.

(59) *WH agreement* (final version):

In the S-structure domain between an A' binder and its variable, Inflection agrees with

a. the Case of the argument containing the variable, or

b. the Case of the variable.

Clauses (a) and (b) are disjunctively ordered within (59): (b) applies only where (a) does not.

3.2.2. *Relevance in Other Theories*

It is worth noting in passing that a phenomenon like WH agreement, which can be triggered by a subject gap, allows a substantive distinction between GB and theories like Generalized Phrase Structure Grammar (GPSG). While GB stipulates that all clauses have subjects, even when the subject is empty, in GPSG a clause with a 'missing' subject is analyzed as simply a tensed VP — there is no subject position at all in such a clause. But if there is no subject variable to trigger WH agreement, the realis/irrealis morphology must be accounted for by some other feature or device; such a device, it seems to me, must be the equivalent of assuming the presence in the clause of a Nominative element, i.e. of a subject.

WH agreement also bears on the claim in Lexical Functional Grammar (LFG) that grammatical functions are not referred to by the morphosyntax of "unbounded dependencies" (Zaenen 1983). In Palauan (and Chamorro), WH agreement, certainly central to the morphosyntax of these structures, is controlled precisely by the grammatical function (or, in our terms, the Case) assigned to the extraction site. (These facts are discussed in detail in Chung and Georgopoulos 1988.)

3.3. *Multiple Variables*

WH agreement has a further effect which is not immediately obvious, but which in fact is predicted by the rule as it is formulated in (59). The productivity of extraction structures in Palauan extends to sentences in which a clause may contain more than one extraction site. For example, a relative clause may contain a topic (see note 2), or a matrix topic may be linked to a position within a clause also containing a WH extraction site, and so on. It is relevant to ask, then, in cases of multiple extraction sites, which site triggers WH agreement locally. In other words, in the configuration (60),

(60) $A' \ldots A' \ldots [_{IP}$ variable $\ldots$ variable $\ldots]$

is WH agreement unambiguously determined? Note that in (60) the dependencies may be either nested or crossed, as in (61a or b):

(61) a. $A'_i \ldots A'_k \ldots [_{IP}$ variable$_k \ldots$ variable$_i \ldots]$

b. $A'_i \ldots A'_k \ldots [_{IP}$ variable$_i \ldots$ variable$_k \ldots]$

Nesting dependencies have been shown in many languages to be grammatical, while crossing dependencies are usually not tolerated (see, e.g., Chomsky 1977, Fodor 1978, Pesetsky 1982b). Various explanations have been offered of this difference, both in pragmatic terms (parsing considerations) and in terms of formal syntactic principles (the ECP, conditions on paths). In Palauan, however, both nesting and crossing are allowed.[21]

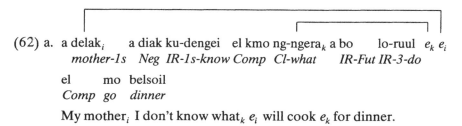

(62) a. a delak$_i$ a diak ku-dengei el kmo ng-ngera$_k$ a bo   lo-ruul e_k e_i
       mother-1s   Neg IR-1s-know Comp Cl-what   IR-Fut IR-3-do
       el   mo   belsoil
       Comp go   dinner
       My mother$_i$ I don't know what$_k$ e_i will cook e_k for dinner.

(62) b. ng-te'a a milde'emii . . .
   Cl-who   R-caught-3s

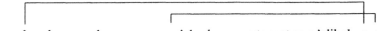

   a uel$_i$ el   mulmes   er a rese'al$_k$ el   omtanget er a 'elibel e_i e_k
   turtle Comp IR-2-saw P boys   Comp R-polish P   shell-3s

   Who caught the turtle that you were watching the boys who were polishing its shell?

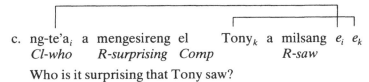

c. ng-te'a$_i$ a mengesireng el   Tony$_k$ a milsang e_i e_k
   Cl-who   R-surprising Comp   R-saw

   Who is it surprising that Tony saw?

That is, both configurations (61a) and (61b) are possible. It then becomes necessary to know which variable the most embedded verb in (62a–c) agrees with. How does WH agreement resolve this potential conflict of triggers of agreement?

In fact, it is the variable of the *closest* binder that determines WH agreement. This we see in (62) above. In (62a), the variable of the nonsubject **ngera** 'what' triggers irrealis morphology, even though this clause also contains the variable of a subject, **delak** 'my mother'. The head of the relative clause, **rese'al** 'boys', is the nearest binder in (62b), and triggers realis morphology even though there is also a relativized position of a possessor, **uel** 'turtle'. Similarly in (62c), the embedded subject topic **Tony** is closer to the realis verb **milsang** than it is to the matrix WH object phrase, **te'a** 'who'. It is the closest c-commanding A' binder that ultimately determines WH agreement in each clause. Note that these facts do not entail any revision of the formulation of WH agreement: the c-command domain of application is automatically defined by the closest A' binder.

The facts of WH agreement in multiple variable binding also provide further evidence that realis morphology associated with subject extraction is part of the WH agreement system (cf. above at section 3.1). If it were not (i.e. if *subject* extraction did not trigger WH agreement), there would be no explanation for why the embedding in (62b) is *realis*.

4. SUMMARY: CHAPTER THREE

This chapter has demonstrated that Palauan syntax permits an unusually wide range of A' binding structures, and that these structures form a natural class, as defined by a set of uniquely shared properties. In all of the structures described here, we saw that an extraction site following

98   CHAPTER THREE

Palauan's only preposition, **er**, contains an overt resumptive pronoun, while other extraction sites are empty. This complementarity of overt and null variables was shown to be independent of the distribution of agreement morphology, despite first appearances.

We then observed that island violations do not result in ungrammaticality in Palauan (or rather that the predicted violations do not occur), and that they occur with *either* an overt pronoun or a gap. The productivity of resumptive pronouns, their occurrence across the whole range of structures, including purely *local* binding, and the irrelevance to the island facts of *either* strategy led us to conclude that all the structures in question are base generated. Thus Palauan has no syntactic WH movement. The null and overt elements at the extraction site are both pronominals at D-structure (or at S-structure), and both types are resumptive pronouns, null or overt, at the point where coindexing establishes the A' binding relation.

Earlier in the chapter we came to the conclusion that the basic structure in all Palauan A' binding is the relative clause. It was hypothesized that there is a natural connection between the lack of movement and the relative clause characterization of variable binding in Palauan, since the relation between the head NP and the extraction site in a relative clause is analyzed, in GB, as the output of an interpretive rule rather than a movement rule. Furthermore, there is no operator movement possible in the nominalized clause, which is a bare IP.

Finally, we worked through example sentences that reveal how the WH agreement rule works in Palauan. We saw that the system of mood morphology was used to distinguish a clause in which a Nominative NP is extracted from a clause in which a non-Nominative NP is extracted. Furthermore, we saw that WH agreement applies in every clause between an A' binder and its variable, relying on two categories of controller, NP and CP. It was shown that WH agreement applies only in the surface A' binding domain, not above it in the tree or below it. Finally, in cases of multiple dependencies into a single clause, it was seen that the closest antecedent determines the WH agreement form, an implicit prediction of the statement of the rule.

The next chapter will go more deeply into the properties of these structures, considering such issues as the level of representation at which A' binding is effected, and the mechanisms which accomplish it.

NOTES

[1] I will occasionally use the familiar descriptive terms 'long-distance' or 'unbounded dependency', 'extraction', and 'extraction site' in describing A' binding constructions, even those containing resumptive pronouns. Use of this terminology is for convenience only.

VARIABLE BINDING STRUCTURES 99

[2] Topicalization within the embedded clause is grammatical.

(i) ak-medengel-ii a 'ekabil [_{CP} el   se'al [a mil'erar   a ngokel ___]]
     R-1s-know-3s   girl   Comp man   R-bought-3s   flute-3s

     I know the girl whose flute that guy bought.

We will see more examples of such a construction below.

[3] Abbreviations in the glosses are explained in the Appendix.

[4] Cf. Bresnan and Grimshaw (1978), who hypothesize this structure for free relatives in English, citing as motivation the lack of a complementizer (n. 10). See also Groos and van Riemsdijk (1979), for counterarguments. Since Palauan has neither WH relative pronouns nor pied piping, and since Palauan WH phrases and topics cooccur with overt complementizers, most of Groos and van Riemsdijk's arguments do not apply to Palauan.

[5] I have not investigated the possibility of these clefts (outside of WH contexts) in embedded clauses (see Chapter Five).

[6] This analysis of clefts supports Pinkham and Hankamer (1975), who claim that a grammar must have a headless relative construction in order to have a "clefting rule".

[7] S. Chung (personal communication) first suggested to me the possibility of the cleft analysis of Palauan WH questions. See Anderson (1984) for a similar analysis of WH questions in the American Indian language Kwakwala.

[8] Full pronouns may appear outside of prepositional phrases; for example, they may be conjoined with full NPs in subject or object phrases.

[9] Williams' tests for distinguishing specificational pseudoclefts from predicational pseudoclefts are not applied here, primarily because Palauan does not distinguish morphologically between anaphors and pronominals, so that tests relying on such distinctions would introduce irrelevant complications.

[10] Many Austronesianists reject the term 'subject' as used in Indo-European studies, using instead the term 'topic' to refer to the NP which is focussed by the verb. My use of 'topic' in section 1.4 is not an alternative to 'subject', however.

[11] For further comments on the fact that identification does not uniquely distinguish pronouns from variables, see Chung (1984).

[12] See also Chung (1985), where AGReement is dissociated from government.

[13] The Palauan case supports the view that subjacency must be a condition on movement rules rather than a condition on structures. See the discussion of the proper characterization of subjacency in, for example, Chomsky (1977; 1981 (p. 90 ff.)).

[14] The exception is in subject extraction, where no subject agreement occurs; the lack of subject agreement is perhaps due to the more specific requirements of WH agreement.

[15] This generalization is impossible in the version of GPSG (see, e.g., Sells 1984) that recognizes only A' bound empty categories, not *pro*, and posits only one level of derivation.

[16] See section 2.3 in Chapter Two.

[17] When we consider agreement in long-distance dependencies (below), it will be clear why the agreement rule must refer to the position of the variable, and not to that of the A' antecedent.

[18] The binder is also linked to Spec(C), into which it moves at LF.

[19] Case is not marked morphologically in Palauan.

[20] On the clefting mechanism of Palauan preposing, review sections 1.2 through 1.5.

[21] Regarding (62a): recall that future tense does not condition irrealis mood.

CHAPTER FOUR

VARIABLE BINDING

0. INTRODUCTION

In Chapter Three we investigated the class of A' binding structures in Palauan, and discovered some of their unusual properties. In this chapter we will consider the evidence for another important property of this class, the coindexing of antecedent and variable at S-structure. The analysis in this chapter constitutes the theoretical core of the book, because it substantially advances the claim that the principles governing the binding relation in the non-movement Palauan A' dependencies are syntactically equivalent to the principles governing A' binding in Move α languages. This claim goes rather far, as it includes the claim that locality applies, though subjacency does not. The evidence of the existence of syntactic variables in Palauan underlies analyses of resumptive pronouns and parasitic gap structures (this chapter), embedded questions (Chapter Five), and strong and weak crossover structures (Chapter Six).

In the first section of this chapter, I compare the properties of A' binding in Palauan to those hypothesized in GB, and attempt to justify the approach distinguishing base-generated from movement structures. In section 2 I demonstrate how the facts of WH agreement constitute evidence for S-structure binding of resumptive pronouns. Coordinate structures and parasitic gap structures are then considered and shown to provide further proof both of syntactic binding and of the syntactic equivalence of gaps and overt resumptive pronouns. These cases of multiple variable binding also underlie a proposal for a typology of islands in which subjects pattern with complements rather than adjuncts. Resumptive pronouns are then considered in more detail, and the variable status of Palauan pronouns is shown to argue for a parameter determining the level at which pronouns are A' bound. Finally, I show in section 3 how coindexing of S-structures is subject to A' chain formation. A' chains in Palauan, and the locality condition on them, are the syntactic correlates of the coindexing that arises from Move α and the subjacency constraint.

1. PROPERTIES OF A' BINDING

The list in (1) summarizes the important properties of Palauan A' binding, based on the discussion in Chapter Three:

100

VARIABLE BINDING

(1) a. The dependency is base generated.

b. The extraction site contains a pronoun.

c. The extraction site is subject to a principle licensing empty categories in certain contexts.

d. The domain is subject to WH agreement.

This set of properties can be compared to that attributed to A' binding structures within the framework of generative grammar; see also Chapter One, where the Move α analysis is reviewed:

(2) a. The dependency is generated by Move α.

b. Movement leaves a trace coindexed with the antecedent.

c. The trace is properly governed.

d. The dependency obeys subjacency.

It is clear that the grammars on which the lists in (1) and (2) are based are superficially quite different. Yet for every item on the list in (2) there is some phenomenon in Palauan that corresponds to it. In this chapter we will explore in particular the phenomena that are represented by the (b) and (d) items of each list: the correspondence of pronoun and trace, and the respective locality effects.

1.1. *Movement vs. Base Generation*

Let us consider briefly the manner in which A' binding structures are generated in Palauan and in GB. I have presented in Chapter Three an analysis in which the Palauan dependencies are base generated. Base generation is, of course, an alternative to the movement analysis that has always been available in the theory. In much current work, in fact, the two analyses are not seen as alternatives, but merely as different ways of stating the same claims about the Move α relation. In either analysis the coindexing relation between antecedent and variable observes subjacency and all the other constraints that traditionally hold of movement structures.

In contrast to this view, I analyze the facts of Palauan grammar as motivating retention of a real distinction between movement and base generation. Base generation, in my analysis, does *not* implicate the same set of properties as Move α. If the movement basis of subjacency is abandoned, moreover, the theory of subjacency must be complicated with some auxiliary account of languages, like Palauan, that 'do not have' subjacency.

In the usual case of structures not obeying subjacency, it is assumed that coindexing is carried out in LF. I argue below, however, that the

102   CHAPTER FOUR

binding in Palauan is syntactic. In view of these arguments, no LF rule comes into play, and the absence of the Move α relation in Palauan cannot be accounted for by the usual appeal to different levels of binding.

Rather than suggest that subjacency is not a universal principle,[1] then, I have chosen to represent certain differences between Palauan and English in terms of the traditional distinction between base generation and movement. Thus bounding theory is not part of the analysis of Palauan's particular grammar. We turn now to the arguments for variable binding in the syntax.

2. S-STRUCTURE BINDING

In the Move α analysis, the coindexed relation between the antecedent and its variable arises by movement; by trace theory, the index of the moved phrase is copied onto the trace left behind. This coindexing relation holds at S-structure, the output of (syntactic) movement. In Palauan, however, no movement takes place, so the coindexing relation does not arise in the way hypothesized in trace theory. Therefore we must establish in some other way that there exists a binding relation between an A′ antecedent and the pronoun at its extraction site. Without such binding, these dependencies are not well formed. And, importantly for the theory in general and for the analysis of resumptive pronouns in particular, we must try to discern the level at which this binding is determined.

2.1. *The 'Resumptive Pronoun Strategy'*

In addition to the two views of the Move α relation mentioned above, one in terms of movement and the other of base generation, there is still a third analysis available in GB: the one proposed for resumptive pronouns in a language like English (Chomsky 1982; see Ch. 1). In this analysis, an *un*bounded interpretive rule of LF ensures that antecedent and pronoun have the same index and may thereby enter into the operator-variable binding relation. In a relative clause, for example, the index of the head and that of a resumptive pronoun are matched, making the clause a predication of the head. This approach to the 'resumptive pronoun strategy' distinguishes resumptive pronouns and WH traces in three important ways: they are coindexed to an A′ binder by different types of rule (a movement rule for gaps, and an interpretive rule for resumptive pronouns); they become bound variables at different levels (S-structure for gaps, LF for resumptive pronouns); and resumptive pronouns occur only in structures of predication (e.g. relative clauses, but not WH questions).

VARIABLE BINDING 103

The separate treatment of resumptive pronouns and gaps in GB is intended to reflect their different behavior with respect to the syntax. In English (as in many languages), the use of resumptive pronouns is viewed as a means of circumventing conditions inducing ungrammaticality. The resumptive pronouns are not bound by an antecedent in the syntax, so, as free pronouns rather than variables, they do not violate island constraints.

A number of cases have been described in the recent literature of languages which use resumptive pronouns productively, in contrast to the case of English. In these languages it can be argued that the resumptive pronouns are 'syntactically bound', i.e. that they are variables at the level of S-structure. For example, Zaenen, Engdahl, and Maling (1981) conclude that both resumptive pronouns and gaps in Swedish are bound in the syntax on the basis of two types of evidence: both may be co-indexed with a reflexive properly contained in a fronted WH phrase, and resumptive pronoun and gap may cooccur in coordination. McCloskey (1979, 1989) demonstrates that, in Irish, the binding relation between an antecedent and a gap, as well as that between an antecedent and a resumptive pronoun, must be defined at S-structure in order to account for the morphology of complementizers.

In Palauan, there are several sorts of consideration that weigh against the analysis of Chomsky (1982). First, the analysis, in spirit at least, is meant to distinguish relative clauses from interrogative structures. Relative clauses are subject to an interpretive rule of predication, while WH questions are not (see Huang 1984, p. 569; Chomsky 1982, n. 11). All Palauan unbounded dependencies are, in fact, relativization structures of some kind, yet structures that are semantically interpreted as WH questions are included in this class.[2]

Second, the conventional GB resumptive pronoun analysis is meant to deal with 'marginal' phenomena, and not with the unmarked case. The marginality of resumptive pronouns in a language like English motivates the analysis outlined above. But Palauan resumptive pronouns are not marginal; they are regular and productive. The fact that they occur even in monoclausal A' binding, or in clauses in which they are directly *locally* bound, shows that their distribution is unrelated to bounding phenomena. The facts that motivate the conventional analysis of resumptive pronouns, therefore, are just not facts of Palauan.

There is also the generality of the theory to consider: all Palauan A' binding structures occur as S-structure representations containing resumptive pronouns. A theory that captures the equivalence of these representations and those formed by syntactic movement is to be preferred to one that relegates the binding of the Palauan structures, which are widespread at S-structure, to a late interpretive rule. Thus the more natural analysis, theoretically as well as empirically, is one that parallels the movement analysis by allowing coindexing in the syntax. Such an analysis would then permit linguistic generalizations that hold for *both* Palauan-type and English-type A' binding.

Beyond the observations that the usual analysis of resumptive pronouns is not 'meant' for a language like Palauan, there is solid empirical evidence that Palauan A' binding is generated by a coindexing rule at S-structure rather than an interpretive rule at LF. We turn to that evidence now, and return in section 2.5 to more detailed discussion of the general theory of resumptive pronouns.

2.2. *WH Agreement and S-Structure Binding*

Before considering the facts that argue for syntactic variable binding, we should recall the model of grammar that we are assuming. In this model, D-structures are mapped onto S-structures by Move α, and Phonetic Form (PF) and Logical Form (LF) are components which are derived from S-structures but which are independent of each other:

(3)
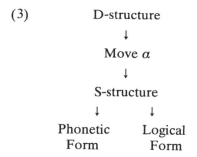

Arguments that distinguish S-structure from LF may build on the fact that syntactic representations bifurcate at S-structure, feeding into the mutually independent PF and LF. Properties that can be attributed to S-structure representations are the output of rules of the syntax (including principles that apply at S-strucutre), and may have effects in both LF and PF. An LF rule would have no effect in PF, however, and vice versa. If A' coindexing is a rule of LF, therefore, it will not be expected to have overt effects. We could show that coindexing in Palauan applies at S-structure, on the other hand, if we could demonstrate that some rule that refers to coindexing has effects in both PF and LF.

WH agreement has the necessary properties, since it has both interpretive and morphological consequences. In addition, it relies on the configuration of S-structure rather than LF representations, and so must apply in the syntax. Observe once again the facts of examples like (4), repeated from Chapter Three:[3]

VARIABLE BINDING

(4) a. t-oumera   a resensei [el   ked-omdasu
        R-3p-believe   teachers   Comp R-1p-think

        [e   ng-mo   er a siabal a **te'ang**]]
        Comp R-3s-go P   Japan   who

  b.   t-oumera   a resensei [el   ked-omdasu
        R-3p-believe   teachers   Comp R-1p-think

        [ng-**te'a**$_i$ a mo   er a siabal ____$_i$]]
        Cl-who   R-go P   Japan

  c.   ng-**te'a**$_i$ [a l-oumera   a resensei [el   d-omdasu
        Cl-who   IR-3-believe   teachers   Comp IR-1p-think

        [e   ng-mo er a siabal ____$_i$]]]
        Comp R-go P   Japan

(All three) Who do the teachers believe that we think will go
to Japan?

The question word **te'a(ng)** 'who' is in situ in (4a), in an A´ position in
the lowest clause in (4b), and in an A´ position in the highest clause in
(4c). These variants are possible because Palauan requires neither that
WH phrases take scope in the syntax, nor that they occupy an A´
position in the syntax. We can confirm that these sentences satisfy WH
agreement (from Chapter Three):

(5)   *WH Agreement*: In the S-structure domain between an A´
        binder and its variable, Inflection agrees with

        a. the Case of the argument containing the variable, or
        b. the Case of the variable.

When a WH phrase is in situ or in cleft position in the lowest clause, as
in (4a, b), the morphology of the higher clauses is unaffected by the rule.
In contrast, when the WH phrase is in the matrix, as in (4c), *every* verb
form in the sentence is affected by the rule. Yet in all the versions of (4)
the WH phrase not only has wide scope semantically but also has wide
scope in LF, due to LF movement of WH phrases to a scope-bearing
position (see Chapter Five).[4] It is evident in (4) that the scope condition
that holds at LF has no effect on WH agreement morphology. Since WH
agreement is triggered exclusively in the S-structure domain between A´
binder and variable, coindexing must be at S-structure.

The significance of the array of facts in (4) is not only that variables
in Palauan are bound at S-structure, but also that the gaps in (4) are
bound at S-structure *despite the lack of movement*. Some rule other than
Move α is therefore responsible for the syntactic binding relation. It is
only the relation of a variable to an A´ antecedent, moreover, that

106 CHAPTER FOUR

triggers WH agreement. This was demonstrated in Chapter Three (section 3).

It is equally important to demonstrate that overt resumptive pronouns, as well as the empty category, are S-structure variables. We have seen that the pronouns are indistinguishable from gaps for all syntactic purposes described so far. This being the case, we predict that overt resumptive pronouns will have the same behavior with respect to WH agreement as gaps. Inspection of the examples in (6) confirms this prediction. These show that WH agreement affects dependencies containing overt resumptive pronouns exactly as it does those with gaps. In particular, its effects extend up the tree only as far as the S-structure position of the antecedent. Compare (4) to (6):

(6) a. ke-dilu   [el   te-mengiil er ngak
       R-2s-said Comp R-3p-wait P me

       [el   mo   meruul er a **ngerang**]]
       Comp R-Fut R-do   P   what

    b. ke-dilu [el te-mengiil er ngak

       [el ng-**ngera**$_i$ a bo   ku-ruul er ngii$_i$]]
       Cl-what   IR-Fut IR-1s-do P it

    c. ke-dilu [el ng-**ngera**$_i$ a lo-ngiil   er ngak
                  Cl-what   IR-3-wait

       [el bo ku-ruul er ngii$_i$]]

    d. ng-**ngera**$_i$ [a 'om-dilu [el lo-ngiil er ngak
       Cl-what   IR-2-said

       [el bo ku-ruul er ngii$_i$]]]

       (All four) What did you say that they're waiting for me to do?

Only in (6d) does the syntactic scope of the WH phrase indicate its scope at LF (and its semantic scope), despite the fact that all of the versions of (6) are direct WH questions. Note, in each case, the correlation between the position of **ngera** and the morphology of each verb in the sentence: again, only the *S-structure* position of the WH phrase is referred to, showing that the binding holds at S-structure.

We may conclude that WH agreement provides firm evidence that both forms of D-structure pronominal, *pro* and the lexical pronoun, are bound by, not just accidentally coindexed with, their A´ antecedent at S-structure.

This finding is not limited to WH questions. In Chapter Three we saw that WH agreement applies in exactly the same way to the class of A´ binding structures as a whole. The LF interpretive rule proposed in

VARIABLE BINDING 107

Chomsky (1982) is therefore not suitable for *any* such structure in Palauan. Rather, WH agreement makes possible an analysis of Palauan resumptive pronouns that is appropriate to their syntactic nature. From this point on I will assume that the claim that resumptive pronouns are coindexed in the syntax is well founded. In referring to 'variable' in Palauan I will henceforth intend a pronoun that is A′ bound at S-structure.

Beyond the evidence of WH agreement, the case for S-structure A′ binding is considerably strengthened in structures in which one antecedent binds multiple variables. Coordination and parasitic gap structures are the typical instances of multiple variable binding. In these structures, not only is WH agreement triggered by both gaps and lexical pronouns, but both types of variable cooccur in the same structure. Since the constraints on these structures hold at S-structure, this cooccurrence strengthens the claim that the syntax of A′ binding in Palauan does not distinguish between gaps and overt resumptive pronouns, but sees them both as variables. The evidence from these structures is found in the following sections. Weak crossover, another case of multiple variable binding, is discussed in Chapter Six.

2.3. *Coordination*

The idea that gaps and overt resumptive pronouns in Palauan are syntactically equivalent, having the same derivation and being bound at S-structure, leads to a definite prediction about their cooccurrence in coordinate structures: coordination of a clause with a gap and a clause with an overt pronoun should be grammatical. If one clause contained a WH trace and the other a pronoun, the structures formed by coordinating them would be ruled out by the Coordinate Structure Constraint (Ross 1967, Williams 1978). The CSC must hold at S-structure, where the binding theory applies and A′-bound positions are identified as variables.

Palauan does in fact observe the Coordinate Structure Constraint, which prohibits extraction from just one constituent of a conjoined structure.

(7) *[a delak [a uleker er ngak [el kmo ng-ngera [a sensei
        mother-1s R-Im-ask P me Comp Cl-what teacher

a milsk-ak a buk] me [a rubak a ulter-ur ___ er ngak]]]]
R-Pf-give-1s book and old.man R-Pf-sell-3s P me

(*My mother asked me what the teacher gave me a book and the old man sold ___ me.)

However, Palauan allows across-the-board extraction (Ross 1967, Wil-

108   CHAPTER FOUR

liams 1978), the general exception to the CSC that allows extraction
from all conjuncts.

(8)   [a delak   a uleker   [el kmo ng-ngera a
          mother-1s   *R-Im-ask*   *Comp Cl-what*

        [l-ulter-ur   ____ a Rose el   me   er ngak] me
          IR-3-Pf-sell-3s   *Comp come P*   *and*

        [a Ioseb a ulter-ur   ____ el mo er a Latii]]]
                 R-Pf-sell-3s   *L go P*

        My mother asked what Rose sold ____ to me and Joseph sold
        ____ to Latii.

The example in (8) appears to be the familiar sort of across-the-board
extraction structure, in which two gaps are bound by a single antecedent.
However, we know that in Palauan these gaps are not WH traces but
rather (null) resumptive pronouns. Since their overt counterparts must
appear as prepositional objects, we predict that structures containing
both a null and an overt resumptive pronoun are grammatical. This
prediction can be tested in the coordination of clauses of different
aspect, for example, since extraction of the object of a perfective verb
leaves a gap, while extraction of the object of an imperfective verb leaves
an overt pronoun. First, (9) shows that coordination of clauses of
different aspect is grammatical:

(9)   [[ak-mil'er-ar   a buk   er a Rose]
          R-1s-Pf-buy-3s   *book P*

        me [a uleme'ar   er a storyboard er a Sam]]
        and *R-Im-buy P*   *P*

        I bought a book for Rose and was buying a storyboard for
        Sam.

Example (10) illustrates across-the-board extraction in sentences containing clauses of different aspect. In (10a), the coordinate structure is
within a relative clause; the first conjunct contains a gap, while the
second conjunct contains an overt resumptive pronoun. In (10b), the
coordintion involves a WH-question; in this case it is the first conjunct
that holds an overt resumptive pronoun, and the second conjunct that
holds the gap.

(10) a. [ak-medengel-ii   a bilas$_i$ el   [le-bil'er-ar   ____$_i$
           R-1s-Pf-know-3s   *boat Comp   IR-3-Pf-buy-3s*

        a Cisco] me [a Ioseb a milngesbereber er ngii$_i$]]
             and   *R-Im-paint   P   it*

        I know which boat Cisco bought ____ and Joseph painted (it).

VARIABLE BINDING   109

(10) b. [ng-ngera*ᵢ* [a lu-ruul   er ngii*ᵢ* a Sie]
    Cl-what   *IR-3-Im-make P it*

    e [a 'o'odal a me'er-ar   _____*ᵢ*]]
    and   *sister-3s*   *R-Pf-buy-3s*

    What did Sie make (it) and her sister buy _____ ?

The examples in (8) and (10) all illustrate extraction of the direct object. The cooccurrence of gap and lexical pronoun does not depend on extraction of NPs of the same grammatical relation from each conjunct, however. In the next example, one variable is a direct object and the other is an oblique object.

(11)   [a buk*ᵢ* [a k-ulnguiu   er ngii*ᵢ*] e
        book   *IR-1s-Im-read P it*   *and*

        [a Sam [a milart   a udoud er a 'als-el   _____*ᵢ*]]]]
            R-Im-hide   *money P* *inside-3s*

    The book, I was reading (it) and Sam had hidden some money inside _____ .

We can assume that these sentences do not violate the Coordinate Structure Constraint only if the A′ binding relation holds in both conjuncts (see Williams 1978). If just the gap in (10) or (11) were bound at S-structure, and the overt pronoun were a referring pronoun at that level, the sentences would be ruled out by the CSC. In other words, the gap cannot be analyzed as a WH trace, coindexed with its antecedent, if the overt pronoun is not so analyzed. The coordination facts therefore confirm the conclusion reached on the basis of WH agreement, that the pronouns in Palauan A′ binding are syntactic variables. These facts also rule out the solution in Chomsky (1982), which was summarized at the beginning of this chapter. That multi-level solution, in which pronoun binding is at LF, does not generalize to a language like Palauan.

Structures like those in (10) and (11) have been observed in other languages. Though the distribution of gaps and resumptive pronouns varies in these languages, their cooccurrence in coordinate structures underlies arguments for the syntactic binding of pronouns similar to those I have presented for Palauan. Engdahl (Engdahl and Ejerhed 1982), for example, shows that, in Swedish, a resumptive pronoun must appear in subject position following a complementizer bearing an index distinct from the index of the subject. A clause with a subject resumptive pronoun may be conjoined with a clause containing a gap ((12) = Engdahl's (74)):

CHAPTER FOUR

(12) jag läste en bok$_i$ som jag redan glömt   [$_{CP}$ vem$_j$ som
      I   read a   book that I already forgotten   who that

[$_{IP}$——$_j$ skrivit ——$_i$]] och [$_{CP}$ hur$_k$ [$_{IP}$ den$_i$ slutar ——$_k$]]
      wrote   and how it ends

In Palauan, the facts of coordination support the claim that both null and overt resumptive pronouns are equivalent in the syntax. In Swedish, it has not been argued that the *gaps* in sentences like (12) are resumptive pronouns; presumably what the Swedish facts show is that WH traces and resumptive pronouns are both A'-bound at S-structure. In general, we would predict that coordination structures like those observed in Palauan and Swedish are possible in any language in which resumptive pronouns are treated as syntactic variables.

Palauan's observance of the Coordinate Structure Constraint is in contrast to its violation of other island constraints. This contrast reflects the fact that the CSC is a constraint different *in kind* from those that are analyzed in terms of bounding theory (i.e. in terms of subjacency). Island violations that result from the crossing of more than one bounding node have been observed in many languages (see, for example, the various articles on extraction in Scandinavian languages in Engdahl and Ejerhed (1982). It seems to be the case, however, that all languages observe the CSC.[5]

2.4. *Parasitic Gaps*

In parasitic gap structures, as in coordination, more than one variable is bound by the same antecedent. Some examples from English are in (13); the second gap is considered to be the parasitic one ((a) and (b) are from Engdahl 1983; as Engdahl notes, speaker acceptance of such sentences varies):

(13) a. Which articles did John file ___ without reading ___?

b. This is the kind of food you must cook ___ before you eat ___.

c. Cannibals are people you should be nice to ___ if you visit ___.

d. That's an analysis that many people adopt ___ without understanding ___.

In this section I will show that Palauan resumptive pronouns participate in the whole range of parasitic gap phenomena. I will appeal to an ECP account of these facts, in particular Kayne's (1983a) CONNECTEDNESS CONDITION.

In the first analyses of parasitic gaps, one of the variables is considered to be 'parasitic' on the other because it occurs in a position

VARIABLE BINDING   111

inaccessible to extraction: in a syntactic island, for example. It would therefore not occur independently (see, e.g., Engdahl 1983; Kayne 1983a). The parasitic gap is 'licensed' by receiving the same index as a legitimate variable left by movement, thereby becoming a variable associated with the coindexed A' antecedent.

In later GB analyses (e.g. Chomsky 1986b; Stowell 1985), a parasitic gap is the trace of WH movement of a null operator. This operator moves to the Comp inside the parasitic gap clause (or to an A' position inside NP), forming a chain. The final term of the chain containing the 'real' gap and the operator of the chain with the parasitic gap must be subjacent. The two chains are composed into a single chain (one with a single index) via a chain composition algorithm (see Chomsky 1986b). The following example is from Stowell (1985); O is the operator, t the 'real gap' and e the parasitic gap:

(14)   who$_i$ does [[everyone$_k$ [O$_i$ who$_k$ [t_k *meets* e_i]]] t_k usually dislike t_i]?

Who$_i$ does everyone who meets ___$_i$ usually dislike ___$_i$?

This coindexing must hold at S-structure, because only variables of syntactic movement, not those arising from movement in LF, license parasitic gaps (see Engdahl 1984). It is assumed that a resumptive pronoun cannot license a parasitic gap, since, according to the usual analysis, it is not a variable at S-structure. The examples in (15) illustrate these facts for English ((15a–c) are adapted from Chomsky 1982).

(15) a. *He's a man who$_i$ everyone who meets him$_i$ knows someone who likes ___$_i$

   b. *He's a man who$_i$ everyone who meets ___$_i$ knows someone who likes him$_i$

   c. He's a man who$_i$ everyone who meets ___$_i$ knows someone who likes ___$_i$

   d. *I threw away that book$_i$ before reading ___$_i$

   e. *I forget who threw away which books$_i$ before reading ___$_i$

   f. Which book did you throw away ___$_i$ before reading ___$_i$?

Palauan allows constructions similar to the English parasitic gap structures; an example is seen in (16):

(16)   a kukau a kall$_i$ [el   kirem   [el   ngikl-ii   ___$_i$
       taro   food Comp 2s-must Comp R-Pf-boil-3s

       [er a u'ei   er a 'o-mekl-ii   ___$_i$]]]
       P   before P   IR-2-Pf-eat-3s

       Taro is food that you must boil ___ before you eat ___.

CHAPTER FOUR

Constructions like this provide us with another context for observing that Palauan resumptive pronouns have the same properties as WH traces in a movement language. In the example in (16), both resumptive pronouns are null. However, in Palauan, an overt resumptive pronoun may also license a gap, and the reverse configuration — in which a gap licenses a 'parasitic' resumptive pronoun —is also possible:

(17) a. [ng-teruata   el 'ad]$_i$ [a m-ulengede'edu' er tir$_i$
       Cl-which(pl) L person   IR-2-Im-talk   P   them

   [e   dimlak mes-terir   ___$_i$]]
   Comp Pst-Neg IR-2-Pf-see-3p

   Which people did you talk to ___ without seeing ___ ?

 b. [ng-teruata   el 'ad]$_i$ [a 'o-muls-terir   ___$_i$
    Cl-which(pl) L person   IR-2-Pf-see-3p

   [e   dimlak mo-ngede'edu' er tir$_i$]]
   Comp Pst-Neg IR-2-Im-talk   P   them

   Which people did you see ___ without talking to ___ ?

In (17a), the first variable is a lexical pronoun, the object of the preposition **er**, which the second variable is a null pronoun, governed by a perfective verb. The converse holds in (17b).

To complete this paradigm, I include the following example, in which a lexical resumptive pronoun licenses a parasitic lexical resumptive pronoun (compare (16)):

(18) a kukau a kall$_i$ [el   kirem   [el   meliokl   er ngii$_i$
       taro   food Comp 2s-must Comp R-Im-boil P   it

   [er a u'ei   er a 'omonga   er ngii$_i$]]]
   P   before P   IR-2-Im-eat P it

   Taro is food that you must boil ___ before you eat ___ .

Thus the parasitic gap structures present the same type of evidence for syntactic binding of pronouns that coordination does.[6] Lexical and null pronouns may freely occur in structures in which their binding properties are determined at S-structure.

In analyzing constructions such as these, we must keep in mind the properties that we have attributed to all A' binding in Palauan, and which apply to these constructions as well. First, movement is not involved: all extraction sites contain base-generated pronouns. And second, we have so far observed that practically any NP position in Palauan is accessible to extraction. In view of these facts, it is not clear

VARIABLE BINDING

that the gap in (17a) or the overt pronoun in (17b) can be identified as 'parasitic' in the way that Engdahl identified parasitic gaps in English.[7]

Even within current theory, it is far from clear what a truly general analysis of parasitic gap structures would look like. Recent analyses claim that the parasitic gap is generated by movement (Stowell 1985; Chomsky 1986b), in contrast to Engdahl's original analysis in which parasitic gaps are base-generated pronominals rather than WH traces. Another defining property of parasitic gaps in the earlier analysis was that the 'real' gap did not c-command the parasitic gap; this criterion, too, has been argued not to hold (e.g. Contreras 1984). The following examples illustrate well-formed parasitic gap constructions ((19a) is from Engdahl 1984; (19b), also from the work of Engdahl, is taken from Chomsky 1986b):

(19) a. en mann som vi forspeilet t at e ikke ville bli arrestert
a man who we promised that not would be arrested

a man that we promised would not be arrested

b. Who did the police warn
t [O that they were going to arrest e]?
└──────── c-command ────────┘

In these examples, the 'real gap' (t) c-commands the parasitic gap (e). In the analysis of cases like (19), the strong crossover violation that would result from t's c-command of e (on the assumption that e is a variable) is avoided by the presence of the null operator in the lower clause (but see Chomsky 1986a).

Since one gap is no longer analyzed as 'parasitic' on the other, the terminology applied to these phenomena is no longer appropriate. What remains constant in the analysis, however, is the assumption that the 'parasitic' gap occurs *only* when there is a normally occurring gap somewhere else in the sentence. The idea of one gap sanctioning the other, and of both occurring in a single chain, therefore, remains important to the analysis. This licensing condition must hold at S-structure, to account for the distribution in (15d–f).

As we noted above, current accounts concentrate on the *bounding* properties of these structures. The focus on subjacency as the primary constraint on parasitic gap structures poses a problem for analyzing the Palauan facts, since, as I have argued, subjacency cannot be appealed to as a constraint on Palauan A' binding.[8] However, it is suggestive that Palauan sentences like those in (16) through (18) are ungrammatical when the 'licensing' variable is replaced by a lexical NP. This is one of the tests that has been used to identify parasitic gaps:

114 CHAPTER FOUR

(20) a. *a kukau a kall$_i$ [el kirem [el meliokl a
        taro   food Comp must-2s Comp R-cook

meduu er a u'ei er a 'omo-nga er ngii$_i$]]
breadfruit   before   IR-2-Im-eat P it

(Taro is the food$_i$ that you must cook breadfruit$_k$ before you eat ___$_i$.)

b. *tia kid a buk$_i$ [el kirem [el 'uiu-ii
    Dem   book Comp must-2s Comp R-Pf-read-3s

a newspaper [a 'omo-me'ar ___$_i$]]]
          IR-2-Im-buy

(This is a book$_i$ that you have to read the newspaper$_k$ if you buy ___$_i$.)

Conversely, the structure is grammatical when the 'licensing' element remains but the 'parasitic' element is replaced by a lexical NP:

(21) a. a kukau a kall$_i$ el kirem el meliokl ___$_i$
        taro   food Comp must-2s Comp R-Im-cook

er a u'ei er a monga a malk
P before   IR-2-Im-eat chicken

Taro is food you have to cook ___ before you eat chicken.

b. [aika kid a 'alde'edu' el 'elid]$_i$ el ble'oel
    these   stories   Comp always

el mo-ngede'edu' ___$_i$ a 'omo-dengel-ii a ulebengelel
Comp IR-2-Im-tell   IR-2-Pf-know-3s end-3s

These are stories that you always tell ___ if you know the end.

Now, it should be noted that the cases of illegal binding all involve *adjuncts*, categories that are not subcategorized by/not governed by the verb. In (20a) the coindexed pronoun is in an adverbial clause introduced by **u'ei** 'before', and in (20b) it is in an *if*-clause (recall that conditional clauses take irrealis morphology). These facts suggest that adjuncts, along with coordinate structures, are islands in Palauan (on adjuncts, see Huang 1982, Lasnik and Saito 1984). Let us explore this possibility in more detail.

VARIABLE BINDING 115

First, we note that 'short' extraction within the adjunct clause is possible:[9]

(22) a. [til'a el buk]$_i$ a u'ei   er a 'om-'iu-ii   ———$_i$,
    this L book   *before*   *IR-2-Pf-read-3s*

    e besk-ak   a ole'es-em
    IR-2-Pf-give-1s   *pencil-2s*

This book before you read, give me your pencil.

b. ng- [ngera el buk]$_i$ a u'ei   er a 'om-'iu-ii   ———$_i$,
    Cl- what L book   *before*   *IR-2-read-3s*

    e ng-kirem el   lu'es-ii   a ngklem
    2s-must   Comp R-Pf-write-3s   name-2s

Which book before you read do you have to sign (for)?

c. [a kall   er a Mexico]$_i$ sei   el monga   ———$_i$
    food P   *which   IR-2-Im-eat*

    e ng-kirem el   melim a betok el ralm
    2s-must   Comp R-drink   much L water

Mexican food when you eat, you have to drink a lot of water.

I assume that the extracted phrase is adjoined within the adjunct clause, though it precedes the adverb. That is, the extractee is in the S-structure position usually taken by WH phrases or topics in Palauan. When an adjunct phrase is not preposed (as it is in (22)), the adverb may follow the preposition **er**, indicating that it is not a complementizer but rather a head of PP (see the examples in (24)).

In contrast to what we see in (22), long extraction out of adjuncts is not possible:

(23) a. temlarngii   a betok el 'ad   el   mle songerenger
    R-3p-Pst-be   many L man Comp Aux starving

    se   er a mekemad
    when   war

There were many people who starved when the war (was going on).

116 CHAPTER FOUR

(23) b. *a mekemad temlarngii a betok el 'ad el mle songerenger (se er ngii)

(The war, were there many people who starved (then)?)

c. *ng- oingerang a mlarngii a betok el 'ad el mle
   when

songerenger (se er ngii)?

(When were there many people who starved (then)?)

(24) a. ng-liluut el mei a Costa [er a u'ei   er a kungede'edu'
    3s-again L come   *P   before*   *IR-1s-Im-talk*

er a Sandii]
P

Costa came back before I talked to Sandy.

b. *a Sandii a liluut el mei a Costa er a u'ei er a kungede'edu' er ngii

(Sandy, Costa came back before I talked to (her).)

c. *ng- te'a a liluut el mei a Costa er a u'ei er a
   who

kungede'edu' er ngii

(Who did Costa come back before I talked to (her)?)

(25) a. ak-mirrael er a party le u'ul
   1s-left   P   party because

a di mla se'elik   el se'al a mla er ngii
    Pst friend-1s L boy   Pst P there

I left the party because my old boyfriend was there.

b. *[a   di mla se'elik   el se'al] a ku-rael   er a party
   my   old boyfriend   *IR-1s-left*

le u'ul ng-mla er ngii
because 3s-was P there

(My old boyfriend, I left the party because (he) was there.)

c. *ng- te'a a 'omu-rael er a party le u'ul ng-mla er ngii
   who IR-2-left

(Who did you leave the party because (he) was there?)

VARIABLE BINDING

117

(25) d.*ng- ngera a 'omurael er a party le u'ul rebek. el 'ad
       what   *IR-2-left*   *because every L man*

   a meruul
   R-do

(What did you leave the party because everyone was doing
___?)

These examples contrast with other cases of long-distance extraction, which we have observed up to this point to be very free. It appears, therefore, that the account of the ungrammatical sentences in (23) through (25) above, parallel with the ungrammatical parasitic gap structures in (20), must take note of the fact that the extraction site is in an adjunct. This elicits an ECP account, and subjacency is not relevant.

The impossibility of extraction out of adjuncts has been analyzed in terms of the theory of government, notably in such works as Kayne (1981), Belletti and Rizzi (1981), Huang (1982), and Chomsky (1986b). These authors all distinguish between arguments and adjuncts on the basis of government: arguments are governed, adjuncts are not. Huang (1982), for example, proposes to account for the facts of extraction from adjuncts in terms of the requirement that the *domain* containing an extraction site be properly governed (formulated as the Condition on Extraction Domain (CED)). Kayne's theory of government and the ECP is perhaps most appropriate to the Palauan case, since it is stated on S-structure representations without reference to movement, and refers to government within both subtrees containing variables.

Kayne's (1981) ECP restricts extraction to positions which the antecedent governs directly or positions whose antecedent is contained in a percolation projection of the structural governor. A percolation projection is a series of co-superscripted (= governed) nodes beginning with the governor of an empty category and projecting up the tree to the node immediately dominating the antecedent. A node that is not co-superscripted breaks this projection, so that empty categories within ungoverned domains fail to satisfy the ECP.

The example in (26) illustrates the phenomena that Kayne's theory accounts for. It calls attention to the contrast between extraction from governed PPs and extraction from non-governed PPs (for 'governed' read 'subcategorized' here). ((26) = Kayne's (28), (29)):

(26) a. How many boys did she smile at?

   b.*How many reasons did she smile for?

The claim is that *smile* subcategorizes an *at*-phrase but not a *for*-phrase,

118   CHAPTER FOUR

which is an adjunct. Since the *for*-PP is therefore not governed, it does not initiate a percolation projection and the extraction in (26b) is not grammatical.

Thus Kayne's ECP, like Huang's CED, constrains not only the extraction site but also the path to the antecedent. In addition, these theories collapse some cases attributed to subjacency: since subjects and relative clauses are not properly governed in English, for example, the Sentential Subject Constraint and the Complex NP Constraint are claimed to follow from the ECP/CED.[10]

The islandhood of adjunct clauses is also captured in these proposals, since adjuncts are not subcategorized and therefore not governed. The finding that adjuncts in Palauan are islands provides further support for the ECP approach (rather than a movement approach) to islandhood. (An account of extraction from complex NPs and sentential subjects is proposed in Section 2.7 below.) We can now attempt to find a way to incorporate some version of this approach into the analysis of the Palauan 'parasitic gap' structures.

Kayne (1981) stipulates that V does not superscript NP, so that NPs and relative clauses remain islands. The refinement of the ECP in Kayne (1983a) dispenses with superscripts and also with the requirement that each node on the path between antecedent and variable must be governed. The path is now defined in terms of 'g(overnment)-projection' rather than 'percolation projection'. G-projection is defined as follows (= Kayne's (8)):

(27)   Y is a *g-projection* of X iff

    a. Y is a projection of X or of a g-projection of X, or

    b. X is a structural governor and

       Y immediately dominates W and Z, where Z is a maximal projection of a g-projection of X, and W and Z are in a canonical government configuration.

W and Z are assumed to be in canonical government configuration iff (= Kayne's (9)):

(28) a. V governs NP to its right in the grammar of the language in question and W precedes Z, or

    b. V governs NP to its left in the grammar of the language in question and Z precedes W.

Canonical government configuration in a VO language like English or Palauan reflects government by the head to the right.

The ECP is now formulated as the Connectedness Condition (Kayne, p. 239):

Let $\beta_1 \ldots \beta_j, \beta_{j+1} \ldots \beta_n$ be a maximal set of categories in a tree T such that $\exists \alpha, \forall j, \beta_j$ is uniformly bound by α. Then $\{\alpha\} \cup (\bigcup_{1 \leq j \leq n} G_{\beta_j})$ must constitute a subtree of T.

By (27), (28), and the Connectedness Condition, any node can participate in the ECP projection path, even when it is not governed, as long as it dominates some maximal projection of the g-projection of the governor of a legitimate empty category, and that maximal projection is right sister to another node. This is illustrated in (29) (adapted from Kayne). Here, the NP in boldface represents a left-branch maximal projection that is a g-projection of *of*. Normally, extraction is not permitted out of an NP in this configuration. The bold NP, however, has a right sister which is a g-projection of *admire*, the governor of a legitimate empty category.[11] Thus the subtrees containing the empty categories are sisters, and the path continues up through IP to reach the antecedent:

(29)

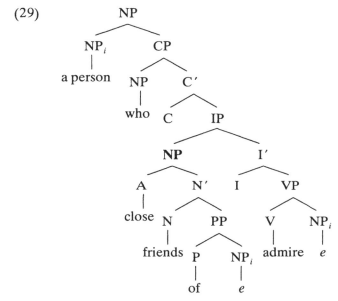

a person who close friends of *e* admire *e*

In other words, in a VO language, an empty category cannot be free within a left branch that is a maximal projection unless that maximal projection is sister to a legitimate g-projection path. In (30), in contrast, the left-branch g-projections of *of* stop at the boldface NP because that NP has no sister on a legitimate projection path, so (30) is worse than (29):

(30)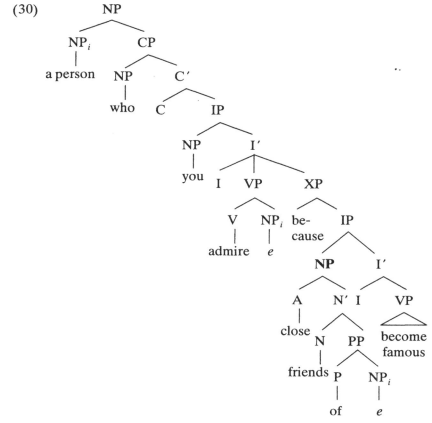

* a person who you admire *e* because close friends of *e* become famous

Put more simply, the fact that the two g-projections in (29) *form a subtree* at IP allows both empty categories to reach the antecedent; the lack of such a subtree in (30) prevents the empty category on the left branch from connecting with its antecedent.

This theory naturally accounts for the fact that adjuncts are islands, without appeal to subjacency. Since the IP node in the adjunct is ungoverned, it breaks the g-projection path of any empty category it contains. However, this theory also allows for the somewhat weaker island effects in parasitic gap structures. In these an empty category in an adjunct is accepted if the adjunct node is sister to a projection path of a legitimate variable, i.e. if together the two projections form a subtree. For Palauan we need make only the natural additional assumption that resumptive pronouns have g-protection paths, just as gaps do, since in this language resumptive pronouns are S-structure variables. Thus (31)

VARIABLE BINDING 121

(= (16) and (18)) is a grammatical structure: the adjunct node XP (in boldface) is right sister to V´, which is on the projection path of NP_i in the complement of **kirem** (some detail omitted):[12]

(31)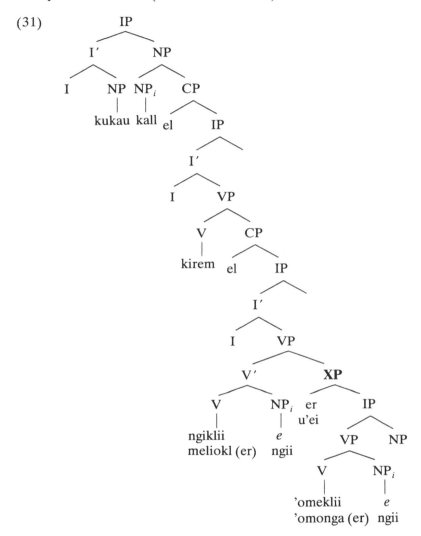

(16) a kukau a $kall_i$ [el   kirem [el   ngikl-ii   ___$_i$
      taro   food   Comp 2s-must Comp R-Pf-boil-3s

[er a u'ei   er a 'o-mekl-ii   ___$_i$]]]
P   before P   IR-2-Pf-eat-3s

Taro is food that you must boil ___ before you eat ___.

122   CHAPTER FOUR

(18) a kukau a kall$_i$ [el   kirem   [el   meliokl er ngii$_i$
     taro   food Comp 2s-must Comp R-Im-boil P it

[er a u'ei   er a 'omonga er ngii$_i$]]]
 P   before P   IR-2-Im-eat P it

Taro is food that you must boil ___ before you eat ___ .

(32) (= (20a)), on the other hand, is not grammatical: there is no legitimate projection path which unites with XP to form a subtree:

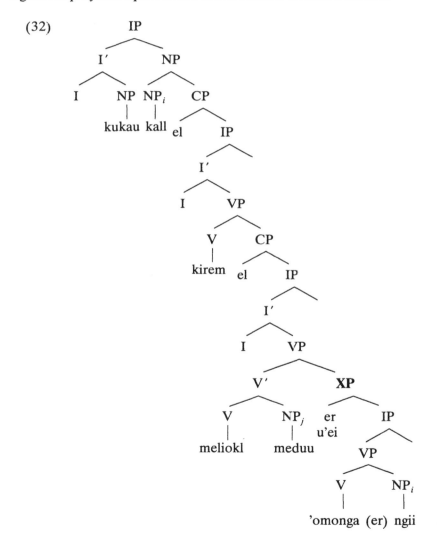

VARIABLE BINDING

123

(20) a.*a kukau a kall$_i$ [el   kirem   [el   meliokl a
      taro   *food*   *Comp*   *must-2s*   *Comp*   *R-cook*

meduu   er a u'ei   er a 'omo-nga   er ngii$_i$]]]
breadfruit   *before*   *IR-2-Im-eat*   *P*   *it*

(Taro is the food$_i$ that you must cook breadfruit$_j$ before you eat ——$_i$.)

Thus Kayne's theory of government accounts for the ungrammaticality of the examples in (20) in a manner similar to the way it accounts for the English facts.[13] The only additional assumption we made for Palauan was that resumptive pronouns, as syntactic variables, have g-projection paths, an assumption well motivated on other grounds.[14] It should be kept in mind, however, that, as a reviewer has pointed out, my analysis differs *in spirit* from Kayne's: Kayne's object is to reduce Subjacency to (his) ECP, while my claim is that connectedness (the ECP) applies even to structures that cannot be analyzed in terms of Subjacency.[15]

This position may seem in some respects like that taken in Cinque (1984), where it is argued that parasitic gaps, gaps of apparent extraction from islands, and gaps in 'object deletion' constructions are actually A′ bound *pro*. In Cinque's analysis A′ bound *pro* is a 'pronominal variable' that is defined as a variable in the conventional way: a locally A′ bound position that satisfies the identification requirement on *pro* through its relation with the A′ antecedent. The *antecedent* supplies the required grammatical features for the A′ *pro*, just as *agreement* in *pro*-drop languages supplies the grammatical features of referring *pro*.

If this variable really is *pro*, however, it is not clear why it is not identified like any other *pro* is presumed to be, via agreement or by the lexical governor. Furthermore, the hypothesis that *pro* must be identified is flawed. As we have already noted, the distribution of *pro* in many languages is unrelated to the presence or absence of overt agreement. Even in Palauan, where identification plays a major role, empty categories regularly occur in positions where identification fails (see Chapter Three). In addition, Palauan has lexical pronouns which function as variables, and lexical resumptive pronouns presumably do not require 'identification' by an antecedent. I therefore do not adopt the identification analysis proposed by Cinque. In Chapter Six I argue that all variables, even resumptive pronouns, are [−pronominal] once they are A′ bound; thus a real resumptive pronoun in my view would not necessarily have any of the syntactic properties of pronominals.

A number of other important issues accompany the analysis of pronouns as variables. Some of them, such as the theory of resumptive pronouns, locality, and formation of A′ chains, are pursued in the

124   CHAPTER FOUR

remainder of this chapter. I leave the issue of whether or not these variables are intrinsically or contextually identified as such to Chapter Six, where the question becomes particularly relevant to the analysis of crossover constructions. We turn first to the treatment of resumptive pronouns.

2.5. *The Theory of Resumptive Pronouns*

In Chapter One and earlier in this chapter I have reviewed the standard analysis of resumptive pronouns, and described the interpretive coindexing rule that is assumed to apply to them in LF. I have now presented conceptual and empirical grounds for rejecting this analysis, and showed that the binding of Palauan resumptive pronouns is at S-structure. Later chapters will demonstrate the nonmarginality of resumptive pronouns in Palauan over an even greater range of A′ binding structures. Clearly, resumptive pronouns may have a syntactic nature quite different from that claimed for them on the basis of English.

There are two issues in the treatment of resumptive pronouns that should be kept distinct: one is their behavior with respect to bounding constraints, and the other is the local conditions which account for their properties. Palauan represents a language in which resumptive pronouns are dissociated from the theory of islands, that is, from bounding, and are more directly associated with phrase-internal conditions on the properties of arguments. That is, they reflect a condition on what occupies the *extraction site*, rather than a condition on the A′ binding *path*.

Many languages use resumptive pronouns productively, though the distribution and function of resumptive pronouns varies widely. Swedish, for example, requires resumptive pronouns in subject position under a lexically filled Comp (an ECP effect) (see also Engdahl in Engdahl and Ejerhed 1982), while other Scandinavian languages allow the subject to be empty in this context (see Engdahl). Hebrew allows resumptive pronouns in relative clauses but not in questions (Borer 1984a), while Irish allows them in both relative clauses and questions (McCloskey 1979). In Welsh, the NP complement case of the Complex NP Constraint is violated with *either* gap or resumptive pronoun, and the relative clause case of the CNPC is *observed* with either (Tallermann 1983).[16] In Igbo (data from Goldsmith 1981), resumptive pronouns are obligatory in a number of positions in the sentence, including NP specifier, PP object, and subject of a tensed clause under a complementizer; interestingly, *both* gaps and resumptive pronouns obey island constraints in Igbo. Thus not all languages with a productive resumptive pronoun option use the pronouns for the same purposes. Many of these languages are analyzed as having *both* movement and nonmovement (RP)

VARIABLE BINDING 125

strategies (e.g. Irish), and others (e.g. Igbo) dissociate resumptive pronouns and movement issues. Presumably English resumptive pronouns are not productive. In Palauan, resumptive pronouns appear in all NP positions in all A′ binding structures, and none obey the movement constraints;[17] as in Swedish, they seem instead to reflect an ECP constraint. In sum, the theory of resumptive pronouns has a good deal of surface variation to account for.

Besides Chomsky (1981, 1982), the only other full-scale attempt to deal with resumptive pronouns within the GB framework is Sells (1984, incorporating Chao and Sells 1983). Quite rightly, Sells rejects the common claim that resumptive pronouns occur only or primarily in relative clauses. He formulates instead a typology of languages, rather than structures, that have, or do not have, resumptive pronouns. For Sells, a language with 'true' resumptive pronouns allows pronouns to be operator-bound at S-structure; that is, it allows free indexing of A′ positions at S-structure. Such indexing is impossible in English, according to Sells, as it would derive island violations. Languages like English do not have true resumptive pronouns at all, in Sells' view. In denying that English has resumptive pronouns, however, this approach seems less than explanatory of the relevant differences among languages.

In order to account for the relation of resumptive pronouns to island phenomena in English and Palauan, I will modify Sells' theory a bit and hypothesize a parameter that sets the level of representation at which pronouns are bound to A′ positions. The syntactic properties of Palauan resumptive pronouns that we have observed follow from such a parameter, if (along with conditions on chains) the Palauan setting allows binding of pronouns at S-structure. This parameter allows resumptive pronouns in English too, however, as A′ bound elements coindexed only at LF (as Chomsky 1982, p. 60, suggests). In general terms, a parameter that refers to levels of binding in this way is capable of deriving the necessary typology with respect to subjacency effects.[18] Pronouns that are not bound variables at S-structure are excluded from participation in A′ binding, while pronouns bound at S-structure are treated on a par with traces. This appears to be a crucial difference.

A necessary correlate to the binding of a variable to its antecedent, but one generally not referred to, has to do with the syntactic features [±anaphor, ±pronominal]. In Chomsky (1982), all NPs, null and overt, are partitioned according to these feature values. A variable is [−anaphor, −pronominal], feature values which not only define the notion 'variable' (whether contextually or intrinsically), but which also match, necessarily, those of the NP antecedent. In particular, once a pronoun is bound, it is [−pronominal]. (An empty category that is not bound is interpreted as [+pronominal].)

This analysis of variables receives a much fuller justification in the

126   CHAPTER FOUR

chapter on crossover (Chapter Six), but is also relevant here as a property of resumptive pronouns derived from the proposed parameter. Recall that one property of Palauan subject resumptive pronouns is that they can be locally bound. That is, in Palauan, a question like *Who$_i$ did she$_i$ see Bill?* is grammatical. There is no principle B binding condition on such pronouns, contrary to predictions of McCloskey (1989) and Aoun & Li (1989). But this follows, if the resumptive pronoun in Palauan is in fact [−pronominal] at S-structure, consequent upon A′ chain binding. We have described the same effect in Swedish, which also has locally bound subject resumptive pronouns.[19]

Returning to the issue of where resumptive pronouns can occur *within* the clause, it must be remembered that resumptive pronouns can be null or overt. Thus overt resumptive pronouns must occur in positions where an empty category cannot be licensed, regardless of its status with respect to A′ binding. This is especially clear in Palauan, where resumptive pronouns are simply pronouns, overt or empty, that have been A′ bound. Sells attempts to account for the structural distribution of (overt) resumptive pronouns in terms of the notion 'Case domain' of INFL, V or Tense: if one of these elements assigns Case, a resumptive pronoun does not occur in the Case domain. This notion presumably refers to the government properties of heads within such domains. Contrary to this theory, Palauan allows *pro*, and therefore a resumptive pronoun, within the stipulated Case domains. In a sense, Sells' theory fails for Palauan because it fails to take full account of the possibility that resumptive pronouns may be represented *either* by gaps or by overt pronouns; it founders on the overt/nonovert distinction, which is probably irrelevant to the actual assignment of Case (though, conversely, the *lexicality* of an NP with Case is not irrelevant to Case theory).

On the analysis presented here, a resumptive pronoun appears wherever a pronoun can appear (modulo language-specific conditions, like the level at which A′ positions are coindexed with A positions). In particular, a null resumptive pronoun appears where *pro* can appear, and an overt one where overt pronouns appear. The conditions that determine the distribution of empty (vs. overt) categories are independent of the resumptive pronoun issue.

2.6. *Parallelism*

The significance of the coordination and parasitic gap structures described above to our main theme is that they are instances of multiple variable binding which applies indifferently to gaps and lexical pronouns. But the cooccurrence in one structure of coindexed null and overt variables is contrary to certain other assumptions about variables in GB. Safir (1984), for example, pursuing the EST concept of *paral-*

VARIABLE BINDING 127

lelism in variable binding, proposes the Parallelism Constraint on Operator Binding (PCOB):

(33)   *Parallelism Constraint on Operator Binding*:

If O is an operator and x is a variable bound by O, then for any y, y a variable of O, x and y are [α lexical].

This constraint is intended to replace the Bijection Principle (Koopman and Sportiche 1983), which requires that operators and variables be in a one-to-one relation. The PCOB allows an antecedent to bind more than one variable but requires it to bind only gaps, or only overt pronouns.

The PCOB analysis accounts for the facts of languages like English, and allows the separate treatment of resumptive pronouns to be preserved. It is not entirely clear, however, how it applies to the Palauan data here. The spirit of the PCOB is clear in Safir's examples, in which multiple variable binding involving a WH trace and a resumptive pronoun is ruled ungrammatical. In spirit then, the PCOB (incorrectly) rules out the Palauan sentences in (10) and (17), since *pro* and the overt pronoun are not [α lexical]. On the other hand, if parallelism can be satisfied via the fact that Palauan variables are all [−pronominal], then Palauan does observe something like the PCOB. This interpretation is ruled out as the PCOB theory stands, however, since Safir does not recognize the possibility that *pro* may be a variable: he limits the distribution of *pro* to clitic constructions and expletives (p. 620). In addition, a precise definition of the term 'lexical' in the formulation of the PCOB is crucial to the viability of this constraint. As it stands, the Palauan facts cannot be said either to support or to contradict the PCOB.

The issues involved in multiple variable binding are pursued in depth in Chapter Six, on crossover constructions.

2.7. *Subjects, Adjuncts, and Relative Clauses*

Though we were able to account above for the failure of extraction from adjuncts in Palauan, the fact remains that Palauan allows extraction out of other structures which are not subcategorized, such as (sentential) subjects and relative clauses. We will again find certain notions of Kayne (1983b) useful in accounting for these facts, especially the notion 'canonical government configuration'. Palauan is a VOS language in which government is uniformly to the right, and in which subjects are on a right branch. Since subjects, in contrast to adjuncts, are properly governed (by Inflection), the subject node in Palauan will always have a left sister (I′) that is a projection of its governor. The projection path above a subject containing a variable will always include IP and therefore CP, and so on

128   CHAPTER FOUR

up the tree to the node dominating the lexical antecedent. That is, extraction from a right-branch subject should always be possible.

In the case of relative clauses, we can account for the possibility of extraction by assuming that they, too, are governed domains in the sense of Belletti and Rizzi (1981) and Huang (1982). This is structurally a reasonable assumption, since a relative head and its modifying clause are immediately dominated by an NP node with the same index as the head, and NP and CP are sisters, in the usual government configuration. This proposal depends on the government properties of N, of course. Government of CP by N is a natural situation in Palauan since, as we have seen elsewhere, N is one of the class of governors in this language (cf. extraction of Spec(N), illustrated in Chapter Three).[20] These considerations, combined with Palauan's lack of subjacency effects, will allow extraction sites in relative NPs. In fact, we could assume that the head of NP in the structure $[_{NP}$ NP CP] governs its CP universally. Movement out of relative clauses would still be impossible, since both the relative NP and the matrix IP must be crossed in one movement, in violation of subjacency. The trace would also fail to satisfy head-government in a language like English, where N is not a proper govenor. Since Palauan does not have WH movement, however, the bounding constraints do not apply, and, in Palauan, N is an ECP governor.

As we have noted, adjuncts are opaque domains because they do not satisfy the ECP. Subjects and adjuncts therefore do not pattern together in Palauan, since subjects are always properly governed. This difference appears to argue against Huang's analysis, which unifies subjects and adjuncts, but actually supports it in showing the crucial factor to be whether or not the subject is properly governed. It also supports Huang's position in that it distinguishes between the ECP and Subjacency analyses of the Subject Condition.

In the final analysis, the fact that Palauan observes the adjunct island but not the islands conventionally subsumed under subjacency constitutes another reason to maintain the distinction between movement- and base-generated structures. This is especially clear in the difference between the SSC and the so-called adjunct island. The lack of sentential subject effects in Palauan can only be analyzed in terms of government, and not in terms of subjacency. Without the movement/base generation distinction — that is, if the adjunct island were analyzed in terms of bounding theory — it would be difficult to account for the Palauan facts. Deriving the adjunct effects from government theory *without* reference to bounding allows both the facts about subject extraction and the adjunct facts to fall out.[21]

It is revealing to note that the distinction between arguments and adjuncts is referred to in other ways by Palauan grammar. For one thing, the subcategorized sentential complements of verbs (and predicate

VARIABLE BINDING 129

adjectives) are normally introduced by the complementizer **el kmo**; this complementizer never appears in adjunct clauses (though it sometimes appears in sentential subjects). If verbs subcategorize complementizers as well as complements, then the distribution of **el kmo** falls out: it is a complementizer for *complements*. In my analysis of Palauan, **el kmo** introduces clauses that receive Case from a matrix predicate.[22]

Second, argument variables have different agreement properties from variables in adjuncts: the former, including subjects, always trigger WH agreement up to the position of the antecedent, while variables in adjuncts do so only optionally:

(34) a. ke-mo   merek el   melu'es er
     R-2s-Aux finish   Comp R-write   P

     a babilengem er a **oingerang**
       paper-2s   P   when?

b.   ng-**oingera**$_i$ $\left\{\begin{array}{l} \text{e ke-mo} \\ \textit{R-2s-Aux} \\ \text{a 'o-bo} \\ \textit{IR-2-Aux} \end{array}\right\}$ merek el melu'es er a babilengem

     (er ngii$_i$)

     (Both) When will you finish writing your thesis?

c. a Nina a milskau   a buk   er **ker**
         R-gave-2s   book   P   where?

     Where did Nina give you the book?

d.   ng- **ker**$_i$ $\left\{\begin{array}{l} \text{a milskau} \\ \textit{R-gave-2s} \\ \text{lebilskau} \\ \textit{IR-3-gave-2s} \end{array}\right\}$ a buk   er ngii$_i$
     where   *book*   *there*

     Where did (s/he) give you the book?

Recall that the formulation of WH agreement in (5) refers to *arguments*. Since WH agreement makes no reference to adjuncts, no prediction is made about agreement in adjuncts. (The WH agreement rule therefore does not account for the cases in which WH-agreement forms *do* appear in adjuncts.)

Finally, adjuncts that are objects of the preposition **er** only optionally correspond to a resumptive pronoun when topicalized (see (34b)), while arguments do so obligatorily.

It appears, then, that several statements of Palauan grammar distinguish arguments from adjuncts.

130 CHAPTER FOUR

2.8. *Summary*

To sum up to this point, I have demonstrated that both the empty categories and the overt resumptive pronouns in Palauan A' binding are S-structure variables, on the basis of several sets of facts. The primary evidence comes from the fact that they are nondistinct with respect to their interaction with WH agreement. Second, neither has special status with respect to island phenomena. Third, they cooccur in multiple variable binding such as coordination and parasitic gap structures. This distribution is not predicted by the GB analysis of resumptive pronouns, which provides only that the pronouns are bound by a predication rule at LF. Since Palauan extraction is base-generated, however, there is nothing to prevent null and overt pronouns from being freely generated together in any sort of structure. We find no evidence in Palauan grammar that overt resumptive pronouns are coindexed separately from the null resumptive pronouns, or that either type of pronoun is co-indexed only at LF. On the contrary, the evidence is conclusive that both are coindexed at S-structure.

Since Palauan does not have WH movement, it instantiates the negative value of the [±WH movement] parameter, proposed recently in various works. A language without WH movement would be expected to have an impoverished system of A' binding at S-structure. Chinese has been described as such a case (Huang 1982). In Palauan, however, the entire range of A' binding is present at S-structure, showing again how the setting of one parameter interacts with other parameter settings to determine a particular grammar. In this case, the parameter most involved in generating Palauan A' binding is the one allowing binding (A' chain formation, below) of resumptive pronouns in the syntax. Important associated effects derive from the setting of the word order parameters (Chapter Six), determining the ways in which the ECP applies to the output of binding.

The findings of this section therefore advance our overriding claim, that Palauan A' binding is syntactically equivalent to A' binding in Move α languages: A' binding constructions are a productive syntactic class; the extraction site is constrained by a principle that licenses empty categories; and the binding holds at S-structure. We turn now to a description of the S-structure coindexing mechanism and the presence of a unique locality effect.

3. A' CHAIN FORMATION

The discussion up to this point has presupposed that the Palauan sentences under consideration have fully indexed S-structures, in which both A and A' positions have an index, and that the syntax has a way of

VARIABLE BINDING

131

determining that the indices of the A′ binder and its bindee match. However, the usual mechanisms of coindexing cannot be appealed to, since Move α is not involved, and LF interpretation comes 'too late'. WH agreement and the conditions on coordination and parasitic gaps rely crucially, however, on the mechanism that ensures coindexing in the syntax. Such a mechanism is available in the notion of **chain**, mentioned in Chapter One (although other views of coindexing are also possible; see, e.g., Bresnan and Grimshaw 1978; McCloskey 1979; Huang 1982). Simply put, a chain is a (maximal) sequence of coindexed positions; it should therefore serve our purpose quite naturally.

The notion of chain is first elaborated in Chomsky (1981, chapter 6), and extended to the analysis of parasitic gaps in Chomsky (1982). A chain (alternatively, an index) is an entity that receives the Case and θ-role assigned to some argument position, and accounts for inheritance of these properties by the antecedent. As a part of Theta Theory, the chain ensures that θ-roles assigned to argument positions in D-structure remain attached to those arguments after syntactic and LF movements. The θ Criterion filters out chains that are not well-formed in terms of the biuniqueness requirements, i.e. one θ-role :: one argument :: one chain. In Chomsky's view, chains encode the results of movement: they are not defined directly on coindexed S-structure positions, but rather represent the derivational history of S-structures generated by Move α. All coindexed positions thus represent landing sites, except for the extraction site at the tail.

Rizzi (1982b) develops a theory of chains that are independent of Move α, and are read directly off S-structures. This is the sort of mechanism that we need to incorporate into the analysis of Palauan, since the Move α interpretation of the chain is excluded a priori. Rizzi's formal characterization of the chain is given below, along with his definition of *binder* and *local binder* (Rizzi 1982b, p. 2).

(35) $C = (a_1 \ldots a_n)$ is a chain iff, for $1 \leqslant i \leqslant n$, a_i is the local binder of a_{i+1}.

A is the *binder* of B iff, for A, B = any category, A and B are coindexed and A c-commands B.

A is the *local binder* of B iff A is a binder of B and there is no C such that C is a binder of B and C is not a binder of A.

Chain formation is free (any sequence meeting the definition is a chain).

Rizzi argues that his *representational* characterization of the chain is superior to Chomsky's *derivational* characterization because the former has greater empirical coverage: it rules out certain representations on purely structural grounds. To see how the chain formation algorithm works, consider Rizzi's example in (36):

(36) *Gianni$_i$ [$_{VP}$ si$_i$ è stato affidato]

(*Gianni to-himself was entrusted*)

The occurrence of the reflexive clitic **si** is incompatible with derived subjects in a range of structures: passives (as in (36)), impersonal passives, unaccusatives, and raising. In these structures, **si** and the trace of the derived subject block chain formation ((37) =(36)):

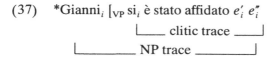

(37) *Gianni$_i$ [$_{VP}$ si$_i$ è stato affidato e'_i e''_i

In terms of Move α, (37) contains two chains: (**Gianni**, e') and (**si**, e''). These two chains also are the only chains in (37) that are allowed by the θ Criterion: each empty category is in a θ-position and a chain may contain only one θ-position. Since both movements are well-formed, the Move α characterization of the chain does not account for the ungrammaticality of such sentences. In representational terms, on the other hand, these two chains cannot be formed: the trace of **Gianni** (e') is the local binder (see the definition above) of the trace of **si** (e''), and therefore blocks the chain (**si**, e''). Likewise, **si** blocks the chain (**Gianni**, e'). A chain containing all four coindexed elements, furthermore, is in violation of the θ Criterion, as it contains two arguments and therefore two θ-roles.

In the early literature on chains, it was argued that chains are only formed on A positions (or on clitic positions) and do not apply to WH operators in Comp. This view stems from the original concept of the chain, which was intended to distinguish A' binding from A binding, and to account for the sharing of θ-roles between argument positions. Chomsky and Rizzi take this view. See Chomsky (1982); Rizzi (1982b); Safir (1982); Kayne (1983b); and Brody (1984). No principle of UG has been called upon to exclude operators from chains, and thus no principle is at stake in including them.[23] In the recent literature, a number of researchers have presented arguments for including A' chains in the grammar; see Chomsky (1986a); Barss (1985); Haïk (1985); Carstens (1985); McCloskey (1989); and others. Below I will demonstrate how the notion of chain can be profitably incorporated into the grammar of Palauan A' binding.

First, we note that all Palauan A' binding structures meet Rizzi's definition of chain. This is a simple matter, since chain formation is free, and in all cases there is a c-commanding binder of a_{i+1}. I assume that both the binder and the NP in argument position have an index at

VARIABLE BINDING   133

S-structure as a result of free indexing. Whether this index is assigned at D-structure or at S-structure is immaterial here, and Palauan grammar does not, in any case, provide evidence to distinguish the two levels. The important point is that by S-structure all NPs have an index.

The chain algorithm does not *assign* indices, therefore, but rather *reads* the indices of members of the set it defines, and ensures that all members have the same index. In this light, it acts as a filter on indexed S-structure representations. Thus an A' chain is freely formed between the binder and the argument position when these two elements have the same index.

Since the variables in Palauan are pronouns rather than traces, a structure may contain more than one potential extraction site. In such cases, if one pronoun c-commands another, the c-commanding pronoun must be construed as the variable in order to avoid a strong crossover violation. Where c-command does not hold between two potential variables, either may be taken as the actual variable (this optionality is discussed in Chapter Six). I will assume, further, that A' chains in Palauan have exactly two members, the antecedent and the variable. This assumption rests primarily on the lack of WH movement, excluding the existence of intermediate traces. It also depends on the crossover analysis and will be more fully motivated in Chapter Six.

3.1. *Chains and Resumptive Pronouns*

One problem in adopting the theory of chains is the claim that (empty) pronominals do not participate in chain formation (Chomsky 1986a). Extension of the notion of chain to pronominals in the Palauan case, however, is entirely compatible with other extensions of the theory I argue for here, and indeed necessary. The only possible candidates for variable status in Palauan are pronouns. Since the evidence that these pronominals are also syntactic variables is conclusive, we naturally expect them to participate in any syntactic phenomena hypothesized of empty categories in other languages. Thus we may assume that Palauan grammar does *not* exclude resumptive pronouns from chain formation. Finally, since overt pronominals are equivalent to *pro* in all the structures we have studied, including coindexing in multiple variable binding, extension of chain formation to the empty resumptive pronoun is not possible without simultaneous extension to the overt resumptive pronoun. In sum, in a language in which syntactic A' dependencies are productive but in which resumptive pronouns are the only variables, the definition of chain can very naturally be employed as a filter on S-structure coindexing of A' bound pronouns.

3.2. *The Chain and WH Agreement*

In A' chain formation we now have a means to ensure that antecedent and variable(s) share indices. It is natural to suppose that WH agreement depends on this process of chain formation: it applies only in the domain of the coindexed A' relation. In fact, we may view WH agreement as consequent on the formation of chains (= the coindexing rule). That is, the existence of the coindexed relation is prior to and a necessary condition for the application of WH agreement.

In this view of WH agreement as contingent on A' chain formation, WH agreement is less of an oddity among agreement rules. It is triggered by a variable whose structural relation to an A' binder has been specified, its target is I, and its domain of application is each local link in the chain.

Consider, now, the mechanisms by which the features relevant to WH agreement might be determined.[24] First, by specifier-head coindexing, I and its specifier (the free relative) are always coindexed. Within the free relative, the (empty) head and the variable are coindexed by chain binding in relativization, and Case is assigned to the chain. The Case feature is passed to the matrix NP. That NP and I then share the Case feature by specifier-head coindexing, triggering WH agreement on I. Schematically,

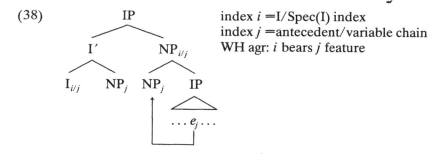

(38)   index i = I/Spec(I) index
    index j = antecedent/variable chain
    WH agr: i bears j feature

In long-distance WH agreement, the argument that contains the variable is assigned NOM or non-NOM Case (cf. earlier discussion about assignment of Case to CPs). That the XP contains a variable is transmitted as a syntactic feature to I in each clause: if the XP is an embedded subject, its Case feature is shared directly with the local I (by spec-head coindexing); if the XP container is a nonsubject, its Case feature is passed along the g-projections of its governor to I. In either case, the feature is ultimately passed to the matrix NP and then to I as in (38). Thus I in each clause is affected by a local trigger of WH agreement, the lowest I by the variable, and higher Is by the container of the variable, as predicted. I provide a representative tree (39) for tracing these mechanisms:

(39)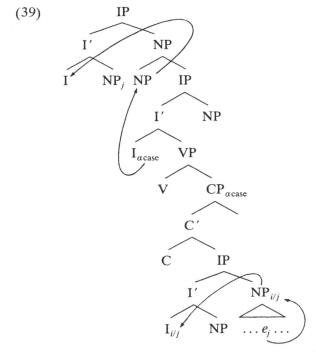

Note that Case probably is not assigned to the A' chain in as simple a manner as generally supposed: both the Case of the variable *and* the Case of the XP containing the variable become features of the chain. The chain formation procedure is necessary to the well-formedness of coindexing between the antecedent and its variable, but Case can be transmitted via other means: specifier-head coindexing and formation of g-projections. These other means appear to subsume some of the functions previously ascribed to chain formation.[25]

An important property of this analysis of index and feature sharing is the fact that movement is unnecessary. Any legitimate coindexing relation can be analyzed in these terms, which, it should be noticed, consist entirely in elements of the theory that are postulated independently of Palauan and WH agreement: predication or chain binding in relative clauses (analogous in another module to lambda abstraction); specifier-head coindexing; feature sharing between heads and their projections; and so on.

3.3. *A Universal Locality Condition*

My main premise has been that Palauan, as an instantiation of Universal Grammar, can be analyzed naturally from within the conceptual frame-

136   CHAPTER FOUR

work of GB. Part of this framework is an account of locality effects in A′ binding. In this section I explore the evidence that Palauan does exhibit such locality effects. The effort to describe a locality constraint parallel to subjacency derives from the attempt to account for Palauan phenomena in terms of universal principles.

In Palauan, A′ binding is subject to WH agreement, and in GB theory, it observes subjacency. Are subjacency and WH agreement in any way grammatically related to each other? On first thought, the answer is no. Subjacency is a condition on a movement path. WH agreement is an agreement rule. The former is a property of Universal Grammar, the latter a property of a particular grammar (or grammars — Chamorro has a similar rule (Chung 1982a)). On the other hand, WH agreement is associated with certain phenomena which mimic a locality effect. These phenomena are the presence of a local controller, and the fact that Inflection *in each clause* in the A′ binding domain must bear WH agreement features. It is of course true that these phenomena, if they do reflect locality, are quite unlike the locality effects usually associated with unbounded dependencies, the island constraints. We have seen that Palauan lacks these island effects, just as it lacks WH movement. Interestingly, the A′ binding relation *does* observe island constraints in Chamorro (Chung 1984). Since Chamorro also has WH agreement, whatever locality effcts underlie WH agreement (in both languages) must be distinct from subjacency effects.

Curiously, the local and clause-by-clause effects of WH agreement parallel the type of evidence that has been appealed to in other languages in order to establish the existence of locality conditions on WH movement. Kayne and Pollock (1978), for example, argue that stylistic inversion in French supports the claim that WH movement is bounded and iterative because extraction from embedded clauses may produce inversion in every clause between the antecedent and the gap. McCloskey (1979, 1989) describes a pattern of complementizer alternation in Irish that affects every clause between antecedent and gap. Reinhart (1981a) notes that in Hebrew a relative pronoun may appear in any Comp between antecedent and gap, and concludes that this is proof of "overt iterative movement to COMP". Finally, Chung (1982a) describes WH agreement in Chamorro extraction, similar to WH agreement in Palauan, which she analyzes as support for her argument that WH-movement is bounded and successive cyclic in Chamorro. (Similar discussions abound in the literature; see also, for example, Taraldsen 1978a; Torrego 1984; Clements 1985; Xu and Langendoen 1985.) In French, Irish, Hebrew, and Chamorro, however, one does not find the lack of island effects or the productivity of resumptive pronouns that is found in Palauan and that forces the nonmovement analysis.

In sum, the Palauan WH agreement effects would provide a strong

VARIABLE BINDING

137

argument for bounded movement, if a movement analysis were tenable to begin with. But they still provide a basis for the proposal that A' binding is locally constrained in this language in a way parallel to the way WH movement is constrained by subjacency. What is crucial is that the entire A' dependency between antecedent and variable in Palauan appears to be broken down into a series of local dependencies just as it is in movement languages. That is, WH agreement involves *subjacent* dependencies. If the relation in Palauan were truly unbounded, we would not expect to find these local effects. If it is in fact bounded in some way, such local effects are to be expected.

That the A' binding of resumptive pronouns does rely on discrete, subjacent steps in this way argues for a universal locality condition on all A' binding. In fact, this aspect of Palauan grammar suggests that the existence of locality effects specific to the A' binding relation can be dissociated from the WH movement transformation and the Subjacency Condition. That is, subjacency is perhaps not a *necessary* attribute of A' binding. Chomsky (1979, p. 27) speculates that

the principle of subjacency is ... a rather natural condition, which one might hope to relate to more general principles of mental processing: perhaps rules of "mental computation" are in general bounded in some manner, as the rule Move α is bounded by the bounding categories.

Palauan appears to confirm this speculation about "rules of mental computation", in that both subjacency and WH agreement may be subcases of a more general locality principle whose reflexes vary among languages. This finding will perhaps advance the project, begun in Koster (1978) and continued elsewhere (e.g. Chomsky 1986b), of formulating a theory of locality of enough generality as to encompass in one statement the constraints now included in individual grammars of A' binding.

If observance of subjacency is only a contingent property of A' binding, then the most important attribute of the class of A' binding relations is the operator-variable relation. The similarities between WH binding and quantification in predicate logic have led to the EST hypothesis that a WH phrase is a true quantifier in LF, taking logical scope over its variable, and participating with the variable in the same relation as does an existential quantifier and its variable. What we have seen of Palauan grammar supports this hypothesis about WH quantification: if A' binding is really independent of subjacency, then it is *more* like the logical relation, to which bounding theory does not apply.

NOTES

[1] ... or propose some alternative to the bounding theory of Chomsky (1986b) ...

[2] The fact that the *form* of a WH question in Palauan is based on relativization can be taken as support of an idea articulated in Grimshaw (1979) and Williams (1983a) that

138   CHAPTER FOUR

the relation between the syntactic category of a construction and its semantic type is not necessarily fixed.

[3] In the case of clausal objects, the subject may precede the object. I assume that this is a case of leftward movement of the subject.

[4] That the WH phrase in the examples in (4) has wide scope is demonstrated by the fact that the examples all translate semantically as questions formed on the WH constituent, and elicit an answer that provides a constant for the NP that is WH-questioned.

[5] It is not altogether clear what principle underlies the phenomena referred to as the CSC. The constraint appears to result from some universal *matching* requirement on the conjuncts (see Williams 1978, Goodall 1984). Such a requirement would, intuitively, derive from the nature of coordination itself. Goodall (1984) argues that coordination is the union of simple clauses, in which each conjunct is independently well formed. In (7), for example, the conjunct '. . . what the old man sold me' is well formed, but the conjunct '. . . what the teacher gave me a book' is not. At LF, the latter would be an instance of vacuous quantification (and a θ-Criterion violation; see Goodall for details).

[6] Note that the parasitic gap is in a clause bearing irrealis morphology. This mood is introduced by the adverbial head, but one wonders whether the gap would trigger IR forms on its own. This is difficult to test, since (true) irrealis mood takes precedence over syntactic WH agreement (see the previous chapter), so it is not absolutely clear that the gap is not actually a pronoun. The issue might perhaps be resolved by further research.

[7] The elements referred to as 'parasitic' in (16)–(18) and in (20) and (21) could be referring pronuns. The binding properties of elements in these structures are not clear.

[8] S. Chung points out (personal communication) that this fact can be taken to strengthen the case that apparent parasitic elements in Palauan are in fact not parasitic at all.

[9] Sentences such as these led me to conclude in Georgopoulos (1985) that adjuncts are *not* islands to extraction. This conclusion is rejected here.

[10] Though the CNPC is still somewhat intractable — see Kayne's note 5. See also Aoun (1981). The CED presumably does not subsume the N-complement case.

[11] Kayne's account precedes *Barriers* X' theory, and Kayne does not label nodes as I have done. Though I' is not a maximal projection, it is a g-projection of *admire*.

[12] I assume er can be ignored for purposes of the Connectedness Condition.

[13] This account confirms the expectation expressed in Chomsky (1982, p. 58) that a language using the resumptive pronoun strategy freely will not pattern like English with respect to the licensing properties of parasitic gaps.

[14] I will not address here the question of what the resumptive pronoun takes as its antecedent at S-structure. I believe that the question is moot in Palauan in view of the range of A' binding phenomena that resumptive pronouns participate in in this language. See Safir (1986) and McCloskey (1989) for two sides of this issue.

[15] In fact, the most accurate observation to make is probably that connectedness (in terms of graph theory) is a property of structures that is independent of such concepts as Subjacency and the ECP.

[16] I thank J. McCloskey for the reference to Tallermann's work.

[17] I do not consider another set of conditions giving rise to resumptive pronouns, those connected with processing. In some languages (e.g. Swedish and perhaps English), resumptive pronouns appear in any deeply embedded positions, presumably to over-come the effects of distance from the antecedent. I assume these resumptive pronouns are not governed by syntactic constraints.

[18] . . . and, incidentally, parallels the multi-level treatment of A binding facts in, e.g., Belletti and Rizzi (1988).

[19] This argues, contra McCloskey (1989), that resumptive pronouns in Irish are not S-structure bound: if they were, island violations would be generated. Since Irish

observes the island constraints, it seems that Irish resumptive pronouns are in fact not bound until LF.

[20] There is a productive class of predicates in Palauan that are lexically and morphologically inalienably possessed nouns (see Georgopoulos 1991a). These predicates govern arguments within their projection just as verbal predicates do.

[21] This suggestion runs counter to the analysis of Chomsky (1986b) that makes an adjunct node a bounding node for subjacency. Thus movement out of adjuncts always violates subjacency, since the adjunct node and IP (a barrier by inheritance from the adjunct node) must be crossed. This analysis would not allow the proper distinction to be made for Palauan, however. See below.

[22] This analysis accounts for the fact that relative clauses do not receive Case, though they are *governed* by N. Presumably N does not select or subcategorize the relative clause, so Case is not assigned.

[23] The fact that an operator cannot be assigned a θ-role from a matrix clause governor (see Chomsky 1981) may be captured by adding a statement such as (i) to the theory of chains:

i.   An element in an A' position inherits θ-role and Case in a chain containing a θ-position.

[24] Parts of the following are adapted from Chung (1991).

[25] This does not necessarily imply that the chain can be derived from spec-head coindexing, g-projections, or other mechanisms. Though this is an interesting question, I do not pursue it here. The overlap may simply be an instance of the redundancy of natural language.

CHAPTER FIVE

EMBEDDED QUESTIONS AND THE SCOPE OF WH PHRASES

0. OVERVIEW

While all languages have some mechanism for posing constituent (WH) questions, they vary in the mechanisms chosen. English, like many languages, is analyzed as having WH movement in both the syntax and LF: a questioned constituent normally moves into Spec(C), a syntactic position that indicates its semantic scope. Only one WH phrase is allowed in Spec(C) at S-structure, however, and other WH movement takes place in LF. Chinese and Japanese (Huang 1982; Lasnik and Saito 1984), in contrast, do not have syntactic WH movement; all WH phrases are in situ in the surface structure of these languages. Polish (Toman 1981; Lasnik and Saito 1984) takes a sort of middle ground: it requires all WH phrases to move to an A' position above IP, but does not allow extraction from indicative clauses (see Lasnik and Saito, fn. 6); WH phrases in CP therefore occur in a position that both differs from their D-structure position and may not necessarily correspond to their semantic scope. Yet other variants are found in Slavic languages described by Rudin (1988): WH movement may be exclusively syntactic, so that all WH phrases are fronted to their scope position at S-structure, either to Spec(C) or adjoined to IP.

In the generative grammatical approach to the variants on WH questions, certain constants of Universal Grammar are integrated with language-specific properties that reflect the setting of some parameter(s) of UG in a certain way. For example, Move α is a rule of UG: parameters associated with Move α include the options of allowing movement in the syntax, in LF, or in both modules. English allows movement in both (perhaps all) levels, and Chinese and Japanese only in LF. Also parameterized is the ability of Spec(C) to hold more than one WH phrase at a given level; this interacts with the movement parameter(s). Polish has multiple syntactic movement but does not allow 'COMP to COMP' movement in the syntax. Languages like Bulgarian and Romanian allow multiple adjunction to Spec(C) but no LF movement (Rudin 1988). In other words, the grammar of each language sets the parameters associated with Move α, and the movement phenomena that are observed in that language follow from these settings.

In Palauan, equivalents of all these strategies are realized: a questioned constituent with wide semantic scope may be in situ, in some non-matrix A' position, or in an A' position dominating the matrix IP.

140

EMBEDDED QUESTIONS   141

Multiple WH phrases may be fronted. But all the structures involved are realized without movement. In Chapter Four, I argued that the coindexing relation between an A′ antecedent and its variable holds in the syntax. Other issues arise, however. The most obvious theoretical issue is that of specifying how the various options for WH placement in Palauan are related to scope interpretation, that is, how matrix and embedded questions are distinguished, and how scope is related to S-structure position. Another important issue involves the X′-theoretic description of these structures. Finally, if a single language can have (the equivalent of) both + and −WH movement settings, and both + and − 'long movement' settings in the syntax, then how is the analysis of the differences among languages like English, Chinese, and Polish, in terms of single settings of the relevant parameters, to be maintained?

The last question involves cross-linguistic analysis of a number of parameters that would go beyond the bounds of this book. I will narrow the subject matter somewhat by grounding the analysis in issues dealing more directly with the Palauan data. Such grounding is necessary in any event, as there are many *descriptive* problems to be addressed.

The chapter first presents the facts of embedded complements containing single WH phrases, and states the constraints on the scope of such phrases, considering both in situ and preposed WH phrases. An analysis is offered for the cooccurrence of complementizer and preposed WH phrase. I also show here how embedded questions are distinguished from free relatives, a crucial distinction. I then turn to multiple interrogation structures, and discuss how the lexical requirements of verbs interact with scope of WH phrases in these contexts. I will attempt to show how embedded (narrow scope) questions are distinguished from matrix (wide scope) questions, in view of all the positional options available at S-structure. Following this presentation of the data, I address the issues raised for the theory of WH scope in LF. Here I argue that the *designated WH scope position* in UG is Spec(C) and that this scope-bearing position is necessarily on the left edge of the clause, even in a VOS language. From this it follows that the essential distinction relevant to satisfying the [+WH] feature is between WH phrases *in Spec(C)* and WHs in other positions, rather than that between simply *preposed* WH and WH in situ. I show that preposed WH phrases in Palauan are not in Spec(C), and from this derives much superficial variation.

1. EMBEDDED QUESTIONS: THE BASICS OF THE ANALYSIS

In the analysis of WH questions, a WH phrase is said to have 'wide scope' if it is identified by some constituent in the answer to the question. That is, an NP identifying *who* (like *Bill* or *Bill and Jim*)

142 CHAPTER FIVE

substitutes for *who* in the answer, and so on for other WH phrases. Substituting a (non-WH) NP for the WH phrase is analyzed as a kind of logical instantiation: the variable that is the WH phrase is replaced by a constant. This analysis of the scope of WH phrases is part of the general approach that assimilates WH questions to quantifier-variable binding: in the WH question, the WH phrase is a quantifier that binds its variable, the trace, while the answer provides a constant value for that variable. Informally, if the WH phrase can be answered by providing a piece of information that corresponds to it, the WH phrase has wide scope.

Conversely, if a WH phrase cannot be answered — if it is not given a constant value — it has 'narrow scope'. Embedded questions contain (at least) one WH phrase with narrow scope, since a WH phrase embedded in such a construction is not assigned a value. Embedded questions may even be part of a matrix statement, as in *I wonder what's on her mind*, in which case an answer is not called for.

This introductory section describes the theoretical machinery for accounting for the syntax of wide and narrow WH scope. Traditionally, the occurrence of WH phrases in clause-initial position has been accounted for in terms of some feature or morpheme at the head of the clause that triggers movement. In this account, the syntactic position of the moved WH phrase corresponds to its semantic scope. In Palauan questions, in contrast, the position that a WH element occupies in the syntax appears to be independent of its scope properties. Yet Palauan WH questions do conform in some ways to the classical analysis.

Three of the formative papers in the theory of WH scope are Katz and Postal (1964), Baker (1970), and Bresnan (1970). In Katz and Postal's analysis of direct questions, an abstract question morpheme Q is proposed, which "attracts" a constituent that has a WH morpheme attached to it. WH questions are derived by matching the Q and WH morphemes.

Baker (1970) lays out much of what is basic to the analysis of WH binding today. He extends the Q-morpheme analysis to indirect questions, suggesting that Q may also occur clause-initially in embeddings, thus allowing Q-attraction (=WH movement) to be restricted to complement clauses. In this analysis, the scope of a WH phrase depends on the position of the Q to which it is attracted. Baker further proposes (following a suggestion of Bach) that in the input to WH movement Q has the character of an operator which binds one or more WH-NP; both Q and the WH-NP have an index which indicates the binding relation. Only NPs indexed to a *matrix* Q have wide scope, i.e. only these NPs represent a direct request for information and are given a constant value in the declarative answer.

For example, according to Baker, the question in (1) is ambiguous (his (67)),

EMBEDDED QUESTIONS   143

(1)   Who remembers where we bought which book?

in the sense that either *who* alone, or else both *who* and *which book* may have wide scope. In the first reading, only *who* is given a constant value in the answer:

(2)   *John and Martha* remember where we bought which book.

In the second, both *who* and *which book* are assigned a value:

(3)   John remembers where we bought the physics book and Martha remembers where we bought *The Wizard of Oz*.

The ambiguity arises from two distinct deep structures for (1) (an intermediate rule translates quantifiers like *some* or *that* to WH, then WH movement applies):

(4) a. $[_{S1} Q_i [some_i one$ remember $[_{S2} Q_{j,k}$ [we bought that$_j$ book at some$_k$ place]]]]

  b. $[_{S1} Q_{i,j} [some_i one$ remember $[_{S2} Q_k$ [we bought that$_j$ book at some$_k$ place]]]]

Since NP_k is indexed to an embedded Q in both structures, it has only narrow scope. In English this NP must move to the embedded Q. But an NP in the embedded clause that is not indexed to the embedded Q (NP_j in (4b), for example) may be bound by the matrix Q and may remain unmoved in the syntax; such NPs are allowed to take wide scope. (See Kuno and Robinson 1972, for a contrasting view; see also Chomsky 1973.)

In Bresnan (1970), Katz and Fodor's Q is identified with the WH complementizer, one of the expansions of the COMP node introduced by Bresnan's S'-expansion rule in (5):

(5)   S' → COMP S

In question formation, a lexical item bearing the feature [+WH] is substituted for the WH complementizer. For Bresnan, WH movement is universally to the left. Therefore only languages with a clause-initial COMP permit this COMP-substitution transformation (WH movement). (It is claimed that the lack of movement in a language like Japanese follows from this, since in Japanese COMP is clause-final.) Since the S' expansion rule applies in complement clauses as well as matrix clauses, WH movement can be confined to an embedded clause by the occurrence of a WH COMP in the embedding.

Bresnan proposes that verbs like *ask, inquire,* and *wonder*, which require interrogative complements, subcategorize for the WH comple-

144   CHAPTER FIVE

mentizer, while verbs like *believe* and *think*, which do not take interrogative complements, do not (examples from Bresnan):

(6) a.   We $\left\{\begin{array}{l}* \text{ believed} \\ \text{ inquired}\end{array}\right\}$ whether he was there.

b.   We $\left\{\begin{array}{l}\text{ believed} \\ * \text{ inquired}\end{array}\right\}$ that he was there.

The COMP-substitution transformation is obligatory in the clausal complements of verbs like *inquire* and *wonder*.

Bresnan explicitly distinguishes the WH complementizer from the [+WH] feature on the questioned constituent; in Baker, this distinction is implicit in the separation of Q and the quantified NP that undergoes movement. This distinction is crucial to the analysis of WH questions. To see this, note the surface structure position and the extraction site of the WH phrase in (7):

(7)   Who do you believe [that George saw ____]?

The WH phrase *originates* in the embedding, under *believe*, but must take wide scope because *believe* does not select a WH complementizer. The [±WH] character of an embedded clause is not determined by the D-structure presence of a WH phrase, therefore, but by the WH feature of its complementizer (and ultimately the subcategorization of the embedding verb).

1.1. *Embedded Questions in Nonmovement Languages*

From this early work has developed a theory of the scope of WH phrases which is grounded on the following assumptions. First, Comp has a [±WH] feature which subcategorizes complement-taking verbs. Second, the semantic scope of a WH word corresponds to its surface structure position if it is in A' position. And third, a WH word in situ in surface structure does not have its scope restricted to its own clause (cf. the possible scope domains of *which book* in (1)).

This analysis has an obvious extension to languages in which there is no syntactic WH movement: the scope possibilities of unmoved WH phrases in these languages should not be as restricted as in languages that allow WH movement. Hankamer (1974) shows that in Turkish, which has no WH movement, all WH phrases may have wide scope. The Turkish equivalent of (8), for example, has three possible answers: those in (9):

(8)   [Charley who where shot] who remembers?

EMBEDDED QUESTIONS 145

(9) a. I remember.

    b. I remember where Charley shot X, and Jack remembers where Charley shot Y.

    c. I remember who Charley shot in Chicago, and Jack remembers who Charley shot in Peoria.

The matrix 'who' alone may have wide scope (as shown by answer (9a)), both 'who' phrases may share wide scope (answer (9b)), and the matrix 'who' and embedded 'where' may have wide scope (answer (9c)). Hankamer points out that each answer must leave one WH word unaddressed, and attributes this fact to the indexing theory: since Q/WH is present in the complement of 'remember', one WH word must always be indexed to it. Engdahl (1982) reports that in Japanese, another language without WH movement, all three WH words in a question corresponding to (10) may be given a value in a single answer ((11)):

(10)   Who knows where Mary bought which book?

(11)   John knows that Mary bought *Syntactic Structures* in L.A., and Bill knows that she bought *Aspects* in San Francisco.

It seems possible, therefore, that *all* WH phrases in a sentence may take wide scope in a language without a designated syntactic position for WH phrases. (But note, crucially, that the embedded CP must be [−WH] in (11).)

I turn now to the Palauan data. As I noted at the outset, one of the most significant aspects of Palauan WH questions is the fact that, as a class, they instantiate the various positional possibilities for WH phrases that have been observed across a range of typologically different languages, but never before (to my knowledge) attested all together in a single language. An important fact, following from the range of possible structural positions for WH phrases, is that scope interpretation is largely independent of position, as noted above. This gives the data to be presented a special interest, while it considerably complicates the descriptive task. Much of this descriptive complexity will be reduced at the level of theoretical analysis, as we would expect. However, it will become apparent that the complexities of Palauan syntax raise more questions than can be answered here, questions awaiting further work, and which are perhaps answerable only by a linguist who is also a native speaker of Palauan.

2. EMBEDDED QUESTIONS: THE PALAUAN FACTS

To begin, it is comforting to find that the [±WH] subcategorization of

146   CHAPTER FIVE

complement-embedding verbs is the same in Palauan as in English and other languages:

(12) a. ak-medengei el kmo ng-klemerang
       R-1s-know   Comp   R-3s-truth

   I know it's the truth.

   b. ak-medengei el kmo ng-te'a a ulu'ais
      R-1s-know   Comp   Cl-who   R-told

   I know who told (the story).

   c. ak-medengei el kmo ng-ngera a 'om-dilung
      R-1s-know   Comp   Cl-what   IR-2-said

   I know what you said.

(13) a. ak-umera   el kmo ng-klemerang
       R-1s-believe Comp   3s-truth

   I believe that it's the truth.

   b.*ak-umera   el kmo ng-te'a a ulu'ais
      R-1s-believe Comp   Cl-who   R-told

   (I believe who told (the story).)

(14) a. ak-umdasu el kmo ng-klemerang
       R-1s-think Comp   R-3s-truth

   I think it's the truth.

   b.*ak-umdasu el kmo ng-te'a a ulu'ais
      R-1s-think Comp   Cl-who   R-told

   (I think who told (the story).)

   c.*ak-umdasu el kmo ng-ngera a 'om-dilung
      R-1s-think Comp   Cl-what   IR-2-said

   (I think what you said.)

(15) a. ak-uker   el kmo ng-te'a a 'o-milsang
       R-1s-ask Comp   Cl-who   IR-2-Pf-saw

   I'm asking who you saw.

   b.*ng-te'a a l-uleker a Latii el kmo ke-milsang
      Cl-who   IR-3-ask   Comp   R-2-Pf-saw

   (Who was Latii asking you saw?)

EMBEDDED QUESTIONS   147

(15) c.*ak-uker   el kmo ng-klemerang
       R-1s-ask *Comp*   *3s-truth*

(I'm asking that it's the truth.)

The matrix verb **medengei** 'know', shown in (12a) through (c), can embed either a proposition or a question. The verb **oumera** 'believe' and **omdasu** 'think', on the other hand, can embed only non-interrogative complements; this is seen in (13) and (14). Finally, **oker** 'ask' must have an interrogative complement (examples (15)).

Aside from the evidence of selection, (12) through (15) illustrate the invariance of the lexical complementizer. Though Palauan verbs may pattern lexically with verbs in other languages, there is no morphological distinction among [+WH] and [−WH] complementizers in this language: the complementizer in all the examples is **el kmo**. I assume then that this C may bear either the [+WH] feature or the [−WH] feature, the value being determined by the subcategorization of the matrix verb.

Before continuing with the analysis of sentences like (12) through (15), it should be made clear how the sentential complements in such sentences are distinguished from free relative clauses. The free relative construction is omnipresent in Palauan A´ binding (cf. section 1, Chapter Three). It is therefore important to eliminate at the outset the possibility that any construction we refer to as an embedded question is actually a relative construction, in which case it would be irrelevant to the analysis of WH questions.

2.1. *Free Relatives vs. Embedded Questions*

It is often noted in the literature that embedded questions resemble free relative complements in many respects. Baker (1968) attributes the ambiguity of an English sentence like (16)

(16)   I don't know what John knows.

to the fact that the complement may be interpreted either as a free relative (an NP) or as an embedded question (a CP). Baker provides a number of tests to distinguish the two.

In Palauan the possibility for the ambiguity described by Baker is greatly reduced by the very different structure of the two complement types. First, the clausal complements of verbs (including embedded questions) and relativizations involve morphologically different complementizers: verb complements are usually introduced by the quotative complementizer **el kmo**, while this complementizer never appears in relative clauses. Headed relative clauses in Palauan are introduced by the complementizer **el**, the 'linker' appearing within NPs. Though some verb complements are optionally headed by **el** rather than **el kmo**

148 CHAPTER FIVE

(perhaps in this case **el** is a variant of **el kmo**), this is rarely so in the case of verbs that select question complements. I will assume, then, on the basis of their distribution, that **el** is always [−WH] but that **el kmo** can freely be assigned the [+WH] feature. Questions are therefore distinguished from (headed) relatives by the different complementizers that are associated with them (see the examples in (17) and (18) below).

Second, free relatives have no complementizer at all, while embedded questions always have a complementizer. In Chapter Three free relatives were analyzed as involving IP rather than CP, along the lines of Bresnan and Grimshaw (1978). This analysis was shown to account for the lack of a complementizer or a specifier position within them. In complements embedded under **el kmo**, in contrast, both topics and WH phrases are found in A′ position. (Even though neither topic nor WH phrase is in Spec(C) at S-structure, their occurrence appears to depend on the presence of the full CP host; see 2.2.)

Third, no relative constructions in Palauan contain WH relative pronouns, while embedded questions on NPs always contain a WH pronoun. That is, WH pronouns in this language are used exclusively in [+WH] constructions.

Finally, both matrix and embedded questions may contain verb forms which unexpectedly fail to exhibit WH agreement (see below at 2.4). This agreement phenomenon is exclusive to questions, while free relatives uniformly display WH agreement.

To sum up, free relative complements contain no complementizer and no WH pronoun, while embedded questions typically contain both; the complementizer in the latter case is usually **el kmo**. The contrasts between the two constructions can be observed in (17) and (18):

(17)   interrogative ([+WH]) complement:

    a. ak-medengel-ii [el kmo ng-**te'a** a mlo   er a stoang]
      1s-know   *Comp Cl-who R-went P   store*

    I know who went to the store.

    b. ng-diak kudengei   [el kmo ng-**ngera** a bo   ku-ruul
      3s-Neg IR-1s-know Comp Cl-what   IR-Fut IR-1s-do

    er   ngii]
    P   it

    I don't know what I'm going to do.

(18)   free relative ([−WH]) complement:

    a. ak-medengel-ii [a 'omo-ruul er ngii]
      1s-know   IR-2-do P it

    I know what you are doing.

(18) b. ng-diak ku-dengel-ii   [a bo   ku-ruul   er ngii]
       3s-Neg IR-1s-know-3s   IR-Fut   IR-1s-do   P   it

   I don't know what to do.

We return now to the analysis of the structures in (12) through (15).

2.2. The S-Structure Position of the WH Phrase

A significant property of structures (12) and (15), in which a WH phrase may be in an embedded A' position, is that the WH phrase is right-adjacent to the complementizer. This suggests that the WH phrase is not in Spec(C), contrary to the standard analysis. Where, then, is it? Let us look more closely at the structure of (12b) and (15a), repeated in (19):

(19) a. ak-medengei [$_{CP}$ el kmo ng-**te'a** a [$_{VP}$ ulu'ais ___]]
         R-1s-know   Comp   Cl-who   R-told

   I know who told (the story).

   b. ak-uker [$_{CP}$ el kmo ng-**te'a** a [$_{VP}$ 'o-milsang ___] pro]
       R-1s-ask   Comp   Cl-who   IR-2-saw

   I'm asking who you saw.

The WH phrase does not 'replace' the [+WH] complementizer; instead, the two cooccur. Furthermore, the position occupied by the WH phrase is actually the predicate position of the embedded clause, as I demonstrated in Chapter Three.[1]

In order for any A' dependency to be well formed, the antecedent must bind the variable. In Palauan, A' binding gives rise to WH agreement (Chapter Three, section 3). The binding facts provide another way to determine the positions of the complementizer and the WH phrase in (19a, b). In Chapter Three, we analyzed WH questions as constructions in which the predicate nominal (the WH phrase) takes a free relative NP as its subject:

(20)
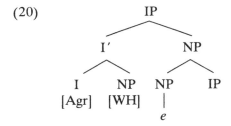

Translating this structure into a tree defined in the extended X' theory of Chomsky (1986b), we get a clearer picture of the relative positions of predicate and subject in these clefts. The tree in (21a) conforms to our earlier analysis, but that in (21b) does not:

(21) a.
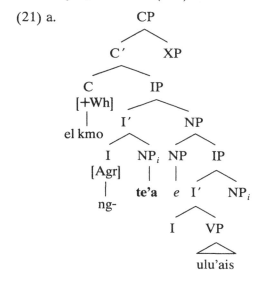

b.
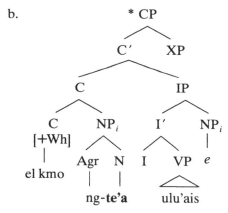

In both trees the WH phrase **te'a** 'who' could conceivably m-command and thus bind its variable.[2] Thus no argument arises to distinguish m-command from c-command in this case. I assume that the WH phrase raises in LF to the *designated WH scope position* (see section 5.2), Spec(C), where it antecedes its variable in the usual way. See Chapter Four, section 3.2, on chain formation in (21a) and the transmission of WH agreement features.

Now, note crucially that only in (21a) is the subject the relative clause structure motivated earlier, and only in (21a) is the WH phrase in the predicate position of IP, where it naturally receives the agreement

EMBEDDED QUESTIONS

151

morpheme **ng-** from I. In (21b), **te'a** is adjoined to C; here there is no account of the presence of the agreement morpheme, and the relativized structure we expect is absent. Without the hypothesized relative clause, i.e. an A' binding structure, the presence of WH agreement on the verb cannot be explained. In addition, adjunction by NP to C is unmotivated on any theory-internal grounds. The same or similar problems would arise if we attempted to adjoin the WH-NP to IP: agreement could not be assigned be normal means, the necessary A' binding structure would be absent, and the adjunction would be anomalous.

To sum up, then, the WH phrase is within IP, not in CP; thus it is naturally preceded, and c-commanded, by the complementizer. In section 4 below I show that a WH phrase in such a position cannot be considered to be in A' position by the grammar of scope assignment. Note especially that the WH is *not* in the specifier of C; this is true of *all* syntactic WH binding in the language.

A further interesting aspect of this analysis is its potential for illuminating structures in other languages in which complementizer and WH phrase cooccur in embedded questions, but in that order and not the reverse. Given the expansion $[_{CP} XP\ C']$, the complementizer is expected to follow its specifier, and given the expansion $[_{CP} C'\ XP]$, not only does the specifier follow the complementizer, but all of IP does too (as in the Palauan trees in (21)). However, in surface sequences Complementizer ... WH phrase, the specifier of CP would be empty and the WH phrase actually clefted or otherwise adjoined to IP, as in Palauan.

In fact, there is no surface evidence that the specifier of C ever occurs at the right edge of the tree — such a rightmost position is never filled. This suggests further motivation for the linear precedence of A' binders, argued for in Georgopoulos (1991b), and for the analysis of scope interpretation developed in section 5 below.[3]

Returning now to the analysis of (12) through (15), the theory presented in section 1 predicts that a WH phrase in A' position has semantic scope corresponding to its surface position. This prediction is based on the assumption that the only A' position available to WH phrases is in Spec(C). Despite the fact that the Palauan WH phrases in (12) through (15) are not in Spec(C), they nevertheless appear to conform to prediction: the WH phrase under a [+WH] complementizer in the examples in (12) through (15a) both is in an A' position (the predicate position) and has narrow scope.

If we make allowance for the special way in which Palauan embedded questions are formed, we can attempt to account for the narrow scope of the WH phrase by reference to its S-structure position, as has been done elsewhere. I assume that a WH phrase moves into the specifier of the embedded [+WH] Comp at LF. That is, the lexical requirements of the matrix verb are satisfied at LF by a lexical WH element in Spec(C)

152   CHAPTER FIVE

(following Chomsky 1973; Aoun, Hornstein, and Sportiche 1981; Lasnik and Saito 1984). The actual mechanism of satisfying this requirement would be the stipulation that Comp and its specifier must agree in the [±WH] feature; such agreement is mediated by spec-head coindexing (Chomsky 1986b; Kuroda 1988). See also section 5.2 below.

If S-structure indicates semantic scope only for a WH phrase that is in A′ position, as the theory claims, then in Palauan as in other languages a WH in situ is expected to be able to take either wide or narrow scope. In the next sections I will describe the range of scope possibilities of WH phrases, for both WH in situ and WH in A′ position. I will then address the ways in which these facts bear on theories of WH scope. The analysis of multiple interrogation structures is taken up separately, in the interests of maintaining clarity.

2.3. *WH in situ*

We know that WH phrases in Palauan may optionally occur in situ at S-structure (see Chapter Three). Therefore it is possible that a WH in situ under [±WH]-selecting verbs has the same scope that it would have if it were clefted. In (22a), the complement of **medengei** 'know' contains a WH phrase in situ. **medengei** subcategorizes either a statement or a question, as we saw in (12). In (22a) the WH phrase takes wide scope. Compare (22b), where it is next to the complementizer, and takes narrow scope:

(22) a. a Joe a medengei el kmo ng-mlo   er a stoang a **te'ang**
             R-know   Comp   R-3s-went P   store   who

Who$_i$ does Joe know ____$_i$ went to the store?

   b. a Joe a medengei el kmo ng-**te'a** a mlo er a stoang
             Comp   Cl-who

Joe knows who went to the store.

The preferred interpretation of the scope of the WH phrase in each case is as in (22): a WH in situ takes wide semantic scope if it can, while a WH in an embedded A′ position can naturally take narrow scope. The scope reading of WH in situ therefore does not necessarily correspond to the scope of a clefted WH, other things being equal. These facts are predicted by the theory as presented in section 1.

Complements subcategorized by **dmu** 'say', 'tell' may also bear either a [+WH] or a [−WH] feature:

EMBEDDED QUESTIONS 153

(23) a. ng-dilu   a   Philips   el   kmo   ng-mo   mekede'or   er   a
     R-3s-said   *Comp*   *R-3s-go*   *R-build*   *P*

     be'es   el   blai
     new   *L*   *house*

     Philip said that he's going to build a new house.

    b. ng-dilu   er   kid   el   kmo   ng-**te'a**   a   mo   er   a   party
     R-3s-said   *P*   *us*   *Comp*   *Cl-who*   *go*   *P*

     He told us who was going to the party.

A WH phrase in situ under **dmu** preferably takes wide semantic scope:

(24) a. ng-dilu   er ngii a Philips el kmo ng-mo   mesuub a **ngerang**
     R-3s-said P him   *Comp R-3s-go study*   *what*

     What did Philip tell him to study?

    b. ke-dilu   el kmo ke-millungel er a   **ngera**   el kuking
     R-2s-said Comp R-2s-smelled P   *what*   *L*   *cooking*

     What did you say you smell cooking?

while a clefted WH phrase under **dmu** takes narrow scope ((23b)). Thus the complements of **dmu** 'say' pattern like the complements of **medengei** 'know', as expected, and the scope taken by WH phrases in the complements of both verbs appears to depend on their S-structure position, as predicted earlier.

The examples in (25) involve verbs which obligatorily subcategorize interrogative complements, and in which a WH phrase must have embedded scope. The preferred configuration is that in which the WH phrase occupies an A′ position indicating its semantic scope (as in (15a)).

But the structures in (25b) and (25c) are also possible. The WH phrase takes narrow scope, whether in A or A′ position:

(25) a. ng-mele'ede' el kmo ng-**ngera** a lo-ngiil   er ngii el
     3s-wonder   *Comp*   *Cl-what*   *IR-3-wait P*   *him Comp*

     bo   loruul
     IR-go IR-do

     He's wondering what she is waiting for him to do.

     (*What is he wondering that she is waiting for him to do?)

    b. ng-mele'ede' el kmo ng-mengiil er ngii el   mo
     3s-wonder   *Comp*   *R-3s-wait*   *P*   *him Comp R-go*

     meruul a **ngerang**
     R-do   *what*

     He's wondering what she is waiting for him to do.

154 CHAPTER FIVE

(25) c. a Latii a uleker   el kmo ng-milnguiu a buk   er
     R-asked Comp R-3s-read book P

  a library a **te'ang**
      who

  Latii asked who was reading a book in the library.

(25) shows that when the complement is obligatorily [+WH], a single WH phrase in this complement may in fact occupy any of the positions that the language independently makes available.

Finally, in the complements of **oumera** 'believe' and **omdasu** 'think', verbs which do not tolerate interrogative complements, a WH phrase has wide semantic scope whether it is in A or A′ position.[4]

(26) a. t-oumera el kmo ngmo er a ngebard a **te'ang**
    R-3p-believe Comp R-3s-go P west   who

  Who do they believe will go to the States?

  (*They believe who will go to the States)

 b. k-umera el kmo ng-**te'a** a ulu'ais
   R-2s-believe Comp Cl-who R-told

  Who do you believe told (the story)?

  (*Do you believe who told (the story)?)

 c. 'om-omdasu e ng-milskak a **ngera** a Basilia
   IR-2-think Comp R-3s-gave-1s what

  What do you think Basilia gave me?

  (*Do you think what Basilia gave me?)

 d. a Roy ng-omdasu el kmo ng-**te'a** a melloms a rengul
    R-3s-think Comp Cl-who smart

  Who does Roy think is smart?

  (*Roy thinks who is smart)

The examples of complements of these two verbs in (27a–c) are taken from Chapter Three. They exhibit the constraints that were observed in the simpler structures above. In (27) the WH phrase **te'a** 'who' is in situ ((27a)), clefted in its embedded clause ((27b)), and clefted in the matrix ((27c)):

(27) a. t-oumera [el ked-omdasu [e ng-mo er a
    R-3p-believe Comp R-1p-think Comp R-3s-go P

  siabal a **te'ang**]]
  Japan who

EMBEDDED QUESTIONS 155

(27) b. t-oumera [el ked-omdasu [e ng-te'a$_i$ a mo   er a siabal ___$_i$]]
            Cl-who   R-go

c. ng-te'a$_i$ [a l-oumera   [el   d-omdasu   [e ng-mo
   Cl-who   IR-3-believe   Comp   IR-1p-think   R-3s-go

er a siabal ___$_i$]]]
Who do they believe that we think will go to Japan?

Of course, pragmatic factors influence which position is chosen in any given situation, but all speakers appear to accept all three possibilities exemplified in (27). The WH phrases in all three sentences have wide scope. Any other scope would be impossible, since neither **omdasu** 'think' nor **oumera** 'believe' takes an interrogative complement. Thus the language allows the WH phrase to be in A′ position under a [−WH] complementizer at S-structure, though the phrase is forced to take wide scope at LF.

What these data tell us about a single embedded WH in situ is that its scope is determined primarily by the selection of the embedding verb and not by its position. A difference in position *can* correspond to a difference in scope interpretation. This is primarily observed with verbs like 'know', which embed either [+WH] or [−WH] complements. Here position is used to avoid ambiguity (but see 2.4). However, examples like (27), as well as the facts of 2.4, show that in general, the correlation between S-structure position (A vs. A′) and LF scope is not strong in Palauan.

Still, the primary problem for the theory, in this and other cases, is to allow a WH phrase in situ under 'say' or 'know' to take wide scope, while preventing a WH phrase in situ under 'ask' or 'wonder' from doing the same. This problem is addressed in section 4. We turn first to the means of dealing with certain cases of potential ambiguity of scope.

2.4. *Resolving Ambiguity*

There is potential for ambiguity in interpreting the scope of a WH phrase under verbs like **dmu** 'say' or **medengei** 'know'. Since a complement of one of these verbs can be either a statement or a question, we must account for the fact that all of the examples in (28) are interpreted as wide scope questions ((28) is taken from Chapter Three):

(28) a. ke-dilu   el   te-mengiil er ngak el   mo   meruul
     R-2s-said Comp   R-3p-wait P me   Comp R-Fut R-do

er a **ngerang**
P   what

156 CHAPTER FIVE

(28) b. ke-dilu el te-mengiil er ngak el ng-**ngera** a bo
                                       Cl-what   *IR-Fut*

    kuruul   er ngii
    IR-1s-do *P* *it*

   c. ke-dilu el ng-**ngera** a longiil   er ngak el bo kuruul er ngii
             Cl-what   *IR-3-wait*

   d. ng-**ngera** a 'om-dilu el longiil er ngak el bo kuruul er ngii
     Cl-what   *IR-2-said*

    What did you say that they're waiting for me to do?

ngera 'what' in (28a) takes wide scope, like other examples of WH in situ we observed above. We might assume that it takes wide scope in (28b) for roughly similar reasons: **mengiil** 'wait' does not subcategorize [±WH] complements, so the scope of **ngera** here is forced to go higher. The syntactic position of **ngera** in (28d) indicates its semantic scope. (28c), however, is ambiguous. It is not difficult to construct a context in which (28c) is construed as containing an embedded question, in which case its gloss could be *Did you say what they're waiting for me to do?*

In the case of (28c), I have nothing further to say. We must simply accept its ambiguity. There is, however, one unusual syntactic device for resolving ambiguity that should be described here. Palauan does not have a [+WH] lexical complementizer like *whether*, but it does have other ways of marking a complement as interrogative. Perhaps predictably, the device in question is encoded in agreement morphology. We first look at this special agreement phenomenon in the context of yes/no questions, where it can be observed in isolation. Its interaction with WH agreement, described next, presents an interesting case in disjunctive ordering of agreement rules.

2.4.1. *Agreement Phenomena in Yes/No Questions*

Simple Palauan yes/no questions that are verb-initial are distinguished from declaratives only via intonation: rising pitch is associated with the question:

(29) a. ng-omele'a a 'elu' er a mlai a Toiu
    3s-put   *gas* *P*   *car*

    Toiu is putting gas in the car.

   b. ng-omele'a a 'elu' er a mlai a Toiu

    Is Toiu putting gas in the car?

Recall, now, the statement of WH agreement, and its morphological effects (Chapter Three, section 3). Briefly, WH agreement distinguishes

EMBEDDED QUESTIONS

157

subjects from nonsubjects: A' binding of any NP triggers WH agreement, but the surface form of the verb varies according to the subject/nonsubject distinction. Subject preposing triggers a realis form bare of person/number agreement, while nonsubject preposing triggers an irrealis form. Compare preposing in yes/no questions, below.

When any NP precedes the verb in a yes/no question, realis subject agreement bearing person and number features is prefixed to the verb (30b) and (31b)); this is in contrast to the usual case of topicalization ((30a) and (31a)):[5]

(30) a. a Toiu a omele'a a 'elu' er a mlai
       R-put   gas   P   car

   Toiu is putting gas in the car.

   b. a Toiu **ng**-omele'a a 'elu' er a mlai
        R-3s-put   gas   P   car

   Is Toiu putting gas in the car?

(31) a. ngkei a mla mo smau el   menga a kukau
       Dem   R.PF R-like   Comp R-eat   taro

   She's getting used to eating taro.

   b. ngkei **ng**-mla mo smau el   menga a kukau
      Dem R.PF R-like   Comp R-eat   taro

   Is she getting used to eating taro?

The preverbal NP is a subject in the examples above, thus triggering a realis form of the verb. Since yes/no questions in Palauan are not themselves semantically irrealis, the form in the (a) sentences is as predicted. The verb form in the (b) sentences is unpredicted, however: WH agreement has not applied. In accordance with the statement of WH agreement in Palauan grammar, the realis mood of the verb in (31a) is [+WH agreement], while the realis form in (31b) is [−WH agreement].

In (32), a nonsubject appears before the verb:

(32) a. a rengalek a lo-ngelebed er tir   a sensei
        children   IR-3-hit   P them   teacher

   The teacher is hitting the kids.

   b. a rengalek ng-mengelebed er tir   a sensei
        children R-3s-hit   P them   teacher

   Is the teacher hitting the kids?

The declarative example (32a) contains a topicalized object NP, while (32b) is the corresponding yes/no question having the same word order.

158   CHAPTER FIVE

A resumptive pronoun, **tir**, appears in both structures, suggesting A'
binding by the topic in both. However, in the statement the verb bears
the expected irrealis WH agreement morphology, but in the question the
verb bears what appears to be the 'normal' subject agreement — the
realis subject agreement that would appear *outside* of A' binding
domains. The examples in (33) illustrate this phenomenon further:

> (33) a. a bangk a l-ulleng   a bebil er a udoud er ngii a demak
>   *bank   IR-3-borrow   some P   money P it   father-1s*
>
>   My father borrowed some money from the bank.
>
>   b. a bangk ng-lileng   a bebil er a udoud er ngii a demam
>   *R-3s-borrow*   *father-2s*
>
>   Did your father borrow some money from the bank?
>
>   c. a demam   ng-lileng   a bebil er a udoud er a bangk ____
>   *father-2s 3s-borrow*
>
>   Did your father borrow some money from the bank?

The preverbal NP is an *oblique* object in (33a) and (33b). (33a) is a
topicalization structure familiar from Chapter Three. (33b) is the corresponding yes/no question, which contains a resumptive pronoun but in
which WH agreement does not apply. (33c) is a paraphrase of (33b) in
which the *subject* is pre-verbal. Yet the form of subject agreement in
(33b) and (33c) is the same. Comparison of (33b) and (33c) demonstrates that in yes/no questions, the morphological mood of the verb is
unaffected by the Case of the NP that precedes it.

In other words, WH agreement does not apply in any of the (b)
sentences above, or in (33c). The NP-initial order and resumptive
pronouns in these examples suggest an A' binding structure, while the
lack of WH agreement contradicts this.

2.4.2. *Two Kinds of Topic?*

It appears that two entirely different structures are involved here. I will
retain the analysis in which the (a) sentences have the structure described in Chapter Three. The subject in this type is a nominalized
clause; as such, it is a subordinate structure. In the (b) and (c) examples,
however, there is no reason to regard the clause following the initial NP
in terms of subordination at all. It is instead most simply analyzed as a
matrix VOS sentence preceded by a topic. The lack of an intonation
break after the initial NP suggests that these structures should not be
analyzed as cases of left dislocation (Ross 1967). It appears, then, that
Palauan has two topicalization strategies — one that involves nominaliza-

EMBEDDED QUESTIONS 159

tion of the clause following the A′ antecedent, and one in which that clause retains matrix status. WH agreement is triggered only in the former case, in embeddings.

There are problems with this analysis. First, if (30) through (33) do involve A′ binding, they violate WH agreement. Second, the proposed analysis gives no reason why topic structures in yes/no questions should be so different from other topic structures. And third, it does not account for the difference between yes/no questions and WH questions:

(34) a. a rengalek ng-mengelebed er tir a sensei
    children R-3s-hit P them teacher

    Is the teacher hitting the children?

b. ng-ruate'a a lo-ngelebed er tir a sensei
    Cl-who(pl) IR-3-hit P them teacher

    Who (pl) is the teacher hitting?

2.4.3. *Yes/No Questions vs. WH Questions*

One promising approach would be to explore the *semantic* differences between yes/no questions and WH questions. One could then assess how the semantics is reflected in their different syntactic behavior. It is likely that the conceptual properties of the two kinds of questions will provide the key to their syntactic analysis. Yes/no questions presuppose a clausal disjunction, while WH questions presuppose the existence of a constituent. For example, yes/no questions do not have a constituent focus, while WH questions do. It may be that the p-or-not-p presupposition of the former, in implicating the truth conditions of a whole clause (proposition), 'overrides' the trigger of WH agreement in a yes/no question with a topic.[6] However this analysis is concluded, it is clear that the two agreement rules are disjunctive, and following the usual case with disjunctive application, the more specific rule — that for yes/no questioning — applies first.

I will assume that some account of these facts is available, and will not pursue the problems posed by (30) through (34) any further here.

The description of agreement in these structures has been included primarily because it plays a role in the overall characterization of embedded WH questions. The interaction of WH agreement and the agreement pattern shown in this section is, in some cases, an overt indication that a particular embedded clause is interrogative rather than declarative.

2.4.4. *Agreement in Embedded WH Questions*

The agreement pattern in yes/no questions also characterizes certain

160   CHAPTER FIVE

WH constructions. For example, a question containing both a preverbal definite NP and a WH phrase in situ may optionally have 'normal' agreement marking rather than WH agreement:

(35) a. a John ng-oureor er ker
          R-3s-work P where

      Where does John work?

   b. a resensei te-kilngei   er a ngerang
          teachers R-3p-accepted P   what

      What did the faculty accept?

   c. a 'ermek   el bilis ng-uleltoir   er a ngerang
          animal-1s L dog R-3s-chased P   what

      What was my dog chasing?

This agreement pattern is therefore not specific to yes/no questions, but applies more generally in interrogatives, except those in which WH agreement applies. Since the WH phrase is in situ in the examples in (35), the characteristic structure and WH agreement of WH binding structures does not arise. It may be that the preverbal NP in (35) is not in a position that triggers WH agreement, or that agreement in (35) depends on some as yet unknown relation between an interrogative Comp and tensed I. In any case, the WH phrase in these structures is regarded as any other NP in argument position would be regarded, and *it* does not trigger WH agreement either.

Both constructions appear to be available in WH questions: a speaker may choose either the familiar topicalized structure, or the alternative structure without WH agreement:

(36) a. a John a oureor er ker
          R-work P where

      Where does John work?

   b. a John ng-oureor er ker
          R-3s-work P where

      Where does John work?

In (36a), the verb bears WH agreement: that is, it has no subject agreement. The second rule applies in (36b).

The failure of WH agreement to apply in a clause that contains an A′ binder can be used as a diagnostic for the semantic scope of WH phrases in embedded configurations. We have already seen an example of this in (26d) (repeated here):

EMBEDDED QUESTIONS

161

(37)   a Roy ng-omdasu el kmo ng-**te'a** a melloms a rengul
       R-3s-think Comp   Cl-who   smart

Who does Roy think is smart?

(*Roy thinks who is smart)

In (37), 'yes/no' subject agreement on the matrix verb **omdasu** 'think' reveals that the sentence is a matrix question. Although the WH phrase is in an A′ position in the embedding, **omdasu** does not subcategorize an interrogative complement, and **te'a** 'who' takes semantic scope over the whole sentence. Though the syntactic position of the WH phrase in (37) is not related to its interpretation in LF, matrix agreement in (37) does seem to be related to the [+WH] feature (or the Q feature). Similarly in (38a), yes/no subject agreement on the intermediate *embedded* verb **mengiil** 'wait for' shows that *that* complement is to be interpreted as the interrogative clause:

(38)   a Tmerukl a mele'ede'   el kmo a Latii ng-mengiil er
       R-3s-wonder Comp   *R-3s-wait P*

       ngii el   mo meruul a **ngerang**
       him Comp go R-do   what

Tmerukl is wondering what Latii is waiting for him to do.

(*What is Tmerukl wondering whether Latii is waiting for him to do?)

In this example the embedding verb **mele'ede'** 'wonder' subcategorizes a [+WH] complement. In both (37) and (38), scope is determined ultimately by the properties of the matrix verb.

The scope of a questioned constituent in situ may also be revealed in this way in cases where it is underdetermined by other properties of the sentence. Observe, for example, the differences among the trio in (39), complements of **dmu** 'say':

(39) a. ng-dilu   a delam   el kmo ng-**te'a** a lilsa   el
       R-3s-said   mother-2s Comp   Cl-who   IR-3-saw Comp

       meskak   a 'ema'el
       R-give-1s   betel.nut

       Who did your mother say that she saw give me the betel nuts?

       Your mother said who she saw give me the betel nuts.

   b. a delak   a dilu   el kmo ng-**te'a** a lilsa   el
       mother-1s R-said Comp   Cl-who   IR-3-saw Comp

       meskau   a 'ema'el
       R-give-2s   betel.nut

       My mother said who she saw give you the betel nuts.

162   CHAPTER FIVE

(39) c. a delam ng-dilu   el kmo ng-**te'a** a lilsa el meskak a 'ema'el
         R-3s-said

Who did your mother say that she saw give me the betel nuts?

Did your mother say who she saw give me the betel nuts?

(39a) and (39c) are ambiguous, while (39b) can only be interpreted as
containing an embedded question. The scope of the WH phrase in (39a),
like that in (28c), cannot be determined syntactically. The matrix in
(39b), however, is clearly non-interrogative: the clause following the
initial NP **delak** is nominalized, and the verb bears WH agreement: it has
no subject agreement. Compare (39c): this is clearly a question (either
WH or yes/no); since the matrix verb bears subject agreement, the
matrix clause must be interpreted as interrogative.[7] Still, the *scope of the
WH phrase* is ambiguous, as it is in (39a).

The minimal pair in (40) involve **omdasu** 'think' and **omdasu** 'wonder'; (40b) must be interpreted as containing an embedded question:

(40) a. ak-umdasu el kmo a Moses a omekde'or er a be'es el blai
        R-1s-think Comp   R-build   P   new L house

    I think that Moses is building a new house.

    b. ak-umdasu   el kmo a Moses ng-omekde'or er a be'es el blai
        R-1s-wonder Comp   R-3s-build   P   new L house

    I wonder if Moses is building a new house.

Though the complementizer is the same in both (cf. the distinction
between English *that* and *if*), the embedded verb form in (40b) shows
that the matrix verb subcategorizes an interrogative complement.

To sum up, embedded WH questions generally have a structure like
that of matrix WH questions. The scope of a WH phrase can be determined by reference to one or more of the following conditions: its
syntactic position (this factor alone is weak, since a WH in A′ position
may take wide or narrow scope, as may a WH in situ); the lexical
requirements of the embedding verb; and the inflectional form of the
embedded verb. The latter two factors also indicate the $[\pm WH]$ feature
of a clause, independently of the presence of a WH phrase. I will now
consider the ways in which these phenomena are interpreted within
theories of scope that refer to LF representations.

3. WH MOVEMENT IN LF

We saw above that the scope of a WH phrase in Palauan is, in general,
determined via the interaction of verb subcategorization and other
properties of the particular grammar. The option for single WH phrases

EMBEDDED QUESTIONS 163

to be in situ in the syntax does not restrict their ability to take wide scope, but such WH phrases may also take narrow scope. WH phrases in embedded A′ position may take wide scope. The mechanisms of accounting for scope are couched in terms of constraints on movement in LF.

3.1. *WH Raising, WH Filters, Spec-Head Agreement*

It is generally assumed that Move α operates in the LF component as well as the syntax. Aoun, Hornstein, and Sportiche (1981; henceforth AHS), for example, assume a rule in LF which raises S-structure WH in situ to a Comp bearing the [+WH] feature. They refer to this rule as WH Raising, though it is simply application of WH movement in LF. Updating AHS to the X′ theory we are assuming here (Chomsky 1986b), WH Raising moves an NP to specifier position of a [+WH] C, written Spec(C). In the following discussion of AHS, Huang, and others, for "COMP" read "Spec(C)".

According to AHS, then, at some level of LF all WH phrases are in COMP, i.e. in a position corresponding to their semantic scope. One of the problems provoked by the WH Raising analysis is that of preventing the movement of WH phrases that are already in COMP at S-structure; that is, the narrow scope of certain WH phrases in embedded questions must somehow be preserved. (41) is an illustration of the problem:

(41) a. Who knows $[_{CP}$ what$_i$ $[_{IP}$ PRO to do $t_i]]$
            [+WH]

    b. Surface structure: Who knows what to do?

    c. Logical form: *$[$What$_i$ who$_j$ $[t_j$ knows $[t_i$ $[$PRO to do $t_i]]]]$

(41c) is ungrammatical because *what* fails to maintain embedded scope. Since WH Raising is in general able to move a constituent into an already filled position,

(42) a. S-structure: $[_{CP}$ who$_i[_{IP}$ t_i bought what$]]$

    b. Logical form: $[_{CP}$ what$_j$ who$_i[_{IP}$ t_i bought $t_j]]$

the prohibition on doubly filled CP does not apply to the output of WH Raising, and will not rule out *(41c).[8] To deal with the problem of (41), AHS propose the principle (43):

(43) WH Raising only affects WH phrases in argument position.

This principle rules out the type of movement suggested in *(41c). However, the fact that the WH phrases in A′ position in the Palauan

164   CHAPTER FIVE

sentences in (26), (27), and (28) (repeated in (44)) have semantic scope wider than their syntactic scope shows that principle (43) is too strong:

(44) a. a Roy ng-omdasu el kmo ng-**te'a** a melloms a rengul
         R-3s-think   Comp   Cl-who   smart

Who does Roy think is smart?

(*Roy thinks who is smart)

b. k-umera   el kmo ng-**te'a** a ulu'ais
    R-2s-believe Comp   Cl-who   R-told

Who do you believe told (the story)?

(*Do you believe who told (the story))

c. t-oumera   el   ked-omdasu e   ng-**te'a** a mo
    R-3p-believe Comp R-1p-think   Comp Cl-who   R-go

er a siabal
P   Japan

Who do they believe that we think will go to Japan?

d. ke-dilu   el   te-mengiil er ngak el   ng-**ngera** a
    R-2s-said Comp R-3p-wait   P   me   Comp Cl-what

bo   kuruul er ngii
IR-Aux IR-do   P   it

What did you say that they're waiting for me to do?

In these examples, the WH phrase is in A′ position, yet it is embedded in a [−WH] complement, and must undergo a rule like WH Raising in LF to reach the wide scope indicated in the English translation. Huang (1982) argues that COMP-to-COMP movement in LF must be allowed in Chinese, so that Chinese, too, violates (43). Lasnik and Saito (1984) show that Polish WH phrases in A′ position at S-structure undergo further movement. WH Raising clearly must refer to both A and A′ positions.

Turning to WH in situ, the AHS analysis also makes the prediction made in Baker (1970) and later writers: a WH in argument position may have a wide scope that is not encoded syntactically. What is not accounted for is how some WH in situ are confined to taking *narrow* scope in LF. Note that AHS's assumption that a [+WH] COMP must actually contain a WH element would not accomplish this, since the proposed filter

(45)   *COMP unless it contains a [+WH] element
        [+WH]

is claimed to be a surface filter, and, as such, applies in PF.[9] In addition, (45) is not universal; as AHS point out, any language without syntactic

EMBEDDED QUESTIONS

165

movement, like Chinese, would not observe it. It would also be possible for (45) to be satisfied in a clause with more than one WH while allowing some WH to 'escape'. This would be a real problem in the Palauan case; see below.

First, Palauan WH phrases in situ violate filter (45), as Chinese does, since in sentences like (25b, c) (repeated below) a [+WH] CP does not contain a [+WH] element at S-structure:

(46) a. ng-mele'ede' el kmo ng-mengiil er ngii el   mo
         3s-wonder   Comp   R-3s-wait   P   him Comp R-go

       meruul a **ngerang**
       R-do   what

       He's wondering what she is waiting for him to do.

    b. a Latii a uleker   el kmo ng-milnguiu a buk   er
            R-asked comp   R-3s-read   book P

       a library a **te'ang**
               who

       Latii asked who was reading a book in the library.

Languages like Polish would be a further problem for AHS, in that a WH phrase may be in a [−WH] CP at S-structure.

Thus both (43) and (45) fail to account for the range of positional and scope phenomena in WH constructions across languages.[10] Clearly, other options are possible.

In Huang (1982), the proposal is made that Chinese satisfies *at LF* the requirement that a [+WH] COMP (CP) actually contain a WH phrase. If the equivalent of filter (45) applies in LF, the problem that Chinese raises for the AHS account dissolves. Since Chinese has no syntactic movement, principle (43) should also be observed in Chinese. Huang demonstrates that the selectional restrictions on the sentential complements of verbs in Chinese are the same as in English ((47) = Huang's (162)–(164), Ch. 4)):

(47) a. [Zhangsan wen wo [shei mai-le   shu]]
            ask   me   who buy-ASP book

       Zhangsan asked who bought books.   (sic)

    b. [Zhangsan xiangxin [shei mai-le shu]]
             believe

       Who does Zhangsan believe bought books?

166 CHAPTER FIVE

(47) c. [Zhangsan zhidao [shei mai-le shu]]
           know

Who does Zhangsan know bought books?

Zhangsan knows who bought books.

Only the verb varies in the surface structure of these sentences. Yet, as in English, the complement of the verb **wen** 'ask' is obligatorily interrogative, the complement of **xiangxin** 'believe' is declarative, and the complement of **zhidao** 'know' may be either interrogative or declarative. Thus the *semantics* of these sentences is the same in English and Chinese, and Huang argues for an account on which the facts of (47) are due to WH movement in LF (following AHS). In Huang's presentation, the grammars of Chinese and English, superficially so different in their interrogative constructions, actually diverge only in the components in which they allow WH movement to apply.

Palauan can be analyzed, to a certain extent, along the lines proposed by Huang. Though Palauan WH phrases can be in an A′ position at S-structure, they are not in Spec(C), nor does their syntactic position necessarily indicate their semantic scope. Thus the constraints on WH scope in Palauan, as in Chinese, are satisfied only after movement to CP in LF. However, the problem of restricting the scope of some WH phrases to embeddings (as must be done for (46), for example), remains.

Lasnik and Saito (1984; henceforth L & S) propose a set of filters to deal with the problems of constraining the scope of WH phrases. They propose that these three filters, which apply at the output of LF, satisfy the $[\pm WH]$ subcategorization requirements of verbs (= L & S (183), (184), (186)):

(48) a. A [+WH] COMP must contain a [+WH] phrase.

b. A [+WH] phrase must be in a [+WH] COMP.

c. A [−WH] COMP must not have a [+WH] head.

L & S claim that these filters overcome the shortcomings of the AHS account. The filters force LF movement into a [+WH] CP, including a matrix CP (filters (48a and b)), force a WH phrase to remain in a [+WH] CP (filter (48b)), and force WH movement out of a [−WH] CP (filter (48c)). The interaction of these filters, the ECP (as formulated by L & S) applying at LF, and the lexical requirements of verbs will produce the correct LF structures, according to L & S.

Recasting L & S in terms of Chomsky (1986b), the filters require matching of the $[\pm WH]$ feature of C and the XP in Spec(C). As suggested earlier, I am assuming that this matching requirement is a type of agreement, based on specifier-head coindexing.[11] The stipulation that

C and Spec(C) must agree in the value of the [±WH] feature would subsume filters (48). Since a head and its specifier are in current theory coindexed, such an apparent stipulation is really a special case of mechanisms existing independently of the analysis of WH questions, and therefore is to be preferred to the filters in (48).[12] In the next section I will show more precisely the role that agreement between C and Spec(C) plays in the overall analysis of WH questions.

I assume that this type of analysis (i.e. matching of the $[\alpha WH]$ feature) works for the cases of single WH phrases in Palauan. Other problems are posed, however, by sentences containing more than one WH phrase. It is in sorting out the scope phenomena of multiple WH phrases that both the descriptive and analytical tasks are the most difficult. Let us begin by looking at the data.

4. MULTIPLE-WH QUESTIONS

Consider again the multiple-interrogative structure (49), taken from Baker (1970):

(49)   Who remembers where we bought which book?

In order to satisfy the subcategorization of *remember*, one WH word must be in the specifier of the embedded CP. Assuming that no CP can contain more than one WH phrase at S-structure, other WH phrases in the same clause remain in situ (in English). Rules of LF (LF Move α) then raise them to either an embedded [+WH] CP or a matrix [+WH] CP. This is the analysis as it applies to movement languages. Languages without syntactic movement, like Turkish and Japanese, it has been argued, allow greater freedom of scope to WH words in embeddings, because all WH items are in situ until LF. Whatever LF movements take place, however, the placement of WH phrases must satisfy the [±WH] feature matching requirement of any C.

In Palauan, as we know, the syntactic representation of WH questions does not conform to the familiar structural notions. WH phrases may be found either in A′ positions or in situ at S-structure. *All* WH phrases in a clause may be in situ. Even under a WH-embedding verb like 'wonder', the scope of the WH phrase might not be indicated in the syntax. In addition, WH phrases in A′ position are not contained in Spec(C), even though the immediately dominating CP may be [+WH]. The predicate position of a cleft, in which WH phrases may be found, does not bear a [+WH] feature. It is therefore unclear what predictions the theory makes for Palauan multiple WH questions.

Unfortunately, this area is as murky in Palauan as in English: though speakers agree on preferred interpretations, judgments as to which embedded WH-NPs can grammatically be addressed in the answers, or

168 CHAPTER FIVE

which NPs *cannot* be (i.e. which of the embedded multiple WH phrases can take wide scope), are not sharp. This section therefore only summarizes my findings, and is provided solely for completeness of descriptive coverage.[13]

First, multiple interrogation is grammatical in Palauan; (50) illustrates a monoclausal structure:

(50) a. ng-**te'a** a **te'ang**
   Cl-who *who*

  Who is who?

  b. ng-**te'a** a meruul a **ngerang**
    Cl-who *R-do* *what*

   Who does what?

As expected, the answer to the multiple WH question in (50b) contains paired NPs, showing that both WH phrases are wide scope operators:

(51) a Peter a melib a belatong e a Sue a meriik er a ulaol
      R-wash *plate* *and*   *R-sweep P* *floor*

  Peter washes dishes and Sue sweeps the floor.

Interestingly, the question in (50b) may occur in several different surface word orders: [14]

(52) a. ng-meruul a **ngera** a **te'ang** (basic VOS order)
   R-do   *what* *who*

   Who does what?

  b. ng-**te'a** a **ngera** a loruul
    who *what* *IR-do*

   Who does what?

  c. ??ng-**ngera** a loruul a **te'ang**
    what *IR-do* *who*

  d. *ng-**ngera** a **te'a** a meruul?
    what *who* *R-do*

All grammatical versions receive an answer like (51b), a paired answer.

4.1. *[± WH] Complements*

(53) illustrates multiple interrogation in a biclausal structure involving **medengei** 'know, remember', which is [± WH]:

EMBEDDED QUESTIONS

(53) a. ng-te'a a medengei   el kmo ng-**te'a** a mil'erar
    Cl-who   *R-remember Comp* *Cl-who*   *R-Pf-bought*

    a **ngerang**
      what

    Who remembers who bought what?

b. ng-te'a a medengei   el kmo ng-**ngarker** a debil'ar
    Cl-who   *R-remember Comp* *Cl-where*   *IR-1p-bought*

    a **ngerang** (er ngii)
      what   *P there*

    Who remembers where we bought what?

The question in (53a) has two preferred answers: one in which only the matrix **te'a** 'who' is assigned a value, and one in which *all three* WH NPs are assigned values:

(54) a.   ng-**te'a** a medengei   el kmo ng-**te'a** a mil'erar
      Cl-who   *R-remember Comp* *Cl-who*   *R-Pf-bought*

        a **ngerang**
          what

      Who remembers who bought what?

b.   ngak *I (do)*

c.   ak-medengei   el kmo a Sabeth a mil'ar   a sasimi
      R-1s-remember Comp   *R-bought*   *sashimi*

      me a Miriam a mil'ar   a rode'
      and   *R-bought*   *fruit*

      I remember that Elisabeth bought sashimi and Miriam bought fruit.

d.   ??ak-medengei el kmo ng-**te'a** a mil'ar a sasimi e a Joe a medengei el kmo ng-**te'a** a mil'ar a rode'

      (I remember who bought sashimi and Joe remembers who bought fruit.)

Similarly for (53b): either the matrix **te'a** alone, or else all three questioned constituents, are spontaneously addressed in the answer:

(55) a.   ng-**te'a** a medengei   el kmo ng-**ngarker** a debil'ar
      Cl-who   *R-remember Comp* *Cl-where*   *IR-1p-bought*

      a **ngerang**
        what

      Who remembers where we bought what?

170 CHAPTER FIVE

(55) b.　ngak *I (do)*

　　c.　ak-medengei　　el kmo kedemil'ar　　a cassette er a K-mart
　　　　R-1s-remember Comp　R-1p-bought　　　　P
　　　　I remember that we bought cassettes at K-mart.

　　d.　??ak-medengei el kmo ng-**ngarker** a debil'ar a cassette . . .
　　　　(I remember where we bought cassettes . . .)

The biclausal question (53a), like the monoclausal question in (50b), may occur in a variety of word orders in the embedding:

(56) a.　ng-te'a a medengei el kmo ng-mil'erar a **ngera** a **te'ang**
　　　　　　　　　　　　　　　　　　　　R-bought　　what　who

　　b.　ng-te'a a medengei el kmo ng-**ngera** a l-bil'erar　　a **te'ang**
　　　　　　　　　　　　　　　　what　　　　IR-bought　who
　　Who remembers who bought what?

The questions in (56) elicit answers as for (54c), in which both embedded WH phrases have wide scope.

Let us focus now on what mechanisms are necessary to account for the preferred readings. Here, if the embedded C is [+WH], then it is a barrier to *all* scope movement; and, of course, if it is [−WH], then *no* WH phrase may have narrow scope. Thus the scope of the embedded WH phrases does not depend on their surface syntactic position, contrary to prediction. Clearly, filters like those in (48), or even the requirement that Spec(C) and C agree in the [αWH] feature, will not account for the fact that *all* WH from a given clause tend to have the same scope. Some other device is needed.

Significantly, the question-answer data displayed so far indicate that, as far as preferred scope interpretation is concerned, an in situ WH and a clefted (A′) WH have the same status. *Effectively, all WH are in situ at S-structure.*

Let us consider this claim. I say "effectively" because, of course, an A′ WH is not in situ. But for scope interpretation, it does not act as though it is preposed. Note, first, that there is no interpretive difference between (54a), (56a), and (56b) (repeated below):

(57) a.　ng-**te'a**　a medengei　　el kmo ng-**te'a** a mil'erar
　　　　C1-who　R-remember Comp　Cl-who　R-Pf-bought

　　　　a **ngerang**
　　　　　what

　　b.　ng-te'a a medengei el kmo ng-mil'erar a **ngera** a **te'ang**
　　　　　　　　　　　　　　　　　　R-bought　　what　who

EMBEDDED QUESTIONS 171

(57) c. ng-te'a a medengei el kmo ng-**ngera** a l-bil'erar a **te'ang**
what IR-bought who

(All three) Who remembers who bought what?

Compare the difference in the English (58):

(58) a. Who remembers who bought what? / Do you remember who bought what?

b. Who remembers what who bought? / Do you remember what who bought?

(58a) can be answered *I remember who bought hotdogs (and Frank remembers who bought steaks)* and (58b) can be answered *I remember what Frank bought (and you remember what Ernest bought)*. That is, wide scope can be given to the WH phrase in situ in the embedding in English, as pointed out earlier. S-structure word order differences signal a difference in meaning, in scope.

But in the variants on the Palauan question in (57), the order of constituents does not determine a meaning difference. Whether 'what' precedes 'who' or 'who' precedes 'what', and whether the WH phrases are actually in situ or not, the question is the same. For example, (57a) is predicted to be ambiguous, in that one of the embedded WH phrases, **te'a** 'who' or **ngera** 'what' should take narrow scope. But instead, if one embedded WH phrase takes wide scope, a narrow scope reading for a clause-mate WH phrase becomes marginal (see (54)), though not impossible.

4.2. *[+WH] Complements*

When we come to study the complements of obligatorily [+WH] verbs like **oker** 'ask' and **mele'ede'** 'wonder', the facts are parallel. In (59), two WH phrases occur under **mele'ede'**; one is in an A′ position and one is in an A position. (59) is construed as a statement, in which *both* WH take narrow scope:

(59)   a Tmerukl a mele'ede' el kmo ng-**te'a** a mengiil er ngii
        R-wonder Comp Cl-who R-wait P him

el mo meruul a **ngerang**
Comp R-Fut R-do what

Tmerukl is wondering who is waiting for him to do what.

(*What is Tmerukl wondering who is waiting for him to do?)

(*Who is Tmerukl wondering is waiting for him to do what?)

There appears to be no possibility for ambiguity in this sentence: neither

172   CHAPTER FIVE

WH phrase can be assigned scope above the embedding. The facts are the same with respect to **oker** 'ask':

(60)　a Tmerukl a oker　el kmo ng-**te'a** a mengiil er ngii
　　　　　　　　　R-ask Comp　Cl-who　　R-wait　P　him

el　　mo　　meruul a **ngerang**
Comp R-Aux R-do　　　what

Tmerukl is asking who is waiting for him to do what.

(*Who is Tmerukl asking is waiting for him to do what?)

(*What is Tmerukl asking who is waiting for him to do?)

In contrast to the monoclausal questions in (50), or the biclausal structures under **medengei** 'know, remember', paraphrases of (59) and (60) in which the object, **ngera** 'what', is clefted and the subject, **te'a** 'who', is in situ are ungrammatical unless they are interpreted as echo questions (in this case it is the in situ WH that might be said to have wide scope):

(61) a. a Tmerukl a mele'ede' el kmo ng-**ngera** a longiil　　er ngii
　　　　　　　　　　R-wonder Comp　Cl-what　　IR-3-wait P　him

el　　bo　　loruul a **te'ang**
Comp IR-Aux IR-do　　who

Tmerukl is wondering *who* is waiting for him to do what?

b. a Dirrabkau a uleker　el kmo ng-**ngera** a lulnguiu a **te'ang**
　　　　　　　　　R-asked Comp　Cl-what　　IR-read　　who

Dirrabkau asked *who* read what?

(61) demonstrates that (except in the context of an echo question) no WH under **oker** 'ask' or **mele'ede'** 'wonder' can be interpreted as having wide scope. I have no account of the difference between (53)/(56) and (61).

Like (56a), the WH arguments under **mele'ede'** and **oker** may both optionally be in situ:

(62) a. a Tmerukl a uleker　el kmo ngmengiil er ngii el
　　　　　　　　　R-asked Comp　R-3s-wait　P　him Comp

mo　　meruul a **ngera** a **te'ang**
R-Aux R-do　　what　who

Tmerukl asked who is waiting for him to do what.

b. a Dirrabkau a uleker　el kmo ng-menguiu a **ngera** a **te'ang**
　　　　　　　　　R-asked Comp　R-3s-read　　what　who

Dirrakau asked who was reading what.

EMBEDDED QUESTIONS

In (62) as in other embeddings under [+WH] verbs, both WH phrases have narrow scope.

In (63), we see that both WH phrases under a question-embedding verb may be fronted within the embedding; in the latter case, the left-most NP is in cleft position and the second one is in topic (= pseudo-cleft) position.[15] Both have narrow scope in all cases:

(63) a. a Dirrabkau a uleker   el kmo ng-**te'a** a milnguiu a **ngerang**
     R-asked Comp Cl-who   R-read   what

   b. a Dirrabkau a uleker el kmo ng-**ngera** a **te'a** a menguiu
        Cl-what   who   R-read

   c. a Dirrabkau a uleker el kmo ng-**te'a** a **ngera** a lulnguiu
        Cl-who   what   IR-read

   Dirrabkau asked who was reading what.

Thus, no matter what their order or S-structure position, all WH phrases in (59) through (63) obligatorily have narrow scope.

4.3. *ECP Accounts*

That *all* WH under a [+WH] verb should take narrow scope is un-expected. Oddly, the intermediate option, represented by English and many other languages described in the literature (see, e.g., Huang 1982), is not available in Palauan: that one WH should attach to an embedded clause while another WH from the same embedding takes wider scope. Schematically, the possibilities for Palauan are as represented below:

$$(64) \quad [_{CP} \ldots V \quad [_{CP} \ldots WH \ldots WH \ldots]]$$
$$+WH \quad \times \quad \longleftarrow ---\rfloor \qquad \rfloor$$
$$\times \quad \longleftarrow ----------\rfloor$$

$$*[_{CP} \ldots V \quad [_{CP} \ldots WH \ldots WH \ldots]]$$
$$+WH \quad \times \quad \longleftarrow ---\rfloor \qquad \rfloor$$
$$\longleftarrow -------------------------\rfloor$$

$$[_{CP} \ldots V \quad [CP \ldots WH \ldots WH \ldots]]$$
$$-WH \qquad \rfloor \qquad \rfloor$$
$$\longleftarrow -----------------\rfloor \qquad \rfloor$$
$$\longleftarrow -----------------------------\rfloor$$

The finding that no WH phrase embedded under a [+WH]-selecting verb may have wide scope suggests at first that movement in LF in Palauan *does* obey subjacency, in particular the WH Island Condition. This would be in contrast to the formation of A′ dependencies in the syntax, which does not obey subjacency. However, a subjacency account

174 CHAPTER FIVE

provides no explanation of (53), for which embedded WH phrases in situ may take wide scope. In addition, it is usually assumed that subjacency does not hold for movements in LF (see AHS 1981; Huang 1982; Chomsky 1986b). For example, Huang (1982) shows that the sentence in (65) (Huang's (1), p. 525) can be interpreted as a direct question on either **sheme** 'what' or **shei** 'who':

(65) a. ni   xiang-zhidao [shei mai-le   sheme]
     you wonder   who buy-ASP what

b. 'What is the thing x such that you wonder who bought x?'

c. 'Who is the person x such that you wonder what x bought?'

In Huang's analysis, extraction of either WH phrase in the embedding should violate the WH Island Constraint at LF, yet (65a) is grammatical. He argues that movement of arguments in LF is sanctioned by a version of the ECP that encompasses WH Island effects, and that the lack of island effects in the syntax in Chinese is due to the lack of movement.

I argued in Chapter Three that Palauan lacks island effects for the same reason that Chinese does: because no movement takes place in the syntax. However, Palauan [+WH] sentential complements behave differently from those in Chinese, in that no WH phrase originating in the complement can have wide scope. Palauan cannot, then, be analyzed in precisely the same terms as Chinese.

Nor do other current approaches offer further insight into Palauan. Consider the rule of Comp-indexing, proposed by AHS. This rule allows Comp to be indexed by a maximal projection it contains at S-structure, and thereby to be a proper governor for the ECP. The rule is stated as in (66), and provides that Comp must not contain a lexical complementizer or contra-indexed elements at the point where (66) applies:

(66) $[_{\text{COMP}} XP_i \ldots] \rightarrow [_{\text{COMP}} XP_i \ldots]_i$

iff COMP dominates only i-indexed elements

A Comp so indexed retains its index at LF, and properly governs a trace in an embedding even after some other phrase has been moved into it by WH raising. (67a) is an indexed S-structure; (67b) its LF structure ((67) =AHS's (58)):

(67) a. $[_{S'} [_{\text{COMP}} \text{qui}_i]_i [_S e_i \text{ fait } \text{quoi}_j]]$
        who   does what

b. $[_{S'} [_{\text{COMP}} \text{qui}_i \text{ quoi}_j]_i [_S e_i \text{ fait } e_j]]$
        who what   does

The i-indexed Comp in (67b) properly governs e_i in subject position, though the antecedent, **qui**, cannot. It is argued that this approach

EMBEDDED QUESTIONS

accounts for the impossibility of extraction from complements of verbs like 'wonder', in which a WH phrase is in Comp at S-structure:

(68) *Who$_i$ do you wonder [$_{S'}$ [$_{COMP}$ e_i what$_j$] [$_S$ e_i saw e_j]]?

The indexing rule cannot apply, since Comp dominates more than i-indexed elements, and a sentence like (68) therefore violates the ECP. (It appears to be grammatical in Chinese, however; see (65).)

The indexing rule cannot account for Palauan, for a number of reasons. First, all A positions including subjects are properly governed (Georgopoulos 1991b; Chapter Six below), so the effect in question does not implicate the ECP. Second, neither subject nor object WH (i.e. no WH) can be extracted from the embedding. Third, since no movement has taken place at S-structure, Comp is not indexed.

Lasnik and Saito (1984) reformulate this indexing mechanism to make it apply to the output of movement in LF as well as at S-structure. Comp is indexed by the first WH phrase that is its head, in L & S's terms, and if this phrase is raised to a higher clause in LF, the [+WH] Comp cannot then accept a WH phrase with a different index. Since a Comp under 'wonder' *must* contain a WH element, however, it may not be empty at LF. (For L & S, traces do not bear a [+WH] feature.) Thus a WH phrase in the Comp under 'wonder' cannot be moved to a higher clause after LF movement.[16] But, as with Huang and AHS, L & S's analysis does not address the particular problems posed by Palauan. All of these theories fail to account for the fact that a *second* WH phrase cannot take wide scope, once one WH phrase satisfies the [+WH] feature of the embedding.

I will assume that subjacency does not hold in LF, so no solution in terms of bounding theory is available to account for the Palauan facts. Nor do the facts suggest a role for the ECP. Earlier predictions about the scope potential of WH phrases in situ simply fail to be confirmed cross-linguistically.

Intriguing as this problem is, I will not attempt to develop a comprehensive solution here. As far as I can see, any solution at this point would be purely mechanical.[17] Rather, in the final section of this chapter, I will attempt to refine the basic terms of the general theory of both direct and embedded questions, in light of distinctions brought into sharper focus by the analysis of Palauan WH structures.

5. ON SCOPE INTERPRETATION FOR WH BINDERS

In Palauan, movement to specifier of C takes place only in LF. As I have pointed out, *no* WH phrase in Palauan is in Spec(C) at S-structure. Yet Palauan has well-formed WH questions, both direct and indirect. At the same time, WH phrases in Palauan have unusual freedom of position.

176   CHAPTER FIVE

The distinction usually made in the theory between WH phrases in situ
and preposed WH phrases does not have much predictive or analytical
value in this language, as far as the analysis of WH questions is concerned. Yet for scope to be ultimately determined, there must be a
designated scope position. What allows the learner/user to interpret
scope?

This question can be answered, in fact, in the same terms for all
languages. The two concepts crucial to the theory of WH question
formation are, first, the agreement between C and its specifier in the
value of the WH feature, and second, the privileged status of specifier of
C relative to other A' binding positions.

5.1. *[± WH] and Agreement within CP*

I have already mentioned the mechanism of specifier-head coindexing
proposed in Chomsky (1986b). This is the basis of certain feature-
sharing phenomena generally, such as subject-I agreement, and 'possessor agreement' within NP (see Georgopoulos 1991a). Within CP this
coindexing underlies agreement in the [±WH] feature, and it is *only* this
agreement, I suggest, that satisfies the [±WH] subcategorization of the
matrix verb. The verb determines lexically that the complementizer has a
particular feature value, but the subcategorization requirement is not
satisfied until LF, where the rule responsible for WH scope interpretation ensures that C and its specifier agree in that value. Assume that the
rule is a statement along the lines of (69):

(69)   *WH scope interpretation*:

        C and the specifier of C are $[\alpha \text{WH}]$.

This rule must apply at LF, because LF is the level of UG where interpretive rules with semantic consequences apply. In addition, the rule
must apply in all languages that have WH questions (most likely this
means all languages), including those languages without movement to
Spec(C) at S-structure.

The other two factors crucial to the WH question analysis are the
settings in a particular grammar for WH movement (obligatory, optional,
or prohibited in the syntax) and the distribution of the [±WH] feature
(satisfied by specifier-head agreement). The movement settings interact
with various other language-particular options and rules to determine
the S-structure facts. The distribution of the [±WH] feature determines
the ultimate scope configurations of LF.

Agreement between C and Spec(C) subsumes the filters proposed by
Lasnik and Saito (1984), as inspection of (48) will show: a [+WH]
complementizer and its specifier must agree, as must a [−WH] com-

EMBEDDED QUESTIONS

plementizer and its specifier. This argument, applying at the output of LF movement, also subsumes most of the content of stipulations (43) and (45) of Aoun, Hornstein, and Sportiche (1981), since it is immaterial whether or not a WH phrase is raised from an A or an A′ position, as long as [±WH] subcategorization is satisfied. That is, a WH phrase in an A′ position at S-structure is free to move to another A′ position in LF, subject to [±WH] requirements.

The agreement analysis proposed here is satisfying in that it is not a system devised especially for WH questions, but is an instance of specifier-head coindexing that is well established for independent reasons to hold in every maximal projection (see Georgopoulos 1991a; Kuroda 1988). It also provides an explanation of why no WH phrase in Palauan can be said to have particular scope at S-structure: no WH phrase is in Spec(C). The problem remains, however, of accounting for multiple WH phrases in a [+WH] complement: in Palauan, [+WH] complements act like islands (cf. AHS's analysis of (68)).

An interesting question is whether or not the [+WH] feature is identical to the Q morpheme postulated by Baker (1970) and others. Lasnik and Saito (1984, n. 5) state that the two are indistinguishable. It seems, however, that they are quite different conceptually, even if they are both intended in practice to be triggers of movement. The [+WH] feature is a property of subcategorization (or of a matrix C) that is satisfied by matching the same feature-value on some moved constituent; any WH phrase can do this. Q, however, is indexed to (binds) *particular* WH phrase(s) (see (4)); thus it chooses, in a sense, which WH will have narrow (or wide) scope. A WH in situ in the Q theory does not *optionally* take wide scope, but does so only if it is indexed to the matrix Q, while a WH in situ in the [±WH] theory does take wide scope optionally.

This may be a trivial difference, and without substance. But the Q theory is better able to explain why all WH phrases in a [+WH] complement in Palauan must maintain narrow scope. A single WH phrase would satisfy the [+WH] feature, while proponents of Q could simply say that *all* WH phrases in this case are indexed to the embedded Q. The Q theory may actually be assimilable to spec-head coindexing, if [+WH] is a property of the index. Whether or not this line of reasoning is worth pursuing depends upon whether other languages can be found to pattern like Palauan.[18]

5.2. The Status of Spec(C)

The analysis of Palauan WH questions has revealed what seems to be a crucial distinction, one impossible to make on the basis of the surface facts of many languages. That is that a WH phrase can satisfy the [+WH]

178   CHAPTER FIVE

subcategorization of a matrix verb *only* by moving into Spec(C). Generalizing from this and other facts described here, I conclude that the *designated WH scope position* in UG is Spec(C).

It is usual in the theory of WH questions (see most of the literature referred to in this chapter) to distinguish between *in situ* and simply *preposed* WH phrases. All predictions made so far have been based on this distinction. But a finer distinction is needed. Whether in situ or preposed, Palauan WH phrases are not in Spec(C) at S-structure, and this seems crucial: [+WH] subcategorization is not involved at that level. I have argued above that Spec(C) is the only position coindexed with C, which has the [+WH] subcategorization feature. C-Spec(C) agreement satisfies that subcategorization. Thus the theory of WH scope must refer to *WH phrases that are in Spec(C)* (at S-structure or LF) *as distinct from those that are not.*

In a theory making this distinction, Palauan and other languages allowing clefting of WH phrases, as well as the IP-adjoined WH phrases described by Rudin (1988), are included.[19] That is, WH binders can be found in a variety of A′ positions, but only the A′ position that is the specifier of C is relevant to WH scope interpretation.

If it is correct that WH scope interpretation depends on specifier-head agreement in LF, the variability in S-structure position of WH phrases, in Palauan *and* cross-linguistically, is to be expected. Any position outside of Spec(C) should be 'effectively in situ', i.e. irrelevant or at least underspecified for scope interpretation, since no other XP position is specified for the [±WH] value and thereby able to agree with C. Even in a language like English, a WH in situ has no designated scope, and can take either wide or narrow scope. This is the general claim made by the traditional analysis summarized in section 1.

It should be noted that the centrality of Spec(C) to [+WH] subcategorization and scope does not carry over to other aspects of A′ binding. A′ binding (operator-variable binding) does not require Spec(C), but only an A′ position. Thus, for example, the analysis of WH agreement (Chapter Three) is not altered by this analysis, since A′ binding does not in general directly involve subcategorization. These conclusions entail, furthermore, that the well-formedness of WH scope constructions and of operator-variable binding is assessed independently.

5.3. *The Orientation of Spec(C)*

In this final section I would like to make a more speculative prediction: that the WH-scope-bearing position (Spec(C)) is necessarily on the left edge of the clause. It was observed in Bresnan (1970), and by others, that WH movement is always to the left. And, as I pointed out above, even though Palauan is a uniformly left-headed language, with specifiers

EMBEDDED QUESTIONS 179

as well as complements in all lexical projections on the right of the head, there is no evidence on the surface that the specifier of C is on the right. Rather, WH phrases and topics are clefted to IP, and follow the complementizer. This leaves open the possibility that, at LF, Spec(C) is actually in a position corresponding to its (potential) WH scope in all languages.

The mechanism responsible for this could be either preposing of Spec(C) (most likely at S-structure, to allow for its position in left-headed languages having overt WH movement) or a special CP expansion rule that universally has the form $[_{CP} XP \, C']$. In Georgopoulos (1991b) I propose a *specifier parameter*, distinct from the head-complement parameter, which sets the position of the specifier relative to the head.[20] Thus a VO language could be either SVO or VOS, and so on. I describe the specifier parameter at the level of the generalized X' schema, as follows:

(70)   *The Specifier Parameter*:

$$XP = X' \, YP \quad or$$

$$XP = YP \, X'$$

In order to account for the (apparent) fact that specifier of C is always on the left, it could be stipulated in the grammar that, when $X = C$, the parameter is set at $XP = YP \, X'$.

This is obviously a set of proposals that need further research, to see if the order of C and IP can be made to follow from something other than a stipulation. I leave the issue here.

6. SUMMARY

In this chapter on embedded questions and the scope of WH phrases, the properties of the resumptive pronoun have taken the back seat. Scope problems do not refer to the properties of the variable, but to those of the binder.

The grammar under scrutiny has nevertheless presented interesting and unusual data and, more importantly, new insights into the traditional terms of the analysis. In particular, we have seen that the specifier of C is the only position that can satisfy the subcategorization feature relevant to WH scope interpretation, with the result that *no* WH phrase in Palauan is ever in the scope position at S-structure. Thus WH scope in Palauan appears to be underdetermined in the syntax. In order to account for the occurrence of well-formed WH questions in Palauan as in other languages, however, I assume that all languages are alike at the output of LF and that WH phrases are in [+WH] specifier positions universally at LF.

180   CHAPTER FIVE

Finally, I suggested that the specifier of C, the eventual landing site of all
WH phrases, is necessarily at the left edge of the clause.

NOTES

[1] As we expect in Palauan A' binding, WH agreement is triggered by the variable
coindexed to the clefted constituent. (19a) contains a Nominative variable, and (19b) a
non-Nominative variable; the morphology of the embedded verb is realis in (19a) and
irrealis in (19b).

[2] See Aoun and Sportiche's (1981) definition of c-command in terms of maximal
projection (Chapter One). Contra m-command in binding, see Rizzi (1990).

[3] And perhaps gives support for the claim in Bresnan (1970) that WH movement is
always to the left, though this should be broadened to include base-generated A' binders.

[4] It is a lexical property of **omdasu** 'think' that it may take irrealis morphology; an
example of this is seen in (26c).

[5] The predicate in (31) has no **a** specifier. The morpheme **a** and demonstratives are in
complementary distribution; see 4.1 in Chapter Two.

[6] Another case of the disjunctiveness of WH agreement and other agreement morphology was described at 2.3 in Chapter Two. Interestingly, in that case, WH agreement
is disjoint with semantic *irrealis* agreement.

[7] Though all speakers consulted agree with the interpretation of these examples, that is,
they agree that realis subject agreement on the matrix verb in (39c) indicates that (39c) is
a question, Palauan speakers are not consistent in using this form. Many are unconscious
of the morphological difference between (39b) and (39c) until their attention is called to
it. Thus my data are inconsistent in this regard, and (39) reveals a general pattern rather
than a pattern without exceptions.

[8] That (42b) is a legitimate LF representation is indicated by the possibility of 'paired'
answers to a question like *who bought what*? If both WH are given a value in the answer,
both are assumed to have wide scope.

[9] Cf. Lasnik & Saito (1984, 238) who describe (45) as an S-structure filter.

[10] Chinese, Polish, and Palauan also represent difficulties for the analyses in Baker
(1970) and Bresnan (1970).

[11] This idea is based on a proposal of Kuroda (1988).

[12] For Polish, there is still no account for the combined multiple preposing and lack of
extraction out of the indicative clause (see first page of this chapter).

[13] One caveat in reading section 4.1 is that I focus on 'preferred' readings, fully aware
that the status of such readings is not totally reliable. In addition, I do not discuss the
extraction of adjuncts at all here, since I do not have a sufficient range of data involving
adjunct extraction. The scope of adjuncts must, however, be considered before any
account of Palauan multiple interrogation is complete.

[14] In (52c and d), the object WH c-commands the subject WH; this presumed Superiority Condition violation is not in itself enough to rule them out, however. Configurations such as this are normally grammatical in Palauan. See, for example, (56b). See also
Georgopoulos (1991b) for arguments that subjects as well as objects are always properly
governed in Palauan.

[15] This order of A' positions is invariant: the position of the lexical complementizer is
leftmost, followed by **ng**-WH cleft position, followed by topic position. See also 2.2.

[16] A WH phrase in situ, like *what* in *Who remembers [$_{+WH}$ who bought what]*?, moves to
the higher clause essentially subjacency-free.

[17] One might initially think that Kayne's (1983a) connectedness theory can be applied
to this question, but the problems with doing so seem serious. First, the [+WH] feature,

EMBEDDED QUESTIONS 181

rather than any actual WH phrase, must be taken as the antecedent (at which the subtree holding both WH phrases is rooted). Second, there seems to be no reason why one g-projection path cannot continue on into the upper clause. Third, there is no sense in which one WH phrase is parasitic on another in this data. Still, the facts are reminiscent of those analyzed by Kayne (see p. 234 ff. of Kayne 1983a).

[18] The Q theory is compatible with the connectedness theory (see prior footnote) in that the node at which WH phrases are indexed is plausibly the node at which the g-projections of the WH phrases meet.

[19] Rudin's analysis includes the proposal that some IP-adjoined WH phrases do not undergo movement to Spec(C) in LF. It is not clear at this point how the two analyses are to be reconciled; perhaps a WH in Spec(C) can be composed with WH adjoined to IP by absorption (May 1977).

[20] A sketch of this parameter is included in section 5.2 of Chapter Six, where it sheds light on the problem of weak crossover.

CHAPTER SIX

CROSSOVER CONSTRUCTIONS

0. OVERVIEW

Since Palauan pronouns have many of the properties that are considered definitional of syntactic variables, the question naturally arises as to what the behavior of these pronouns in crossover contexts might be. It turns out that their properties in these contexts are unusual. Palauan has the strong crossover effect, but in order to account for it, an intrinsic definition of variable must be adopted. Palauan has no weak crossover effects at all, once the influence of a precedence effect is factored out. In attempting to deal with these facts in the light of generative theory, it will become clear that the issues involved are not limited to crossover contexts. The discussion will therefore be extended to a larger range of anaphoric constructions.

In this chapter I will first provide an overview of the general issues involved in the analyses of strong and weak crossover. The Palauan crossover facts will then be presented. Section 1 reviews the arguments for precedence and for c-command in earlier approaches to definite and indefinite NP anaphora. Section 2 summarizes three theories of weak crossover within GB: bijection (Koopman and Sportiche 1982), parallelism (Safir 1984), and various c-command accounts. Section 3 lays out the facts of strong crossover constructions in Palauan. It shows that these constructions behave as predicted, but that this behavior depends crucially on the grammar being able to distinguish bound pronouns (variables) from other pronouns. The hierarchical definition of variable is challenged here, as it is shown unable to account for strong crossover cross-linguistically.

Turning to weak crossover constructions in section 4, I demonstrate the lack of any weak crossover effect in Palauan. The possibility that anaphora in Palauan depends on both precedence and c-command by the lexical antecedent is considered, and these combined conditions are found to account for the lack of weak crossover effects. I then explore the consequences of the apparent precedence condition in other anaphoric constructions; interestingly, this condition appears to hold only between the external and internal arguments of the verb.

Section 5 presents a government-theoretic account of weak crossover: basically, languages in which specifiers are canonically governed, like Palauan (which is VOS), has no weak crossover effects, while SVO languages like English do. Integral to this account is a parameter which,

CROSSOVER CONSTRUCTIONS 183

in Universal Grammar, determines whether or not specifiers are canonically governed. I include here arguments that the ECP, stated as a requirement involving canonical government, applies to resumptive pronouns. This brings us back to the issue of distinguishing a pronoun from a variable, and the definition of variable, issues especially relevant in Palauan. This section once more makes the point that whether or not a category is phonologically empty does not determine its identity as a variable or a pronoun; what is at stake is its *syntactic* identity, in terms of the features [±pronominal, ±anaphor].

The chapter ends by proposing a distinction between extraction site and other A′ bound positions, and a reformulation of the homogeneity constraint on A′ binding.

1. BACKGROUND

The 'crossover' phenomenon was named and first discussed by Postal (1971), and was reanalyzed by Wasow (1972). 'Crossover' in these early treatments referred to the blocking of derivations in which some NP moved across a coindexed pronoun. There are two cases of crossover: 'strong' and 'weak'. The distinction is due to Wasow, and refers to the relative strength of ungrammaticality of the two types. The examples in (1), which illustrate strong crossover, are taken from the discussion in Chomsky (1977):

(1) a. Who ____ said Mary kissed him?

b. *Who did he say Mary kissed ____?

c. Who ____ said he kissed Mary?

In (1a) and (1c), the third-person pronouns *him* and *he* can enter into an anaphoric relation with (= be coindexed with) the variable bound by *who*, but in (1b) *he* cannot have such a relation with the variable of *who*.[1] In movement terms, *who* moves across *he* in (1b), but no such offending movements occur in (1a or c). The relation of the pronouns to the WH extraction sites in (1a–c) is mirrored by the relation of the pronouns to the referring expression *John* in (2); intended coreference is indicated by italics:

(2) a. *John* said Mary kissed *him*.

b. **He* said Mary kissed *John*.

c. *John* said *he* kissed Mary.

The example in (3) illustrates weak crossover, which involves a different structural relation of pronoun and antecedent than in (1) and (2) above:

184   CHAPTER SIX

(3)   *The woman *he* loved betrayed *someone.*

The analysis of sentences such as (3) involves further assumptions which are explored in detail below.

The examples in (1) through (3), involving both definite NP anaphora and bound variable anaphora, illustrate the problem of determining the structural conditions under which a pronoun can be coindexed with some other NP position in the sentence (therefore readings on which the pronoun refers to someone *not* mentioned in the sentences will be ignored). The attempt to specify the syntactic conditions on anaphora is a long-standing project in transformational grammar.

As the term 'crossover' suggests, the directionality of movement in a SVO language like English figured prominently in early analyses. These analyses have evolved through a number of stages during which directionality has been abandoned.

1.1. *Leftness*

Chomsky (1977) observes that the WH traces in (1) appear to function like the names in (2), and concludes that the same PRECEDE AND COMMAND conditions on definite NP anaphora (Langacker 1969)[2] account for the coindexing possibilities in both paradigms. Chomsky also notes that some further constraint is needed for (3), to account for the lack of coindexing between the pronoun and the 'indeterminate' quantified phrase. After LF movement of the quantified NP, there is a trace in the position of *someone* (see (5c) below). In the terms of Chomsky (1977), the pronoun *he* will not command the trace, however, since *he* commands only the material in the embedded clause and is not immediately dominated by the S node that dominates the trace. The sentence is therefore predicted to be grammatical, but it is not. Chomsky proposes that the condition in (4), which refers only to the linear *precedence* relation, is the interpretive principle relevant to crossover cases (= Chomsky's (105)):

(4)   A variable cannot be the antecedent of a pronoun to its left.

(4) has been referred to as the Leftness Condition. It applies to both strong crossover (cases like those in (1), in which the pronoun commands the trace), and to weak crossover (cases like (3)).

According to Chomsky, the Leftness Condition applies in the mapping from surface structures to LF, accounting simultaneously for the cases in (1) and for cases involving logical quantifiers, such as (3).[3] The LF forms of these sentences are seen in (5).

(5) a.   For which person x, x said Mary kissed him

CROSSOVER CONSTRUCTIONS 185

(5) b. *For which person x, he said Mary kissed x

c. *For some person x, the woman he loved betrayed x

The pronoun is to the left of x in (5b, c), but not in (5a).

1.2. *C-command: Strong Crossover*

In the work of Reinhart (e.g. Reinhart 1976, 1981b), a dependency or relation between two positions in a sentence is based on the hierarchical relation C(constituent)-COMMAND:[4]

(6)   Node A c-commands Node B iff the branching node most immediately dominating A also dominates B.

Reinhart employs the notion of c-command in stating two conditions on anaphora. The first is the general condition on definite NP anaphora (from Reinhart 1981b):

(7)   An NP cannot be interpreted as coreferential with a distinct nonpronoun in its c-command domain.

This rule is generally accepted as the most satisfactory account, in structural terms, of (non)coreference of NPs.[5]

The rule applies straightforwardly to the examples with referring NPs ((2)): the pronoun cannot c-command its antecedent. It applies to the WH questions in (1) as follows, assuming the presence of the trace: the pronoun in (1a, c) is c-commanded by the trace and, since it is a pronoun, can be coindexed with the trace. *He* and the trace in (1b) cannot be coindexed, however, since the pronoun c-commands the trace. The coindexing possibilities of the trace in (1) show, furthermore, that the trace is not a pronoun. (In other words, variables are interpreted as nonpronouns.)

In essence, the characterization of the trace as a 'full NP' and thereby subject to a rule of anaphora such as (7) sums up the approach to strong crossover in EST. If a pronoun c-commands the (non-pronominal) trace, anaphora between them is impossible. Assuming that sentences containing quantified NPs (like (3)) undergo a movement rule like Quantifier Raising (May 1977), there is a bound variable in the output that is also subject to Reinhart's rule. However, the rule is in itself not enough to account for (3), since c-command does not hold between the coindexed positions. This is the weak crossover configuration.

1.3. *C-command: Weak Crossover*

The usual paradigm of weak crossover facts is seen in (8) (italics indicate intended coindexing):

186   CHAPTER SIX

(8) a.   *His* mother loves *John*.

   b.   * *Who* does *his* mother love *t*?

   c.   * *His* mother loves *everyone*.

Weak crossover is observed in constructions in which coindexing is prohibited between a pronoun and a bound variable, but in which neither c-commands the other. The structures involving names, as in (8a), do not give rise to weak crossover for most speakers. Those who find (8a) awkward usually accept slight variations on the construction:

(9) a.   The woman *he* married still thinks *Steve* is great.

   b.   The secretary who works for *him* despises *Siegfried*.
     (Reinhart 1983)

In contrast to the case of names, variables in these constructions produce ungrammaticality:

(10) a. * *Who* does the woman *he* married still think *t* is great?

   b.* *Who* does the secretary who works for *him* despise *t*?

(8c) demonstrates that the trace of Quantifier Raising has the same crossover effect as WH trace: anaphora is blocked between the extraction site of *everyone* and the specifier of the subject.

As Reinhart (1976) notes, anaphora in sentences like (8) or (10) is not ruled out on semantic grounds: anaphoric relations between traces and pronouns are possible when the trace c-commands the pronoun (Reinhart's examples, p. 110):

(11) a.   *Who t* insisted that those who like *him* are crazy?

   b.   *Who* did you accuse *t* of killing *his* mother?

The weak crossover facts show that the c-command restriction (7) alone is not sufficient to account for the possibilities of anaphora between pronouns and traces. The Leftness Condition, so far, accounts better than (7) for the lack of coindexing observed in weak crossover.[6]

That Leftness is not adequate over a greater range of cases is shown by sentences such as those in (12) and (13) (from Reinhart 1976):

(12) a. *The fact that *he* lost amused *someone in the crowd*.

   b.*The fact that *someone in the crowd* lost amused *him*.

CROSSOVER CONSTRUCTIONS

(13) a. *The fact that *she* has already climbed this mountain before encouraged *some woman* to try again.

b. *The fact that *some woman* has already climbed this mountain before encouraged *her* to try again.

The pronoun cannot be to the left of its quantified antecedent in the (a) sentences, but neither can it *follow* the antecedent in the (b) sentences. Reinhart therefore proposes a second condition, a rule applying to bound anaphora. This is a stricter rule than the one in (7), and accounts for the examples with what Reinhart terms "nondefinites" (traces, quantified NPs, and focus NPs (p. 126)):

(14)   Nondefinite NPs can have anaphoric relations only with NPs in their c-command domain.

By the earlier rule (7), a trace cannot be coindexed with any pronoun that c-commands it; by the stricter rule (14), a quantified NP or trace cannot be coindexed with any pronoun that it does not c-command.

In GB, two approaches to weak crossover can be distinguished. One is an account based on or derived from Reinhart's rule (14) (e.g. Higginbotham 1980a; Saito and Hoji 1983; Hoji 1985; Stowell 1987; Stowell and Lasnik 1987). The second approach treats weak crossover in terms of the operator-variable relation. Both are described in the next section.

2. CROSSOVER IN GOVERNMENT-BINDING THEORY

In the same work in which he proposes the Leftness Condition, Chomsky restates the condition in terms that describe how a pronoun can itself be interpreted as a variable (Chomsky 1977, p. 37):

(15)   A pronoun P within the scope of a quantifier may be rewritten as a variable bound by this quantifier unless P is to the left of an occurrence of a variable already bound by this quantifier.

Schematically, (15) rules out this configuration:

(16)   *quantifier$_i$ . . . pronoun$_i$ . . . variable$_i$ . . .

This is precisely the configuration that gives rise to both strong and weak crossover effects, i.e. when both the pronoun c-commands the variable and when there is no c-command between them. Despite the suggestion of a unified account raised by (16), however, the two types of crossover are treated quite differently in GB.

Strong crossover is accounted for by Principle C of the Binding Theory, together with the assumption that variables are like names with

188 CHAPTER SIX

respect to binding (Chomsky 1977, 1981).[7] The assimilation of variables to names is based on the facts illustrated in (1) and (2). By Principle C, R(eferring)-expressions (including names and variables) are free: they cannot be coindexed with any c-commanding argument position.[8]

2.1. *Weak Crossover*

· Whereas the treatment of strong crossover is assimilated to the conditions on definite NP anaphora, the primary approach to weak crossover in GB is concerned instead with the conditions on (syntactic) variable binding. A syntactic variable is defined in terms of the tree structure. It is a category whose binder is in a c-commanding A′ position: either a WH quantifier in Spec(C) or a quantified NP adjoined to IP by Quantifier Raising in the mapping to LF. One common definition of syntactic variable is that of Chomsky (1981):

(17)   Variable: α is a variable if α is in an A position and is locally A′-bound.

This definition is interpreted to mean that the closest binder of α is an A′ binder; if α is locally A-bound, even if it is coindexed with a quantifier, it is not a variable. Chomsky (1981) presupposes that α in his definition of variable is an empty category. Any empty category that meets this definition is a variable, although, historically, the definition applies to an empty category at an extraction site.

It can be argued, however, that extraction site variables and other A′ bound positions are not defined in the same way by the grammar. In particular, it can be argued that (17) does not uniquely identify variables, since in any given clause there are n A positions that can potentially be locally A′ bound. Later in this chapter I will present evidence to show that (17) in fact does not uniquely define the notion 'variable'.

The definition in (17) is central to all approaches to weak crossover, as the following sections show.

2.1.1. *Bijection*

In Koopman and Sportiche (1982), the conditions on bound anaphora are formalized in the BIJECTION PRINCIPLE, which requires that operators and variables correspond to each other one-to-one. Koopman and Sportiche's formulation of this principle is given in (18a); a more transparent statement of bijection (from Saito and Hoji 1983) is in (18b):

(18)   *The Bijection Principle*:

a. There is a bijective correspondence between variables and A′ positions.

(Koopman and Sportiche, p. 146)

CROSSOVER CONSTRUCTIONS 189

(18) b. Every operator must locally bind exactly one variable, and every variable must be locally bound by exactly one operator.

(Saito and Hoji, p. 252)

The definition of variable that both sources appeal to is that in (17). Koopman and Sportiche propose to extend this definition to overt pronouns, as it is necessary to account for languages in which resumptive pronouns trigger weak crossover effects. This extension also has the consequence that the Bijection Principle applies not just to resumptive pronouns, but, more generally, to *all* coindexed pronouns within the scope of the local A′ binder. By the Bijection Principle, an operator may not bind more than one variable in a single sentence. If it does, the one-to-one correspondence of operator and variable required by the Bijection Principle is violated. Thus the extension of the definition of variable to A′ bound pronouns outside of an extraction site allows the weak crossover effect to be derived from bijection.

The bijection account and other WCO theories assume May's (1977) Quantifier Raising rule, which creates traces in the mapping from S-structure to LF. WH questions and quantified sentences therefore present equivalent structures to the bijection principle (as they did for Leftness in Chomsky 1977). Bijection is assumed to hold at LF (and at other syntactic levels as well). For example, the LF form of (19a) would be (informally) as in (19b); the LF form of a sentence containing a quantified NP ((20b)) has the same structure:

(19) a. * *Who* do *his* students respect t?

b. For which person x, x's students respect x

(20) a. * *His* students respect *everyone*.

b. For each person x, x's students respect x

In (19b) and (20b), the operator phrase (*for which person x or for each person x*) binds two variables x in the clause, in violation of bijection.

Koopman and Sportiche point out that the bijection principle is stipulated in toto (their note 15). Its formulation rests on the definition of variable and the extension of that definition to pronouns, which is itself a stipulation. No claim is advanced in this theory that an expression containing two (or more) variables bound to the same operator would be uninterpretable semantically. Since there is a range of other structures that have been analyzed in terms of multiple variable binding, including across-the-board extraction in coordination, parasitic gap structures, right node raising, sentences like those of Reinhart in (10), certain multiple WH questions, and others, several have argued that bijection

190   CHAPTER SIX

lacks motivation as a principle of Universal Grammar (see, e.g., Safir 1984, discussed below).[9]

2.1.2. *Parallelism*

Safir (1984) addresses the first of the problems mentioned above — the presumed excessive restrictiveness of the bijection principle. He adopts Koopman and Sportiche's other assumption that an overt pronoun coindexed with a phrase in an A′ position is a bound variable. In referring to structures containing parasitic gaps, such as (21) (Safir's (11)),

(21)   Which report$_i$ did you file e_i without reading e_i?

Safir notes that they should be ungrammatical on Koopman and Sportiche's account for the same reason (19) and (20) are: the WH operator binds more than one variable. But parasitic gap structures are often acceptable while weak crossover structures are not. Since in the latter case one of the variables is a pronoun, Safir hypothesizes that it is the "mix" of pronoun and trace that gives rise to the weak crossover effect. This hypothesis is bolstered by the perfect grammaticality of across-the-board extraction from coordinate structures:

(22)   The student who$_i$ [we really hated e_i] and [the faculty really liked e_i] finally flunked out.

That is, multiple variable binding is obviously allowed, but the variables appear to be under some feature-matching constraint. Safir formalizes this constraint in terms of PARALLELISM in the sense of George (1980). ((23) is Safir's (6)):

(23)   *The Parallelism Constraint on Operator Binding (PCOB)*:

If O is an operator and x is a variable bound by O, then for any y, y a variable bound by O, x and y are [α lexical].

In the context of Safir's discussion, the term "lexical" in the definition of the PCOB appears to refer to items inserted in D-structures.

As we noted in Chapter Four, the "mix" of coindexed empty category and lexical pronoun is perfectly grammatical in Palauan. In addition, Safir's theory relies on the distinction between parasitic gap structures and weak crossover structures: the former contain two gaps, while the latter contain a pronoun and a gap. This distinction disappears in Palauan, since both NP positions contain a pronoun. This means that weak crossover structures in Palauan are not distinct from parasitic gap structures in the way Safir assumes. Safir also relies on the definition of variable in (17), a definition I call into question below. Overall, then, it does not seem that we can take advantage of the PCOB in the analysis of Palauan anaphora. See section 6, however.

2.1.3. C-command Accounts

Many current accounts of weak crossover are based on the c-command analysis initiated by Reinhart (1976). These include Saito and Hoji (1983), Hoji (1985), Stowell (1987), and Stowell and Lasnik (1987).[10] In this approach, a pronoun can be construed as a bound variable when it is coindexed with a c-commanding 'true' variable (the variable which occupies the D-structure position of a quantified NP). The statement below is from Stowell (1987):

(24)   If a pronoun P and a variable V are bound by the same quantifier, then V must c-command P.

Both (17) (Reinhart's rule) and (24) stipulate that a variable must c-command a coindexed pronoun. Weak crossover is then derived when the prescribed c-command relation fails to hold and the pronoun cannot be bound.

There is a substantive difference between the bijection account and the c-command account. In the latter, both pronoun and trace must be construed as variables to avoid the weak crossover effect. For the former, in contrast, it is precisely this construal of both as variables that *produces* the weak crossover effect. The two approaches therefore make different predictions. If for some reason the definition of variable in (17), which the bijection account relies on, cannot be maintained, the lack of c-command between A positions in weak crossover structures should suffice to rule out the coindexing relation. We will see that the Palauan facts distinguish between these two approaches, and that the lack of a weak crossover effect in Palauan will show both to be too strong.

3. STRONG CROSSOVER IN PALAUAN

We begin the investigation of crossover in Palauan with the strong crossover constructions. In strong crossover, a pronoun c-commands a coindexed variable (or name). I will show that Palauan supports the GB account of such cases, in which their ungrammaticality is due to violation of Principle C of the binding theory. I will also show how Palauan's observance of Principle C in crossover contexts argues that (17) is not a definition but simply a description, and that the correct definition of variable is featural.

Typically, since subjects c-command the rest of the sentence, the pronoun involved in strong crossover is in subject position. Since Palauan is a VOS language, the data that follow should provide a crucial

192   CHAPTER SIX

test of the c-command hypothesis as opposed to hypotheses of crossover
that appeal to linear order. If c-command alone can account for the
facts, as Reinhart predicts, the order of the subject in relation to other
NPs in the sentence is irrelevant to the analysis of strong crossover.

Before we consider the data, we should recall the role of Palauan verb
morphology in indicating an extraction site (the full discussion is in
Chapter Three, section 3). If the verb in an A′ binding domain has realis
morphology (glossed R), this indicates that its subject is (or contains)
the extraction site. If the verb has irrealis morphology (glossed IR), the
extraction site is (or is contained in) a nonsubject.

Some Palauan examples of strong crossover involving WH quantification are seen in (25) ('*pro*' refers to an empty pronoun that is *not*
bound, and '___' indicates the null resumptive pronoun):

(25) a. *ngte'a$_i$ [a ldilu   [el kmo ngmerau ___$_i$] pro$_i$]?
     who   *IR-3-said that   R-rich*

     (Who$_i$ did he$_i$ say t_i is rich?)

   b. *ngte'a$_i$ [a lomdasu   [el kmo akmengull er ngii$_i$] pro$_i$]?
     who   *IR-3-think that   R-1s-respect P 3s*

     (Who$_i$ does he$_i$ think I respect t_i?)

In these examples, the surface realization of WH agreement shows that
the variable is not the subject of the matrix verb. The matrix subject
position contains a null pronoun[11] which c-commands the variable; by
Principle C, these two positions cannot be coindexed. In (25a), the
variable is the embedded subject; in (25b), it is the overt resumptive
pronoun **ngii**, both coindexed with **te'a** 'who'. Both sentences are ungrammatical with the coindexing indicated.

In comparison, counterparts of the sentences in (25) are grammatical
when the identity of variable and pronoun are reversed:

(26) a. ngte'a$_i$ [a dilu   [el kmo ngmerau pro$_i$] ___$_i$]?
     who   *R-said that   R-rich*

     Who$_i$ t_i said that she$_i$ is rich?

   b. ngte'a$_i$ [a omdasu [el kmo akmengull er ngii$_i$] ___$_i$]?
     who   *R-think that   R-1s-respect P 3s*

     Who$_i$ t_i thinks that I respect her$_i$?

Here, the reader can verify that the variable is in matrix subject position,
on the basis of the realis morphology of the matrix verb.

It is important to keep in mind that the variable in all cases is a
resumptive pronoun, and that, in fact, all Palauan WH variables are
pronouns (cf. Chapter Four). The contrast in grammaticality between the

CROSSOVER CONSTRUCTIONS 193

sentences in (25) and those in (26) can be attributed directly to Principle C, however. Resumptive pronouns in crossover contexts in Palauan therefore act exactly like WH traces, which is just what we would expect in view of the analysis of resumptive pronouns in earlier chapters.

For completeness, we note that the structures in (25) are grammatical on the *non*-coindexed readings. (27a, b) correspond to (25a, b), respectively:

(27) a. ngte'a$_i$ [a ldilu   [el kmo ngmerau ____$_i$] *pro$_j$*]?
      who   *IR-3-said*   *that*   *R-rich*

      Who$_i$ did he$_j$ say t_i is rich?

   b. ngte'a$_i$ [a lomdasu   [el kmo akmengull   er ngii$_i$] *pro$_j$*]?
      who   *IR-3-think*   *that*   *R-1s-respect*   *P*   *3s*

      Who$_i$ does he$_j$ think I respect t_i?

As in (25), the irrealis morphology of **ldilu** 'said' reveals that the matrix subject is not the variable. Since this position and the extraction site are not coindexed, no rule of sentence anaphora is violated.

We know that Palauan also allows WH in situ (see Chapters Three and Four). Assuming a rule like WH movement in LF, which provides a variable at a stage of derivation later than S-structure, sentences like (25a, b) are also expected to be ungrammatical with the WH phrase in argument position. This is the case, as can be seen in (28):

(28) a. *ngdilu   [el kmo ngmerau a **te'ang$_i$**] *pro$_i$*?
      R-3s-said   *that*   *R-3s-rich*   *who*

      (Who$_i$ did he$_i$ say t_i is rich?)

   b. *ngomdasu [el kmo akmengull   er a **te'ang$_i$**] *pro$_i$*?
      R-3s-think   *that*   *R-1s-respect* *P*   *who*

      (Who$_i$ does he$_i$ think I respect t_i?)

Palauan also allows a WH phrase with wide scope to be in an embedded A′ position at S-structure. Sentences parallel to those in (25), in which the embedded WH operator has wide semantic scope,[12] are seen in (29):

(29) a. *ngdilu   [el kmo ngte'a$_i$ a merau ____$_i$] *pro$_i$*
      R-3s-said   *that*   *who*   *R-rich*

      (Who$_i$ did he$_i$ say t_i is rich?)

   b. *ngomdasu [el kmo ngte'a$_i$ a kungull   er ngii$_i$] *pro$_i$*
      R-3s-think   *that*   *who*   *IR-1s-respect*   *P*   *3s*

      (Who$_i$ does he$_i$ think I respect t_i?)

194 CHAPTER SIX

(25) and (27) through (29) show that, regardless of the S-structure position of the WH phrase, coindexing between the pronoun and the variable it c-commands is impossible. This is as predicted, since strong crossover holds of the output of movement in LF. At LF, (25), (28), and (29) are indistinguishable.

Finally, the counterparts of the sentences in (25), in which a name appears in the place of the variable, are also ungrammatical. (As was the case in (27), these sentences are grammatical if the pronoun and the name are not coindexed.)

(30) a. *ngdilu   [el kmo ngmerau a Ngiriou$_i$] *pro$_i$*
    R-3s-said   that   R-3s-rich

(He$_i$ said that Ngiriou$_i$ is rich.)

b. *ngomdasu [el kmo akmengull   er a Ngiriou$_i$] *pro$_i$*
    R-3s-think   that   R-1s-respect P

(He$_i$'s thinking that I respect Ngiriou$_i$.)

These facts support the claim that variables and names have the same behavior in strong crossover contexts, as the binding theory predicts. No R-expression can be coindexed with a c-commanding pronoun, so the examples in (30) receive exactly the same account as the examples in (25) (and their S-structure variants).

To sum up, Principle C accounts for the cases of strong crossover in Palauan in the same way as in English and other languages. On the account developed up to this point, the S-structure position of the WH phrase itself is irrelevant to the coindexing possibilities for variables and pronouns. Palauan's VOS order does not affect the analysis, and Leftness plays no role. A pronoun simply cannot be coindexed with a variable it c-commands.

Other views of the strong crossover effect have been taken, however; one is described in the next section.

3.1. *The Definition of 'Variable'*

It may not be surprising to find that the strong crossover facts fall out in the way I have described. This is what the theory predicts. But surprise may be appropriate after all. In the structures we have been analyzing, both the position of the variable and the position of the pronoun are occupied by D-structure *pronominals*. This introduces a number of considerations important to the crossover theory.

Obviously, in order to derive the effects illustrated above, the grammar must be able to distinguish between pronouns and variables; that is, between [+pronominal] and [−pronominal] elements. This is precisely

CROSSOVER CONSTRUCTIONS 195

the distinction that underlies strong crossover phenomena. A [+pronominal] element cannot c-command a (coindexed) R-expression. Recall that Reinhart's rule ((7)), which underlies the Principle C account, is violated if the c-commanded element is (interpreted as) a *nonpronoun*. That a trace can c-command a coindexed pronoun shows that the trace is [−pronominal]. The strong crossover facts thus provide fuel for the argument that a critical part of the definition of a variable is [−pronominal], presented in section 5.

Furthermore, the variable cannot be identified on the basis of the overt/nonovert distinction. The possibility in UG of a variable being overt and the possibility of *pro* being bound remove the morphological basis on which pronouns and variables are often distinguished.

To make these points concrete, consider the Palauan contrasts exhibited in (31) and (32) (cf. (28)):

(31) a. ngte'a$_i$ [a dilu   [el kmo ngmerau *pro$_i$*] *pro$_i$*]
          who   *R-said-3s that   R-3s-rich*

      Who$_i$ ___$_i$ said that he$_i$ is rich?

   b. ngte'a$_i$ [a ldilu   [el kmo ngmerau *pro$_i$*] *pro$_j$*]
          who   *IR-3-said that   R-3s-rich*

      Who$_i$ did he$_j$ say ___$_i$ is rich?

(32) a. Who$_i$ did he$_i$ say he$_i$ is rich?

   b. Who$_i$ did he$_j$ say he$_i$ is rich?

The sentences in (32) are literal translations of those in (31); (32a) corresponds to (31a), and (32b) to (31b). The English sentences are both ungrammatical, as English does not allow resumptive pronouns.

Note the realis morphology on the matrix verb in (31a) and the irrealis morphology on the matrix verb in (31b). This tells us that the *matrix pro* is construed as the variable in (31a), and the *embedded pro* as the variable in (31b). If both coindexed pronouns in (31a) were construed as variables, Principle C would be violated, since one R-expression would c-command another and both are in A position. (If neither *pro* is construed as a variable, the sentence is ruled out as an instance of vacuous quantification: the A′ operator has no variable to bind.) Since both sentences are grammatical, no principle is violated. Clearly, when one of two coindexed pronoun forms c-commands the other, the c-commanding position must be taken to be the variable. Palauan grammar therefore confirms the role of c-command in the analysis of binding, while it denies the role of overtness or nonovertness in that analysis.[13]

The question remains of how the variable is defined. Since the variable is a D-structure pronoun, the hierarchical structure of strong

196   CHAPTER SIX

crossover sentences does not alone determine their grammatical status.
And, of course, any A position can potentially contain a variable (cf.,
e.g., (31)). Any A position can potentially be A´ bound (in any language,
modulo the effect of other systems). That is, in order for the usual definition ((17)) to apply, the grammar *must already know* which position,
among several, is A´ bound.

Let us consider, then, in what way a variable is specified by the
grammar of a language like Palauan. As a starting point, I repeat below
the usual definition of variable. With it, I give the accompanying definition of pronominal (see also the contextual definition of empty categories in Chapter One):

(33) a. *Variable*:

α is a variable if α is in an A position
and is locally A´ bound.

b. *Pronominal*:

α is a pronominal if α is in an A position and is free, or
locally A bound by an element with an independent θ-role.

These definitions apply to the sentences in (31) as follows. In (31a), the
pronoun in the matrix is locally A´ bound, so it is construed as a variable. The pronoun in the embedding in (31a) is locally A bound (by the
matrix subject), so it is construed as a pronominal. In (31b), the pronoun
in the matrix is free, and it is the pronoun in the embedding that is the
variable.

Sportiche (1985) suggests that, given the definitions in (33), Principle
C is superfluous to the account of strong crossover. He points out that in
a sentence like (34), it is the pronoun *he* that is locally A´ bound and
construed as the variable, and the empty category *e* is A bound by *he*
and is construed as the pronominal:

(34)   *Who_i did he_i see e_i?

Sportiche argues that the definitions in (33) are sufficient to rule out this
sentence, since English allows neither resumptive subject pronouns (in
such contexts), nor empty object pronominals (see also Chomsky 1986a,
n. 26).

Palauan has both resumptive subject pronouns and object *pro*, both of
which can be locally A´ bound. Sportiche's account of the ungrammaticality of (34) therefore does not generalize. Note that this analysis relies
crucially on the purely contextual definition of variable in (17), which
forces *he* in (34) to be taken as an A´ bound position. The Palauan facts
show reliance on this definition to be mistaken. First, a pronoun in this
position *can* be A´ bound. And second, we still need Principle C to rule
out a sentence in which a pronoun form in this position c-commands a

CROSSOVER CONSTRUCTIONS 197

coindexed pronoun construed as a variable. This is the case of (31), and of the example in (35), which corresponds to (34):

(35) *ngte'a$_i$ a lbilsang   ____$_i$ pro$_i$
      who   IR-3-saw-3s

      (Who$_i$ did he$_i$ see ____$_i$?)

Both subject and object positions contain what is a null pronoun at D-structure. Either could independently be A′ bound. Given *intrinsic* features which distinguish variables (and pronouns), a structure with this coindexing can be ruled out by a principle relying on c-command: the [−pronominal] variable cannot be c-commanded by the coindexed [+pronominal] pronoun). That is, the variable has intrinsic features, features that are visible to the syntax in the same way as such categorial features are visible on any other NP. Both sentences are grammatical.

(35) is not ruled out, however, in Sportiche's analysis. That is, Principle C rules out some configurations of [+pronominal] and [−pronominal] elements, but (33a) does not. The conclusion is that (33a) is an (extensional) description of the syntactic entity 'variable', but not its definition. A variable is indeed locally A′ bound, but it is an intrinsically [−pronominal, −anaphor] element that is locally A′ bound.[14] I therefore do not appeal to (33a) in the analysis of resumptive pronouns.

So far, we have no definition of variable that is general enough to allow for WH traces as well as for all uses of resumptive pronouns. Let us assume for the moment that any position containing a pronoun can potentially be bound in Palauan. In the strong crossover configurations, Principle C will terminate a derivation in which the "wrong" pronoun is chosen, exactly as it terminates the analogous movement derivation. In weak crossover, Principle C does not apply, yet in weak crossover too, the definition of variable is crucial. Consideration of the properties of weak crossover configurations in Palauan will clarify the ways in which a variable is specified. I now turn to these constructions, and will then return in section 5 to this problem of definition. (See also comments on (17) in section 4.5.)

4. WEAK CROSSOVER

In weak crossover, anaphora is blocked between a trace and a pronoun, or a quantified phrase and a pronoun, in sentences in which neither c-commands the other. I repeat in (36) the familiar paradigm:

(36) a. *His* students respect *Steve*.

     b.* *Who* do *his* students respect *t* ?

     c.* *His* students respect *everyone*.

198   CHAPTER SIX

The case of backward pronominalization with a name, (36a), contrasts
with the cases like (36b) and (36c), in which anaphora is prohibited (or
if not prohibited, then marginal). Below we will see that Palauan does
not follow this paradigm at all. I will attempt to show just what the
anaphora conditions are in Palauan, and how they bear on theories of
anaphora in GB.

Since Palauan has no weak crossover effect, all the theories described
above which attempt to derive weak crossover in terms of universal
principles are weakened. The proposal that I offer below is that weak
crossover (WCO) is essentially an ECP effect, that is, that it can be
derived from the theory of government. In order to arrive at that
analysis, the relevant structures of Palauan must be examined carefully. I
will first show that there is a precedence effect in Palauan that initially
clouds the picture, but, once we dispose of the influence of the precedence constraint, the underlying government-theoretic issues become
clear.

4.1. *The Structures*

Consider, now, the sentences in (37):

(37) a. ng-te'a$_i$ a lilsa   ____$_i$ [a retonari   er ngii$_i$]
        who   *IR-3-saw-3s*   *neighbors P   her*
     Who$_i$ did her$_i$ neighbors see t_i ?

    b. ng-te'a$_i$ a longull   er ngii$_i$ [a rengelekel *pro$_i$*]
        who   *IR-3-respect P   her*   *children-3s*
     Who$_i$ do her$_i$ children respect t_i ?

(37) are typical of the weak crossover construction. (That **ngii** in (37b)
is the variable and *pro* the pronoun is demonstrated overtly by WH
agreement.) The bijection theory of Koopman and Sportiche (1982)
requires that both **ngii** and *pro* be bound, and predicts that these sentences are ruled out as a bijection principle violation. The Parallelism
Constraint on Operator Binding (Safir 1984) might be thought to reject
these sentences, since **ngii** and *pro* are not parallel; but the issue is
obscured by Safir's taking resumptive *pro* to be lexical. Finally, the
c-command theory will exclude configurations of this type since the variable does not c-command the pronoun. Unlike (36b), however, and contrary to expectation, the sentences in (37) are completely grammatical.

Now, recall that WH phrases need not be preposed at S-structure, but
can optionally remain in situ. Nothing in the grammar forces Move α to
apply to WH phrases prior to S-structure, so both (38a) and (38b) are
grammatical:

CROSSOVER CONSTRUCTIONS 199

(38) a. ng-omele'a a ngera er a mlai a Sabeth
     3s-put   what? P   car

What did Sabeth put in the car?

b. ng-ngera$_i$ a lomele'a ____$_i$ er a mlai a Sabeth
   what?   IR-3-put   P   car

What did Sabeth put in the car?

This being the case, we would predict that sentences like (37) would be equally grammatical when the WH phrases are in situ. That is, a WH in situ is fully grammatical in itself, and, since the sentences have the same LF, the status of the sentences in (37) above and (39) below should be the same from the point of view of theories of WCO. This is not the case, however:

(39) a. ??temilsa   a te'a$_i$ a retonari er ngii$_i$
         3p-saw-3s   who?   neighbors P   her

(Who did her neighbors see?)

b. ??temengull er a te'a$_i$ a rengelekel *pro$_i$*
    3p-respect P   who?   children-3s

(Who do her children respect?)

With the coindexing indicated, the sentences with WH in situ are marginal, at best, and their counterparts in (37) are strongly preferred. Since (37) are fine, and (37) and (39) have equivalent LF structures, it cannot be the WCO effect that degrades the grammaticality of the examples in (39). Nor is it simply that the WH phrase must be preposed in WCO structures, as we will see.

Interestingly, sentences corresponding to (37) are also less grammatical when the subject is topicalized, a structure otherwise unexceptional:[15]

(40) a. ??[a rengelekel *pro*] a mengull er a te'ang____
         children-3s   R-respect P   who

(Who$_i$ do her$_i$ children respect t_i?)

b. ngte'a a longull   er ngii [a rengelekel *pro*]
    who   IR-3-respect P   her   children-3s

Who$_i$ do her$_i$ children respect t_i?

In (40a) the subject, which contains a *pro* specifier, is topicalized, and in (40b) the WH phrase is topicalized. In both, anaphora between the WH phrase and the pronoun is possible: since these are monoclausal WH questions, the WH phrase can be interpreted as having scope over the

200   CHAPTER SIX

sentence even when it is in situ, by whatever LF rule determines the
logical scope of WH phrases that are in argument position in surface
structure (similarly for (39)). What is odd is that (40b) is the only
fully grammatical structure. The WCO configuration actually improves
grammaticality. Since (40a) and (40b) have the same structure at LF,
again, it cannot be a weak crossover effect that makes (40a) less
grammatical.

Paradigms equivalent to (39) and (40) could be supplied for the
examples in (41), which further illustrate the lack of the weak crossover
effect in WH questions:

(41) a. ngte'a a lilsa   ____ [a retonari   er ngii]
         who   *IR-3-saw-3s*   *neighbors P   him*

         Who$_i$ did his$_i$ neighbors see ____$_i$?

     b. ngdiak kudengei   el kmo ngte'a a lbilsa   ____ a
         Neg   *IR-1s-know Comp who*   *IR-3-gave-3s*

         tiket   [a delal   *pro*]
         ticket   mother-3s

         I don't know who$_i$ his$_i$ mother gave the ticket to ____$_i$.

     c. ngte'a a lbileng'ii   ____ a 'ermel   el bilis
         who   *IR-3-bit-3s*   *animal-3s L   dog*

         Who$_i$ did his$_i$ dog bite ____$_i$?

One way of accounting for the facts might begin with the observation
that the WH phrase in (37), (40b), and (41) not only c-commands but
also precedes the pronoun. That is, even though a WH phrase may
optionally occur in situ, we should consider the possibility that the
Palauan conditions on indefinite NP anaphora require a WH phrase to
be in operator position. Keeping this possibility in mind, we now look at
data involving the logical quantifiers.

There are two lexical items that correspond to the universal quantifier
in Palauan: **bek** 'each, every' (**rebek** when modifying [+human] NPs),
and **rokui** 'all'. They enter into coindexing relations with pronouns in
exactly the same way and can normally be substituted for each other. I
will illustrate their properties with examples using **rebek**. A special
property of these expressions is that they can only be coindexed with a
plural resumptive pronoun:

(42) a. akiulemes   er a rebek el 'ad
         R-1p-watch P   every L person

         We were watching everyone.

CROSSOVER CONSTRUCTIONS 201

(42) b. a rebek el 'ad   a kimulemes   er tir$_i$ /*ngii$_i$
*every L person   IR-1p-watch P **3p   3s**

We were watching everyone.

(43) a. *a rebek el 'ad   a oltoir er [a delal   *pro*] ___
every L person   R-love P   mother-3s

(Everyone$_i$ loves his/her$_i$ mother.)

b. a rebek el 'ad   a oltoir er [a rederir   *pro*] ___
every L person   R-love P   mother-3p

Everyone$_i$ loves their$_i$ mother.

(42) and (43) show that the universal quantifier **rebek** can neither bind a
singular resumptive pronoun nor be coindexed with any other singular
pronoun (the same holds for the quantifier **rokui** 'all'). In the next pair of
examples, I attempt to force the reading 'each NP' by using the quantified expression **ta me a ta el** NP, literally 'one and one of NP'.[16] Even
with this expression, which would seem to represent a distributive reading, a coindexed pronoun must be plural:

(44) a. [a ta me a ta el senator] a dilu   el kmo a Merii
       each   R-said that

⎰ a ulemes   er tir /*ngii
⎱ *R-Im-saw P 3p   3s*
⎰ a milsterir   /*milsang
⎱ *R-Pf-saw-3p   R-Pf-saw-3s*

[Each senator]$_i$ said that Merii saw them$_i$/*him$_i$.

b. [a ta me a ta el senator] a longull   er tir
   each   IR-3-respect P 3p

[a rengelekir *pro*] /*[a rengelekel *pro*]
children-3p   *children-3s*

Their$_i$/*his$_i$ children respect [each senator]$_i$.

The lack of a distributive reading for any of the expressions translating
the universal quantifier shows that **rebek** and similar expressions can
only have a group reading, and a pronoun coindexed with one of them
refers to the same group that is the range of the quantified phrase.[17]
There is no well-formed expression in which **ngii** or singular *pro*, which
range over individuals, can be coindexed with a universally quantified
phrase. This explains the use of singular and plural resumptive pronouns; the difference does not affect the analysis further, however.
   Observe now the facts of coindexing between **rebek el 'ad** and a

CHAPTER SIX

specifier in (45); in the (a) and (b) sentences, the S-structure position of the quantifier varies:

(45) a. *temengull er a **rebek el 'ad**$_i$ a retonari   er tir$_i$
   3p-respect P   every   person   neighbors P   their

   (Their$_i$ neighbors respect everyone$_i$.)

   b. a **rebek el 'ad**$_i$ [$_{IP}$ a longull   er tir$_i$ a retonari   er tir$_i$]
   every   person   3-respect P   them   neighbors P   their

   Their$_i$ neighbors respect everyone$_i$.

Example (45a) is impossible as it stands,[18] but if the quantified object is a topic, as it is in (45b), the sentence is grammatical. Again, (45b) is fine; both examples in (45) have the same LF structure, so there is no account of the ungrammaticality of (45a) in terms of WCO theories. In fact, the weak crossover configuration in (45b) actually *improves* grammaticality, just as we saw, for example, in (40b).

Thus the pattern of binding and coindexing in (37) and subsequent examples has revealed a surprising fact: that grammaticality of these examples depends on precedence (as well as c-command) of the antecedent. Whether or not the WCO configuration is present appears to be irrelevant. This is summed up in the contrasts in (46) and (47):

(46) a. *temengull er a rebek el 'ad   [a retonari   er tir]
   3p-respect P   every L person   neighbors P   3p

   (Their$_i$ neighbors respect eveyone$_i$.)

   b. *temengull er [a retonari   er tir] a rebek el 'ad
   3p-respect P   neighbors P   3p   every L person

   (Everyone$_i$ respects their$_i$ neighbors.)

   c. a rebek el 'ad   a longull   er tir [a retonari   er tir]
   each L person   IR-respect P   3p   neighbors P   3p

   Their$_i$ neighbors respect everyone$_i$.

   d. a rebek el 'ad   a mengull er [a retonari   er tir] ____
   each L person   R-respect P   neighbors P   3p

   Everyone$_i$ respects their$_i$ neighbors.

The first occurrence of **tir** in (46c) is the resumptive pronoun, the second a coindexed specifier of the subject. What is important to note is that while (46c) is a weak crossover structure, (46d) is not.

(47) exhibits the same pattern, this time with a null specifier; that the null pronoun is also plural is demonstrated by the form of NP agreement:

CROSSOVER CONSTRUCTIONS 203

(47) a. *toltoir   er a rebek el 'ad   [a rederir   *pro*]
       R-3p-love P   every L person   mother-3p

(Their$_i$ mother loves everyone$_i$.)

b. *toltoir   er [a rederir pro] a rebek el 'ad
    R-3p-love P   mother-3p   every L person

(Everyone$_i$ loves their$_i$ mother.)

c. a rebek el 'ad   a loltoir   er tir [a rederir   *pro*]
   each L person   IR-3-love P 3p   mother-3p

Their$_i$ mother loves everyone$_i$.

d. a rebek el 'ad   a oltoir er [a rederir   *pro*] ⎯⎯
   each L person   R-love P   mother-3p

Everyone$_i$ loves their$_i$ mother.

The (a) sentences of (46) and (47) are out, as are the (b) sentences; only the (a) sentences, however, potentially implicate the crossover issue. The examples in (46c) and (47c) are predicted to be weak crossover violations, but they are grammatical sentences. And again, (c) sentences are weak crossover configurations but (d) sentences are not. In (46b) and (47b), the subject c-commands the pronoun from its base position. It appears that, in all configurations in (46) and (47) (and in earlier pairs), the antecedent must be in an A′ position for coindexing between subject and object to be grammatical, both when the pronoun is contained in the subject (and the object contains the antecedent) *and* vice versa. Since the same constraints apply to (46c, d) and (47c, d) (and both (46a, b) and (47a, b) are ungrammatical), the phenomenon we are observing has nothing to do with weak crossover, but is instead a more general fact about Palauan grammar.

It is clear that these contrasts are due to a precedence effect, and not to weak crossover. This bears repeating, as it is crucial. The examples in (39), (40a), (45a), and (46a) are *not* ungrammatical because of weak crossover; their status is determined exactly as in (43b), (46d), and (47d), which are not WCO structures: by the requirement that, in cases of coindexing a pronoun, the antecedent precede the pronoun. Thus, the overall pattern displayed in (37) through (47) has *no bearing* on issues of crossover.

4.2. *Topicalizations*

In earlier chapters I have also analyzed topicalization of definite NPs as A′ binding structures involving variable binding. These structures are therefore expected to share properties with (37) through (47) above. As

204   CHAPTER SIX

might by now be expected, coindexing between a pronoun and a name is
affected by topicalization of the name (?? indicates questionable grammaticality on the coreferential reading):

(48) a. ??temengull er a Ngiraklang [a retonari   er ngii]
         3p-respect P   *neighbors P him*

         (His$_i$ neighbors respect Ngiraklang$_i$.)

     b. ??temengull er a Ngiraklang [a rengelekel *pro*]
                                                    students-3s

         (His$_i$ students respect Ngiraklang$_i$.)

     c. a Ngiraklang$_i$ a longull   er ngii$_i$ [a retonari   er ngii]
                          IR-respect P him   *neighbors P him*

         His$_i$ neighbors respect Ngiraklang$_i$.

     d. a Ngiraklang$_i$ a longull er ngii$_i$ [a rengelekel *pro*]
                                                    students-3s

         His$_i$ students respect Ngiraklang$_i$.

     e. *ngmengull er [a rengelekel *pro$_i$*] a Ngiraklang$_i$
         3s-respect P   students-3s

         (Ngiraklang$_i$ respects his$_i$ students.)

     f. a Ngiraklang$_i$ a mengull   er [a rengelekel *pro$_i$*] ____
                          R-respect P   students-3s

         Ngiraklang$_i$ respects his$_i$ students.

The contrast between (48a and b), in which **Ngiraklang** is in an A position, and (48c and d), in which **Ngiraklang** is topic, is exactly like the
contrast observed in WH questions and universally quantified sentences
above. Coindexing is facilitated when the antecedent is in an A' position. The examples in (48c and d) are, again, just the sort of structures
that would be expected to exhibit weak crossover. The sentences in (48e
and f) do not involve weak crossover, though the constraint requiring
topicalization of the name holds in these cases too. Thus, topicalization
follows the pattern of other A' binding constructions.

4.3. *Biclausal Structures*

The analysis of multi-clausal structures in which we might expect to find
weak crossover effects is very complicated. A discussion of all these
complications would only introduce confusion, and I will therefore not
include such a discussion. However, there is no clear evidence of a weak
crossover effect in structures in which a pronoun is contained within a

CROSSOVER CONSTRUCTIONS

clause that does not contain or c-command the antecedent (a structure such as (3), for example). The following examples illustrate this statement. The first example exhibits backward pronominalization controlled by a name, the second by a quantified phrase, and the third by a WH phrase:

(49) a. a 'ais   [el kmo [a ngelekel *pro$_i$* a mlo kot er a skuul]
       news *that*   *child-3s*   *Aux first P   school*

   a uremelii   a **Latii**$_i$ el   ulduruklii el mo er a Hawaii
   encourage-3s   *Comp send-3s   to go P*

   The news that her$_i$ son won first prize at school encouraged Latii$_i$ to send him to Hawaii.

   b. a 'ais   [el kmo ngmengull er tir$_i$ a Ngiraklang]
      news *that*   *3s-respect P   them*

   a ruleterir [a **rokui el 'ad**]$_i$ el mo ungil a rengrir
   made-3p   all   L person L go good   heart-3p

   The news that Ngiraklang respects them$_i$ made everyone$_i$ happy.

   c. a 'ais   [el kmo ngoltoir er ngii$_i$ a Ngiraklang]
      news *that*   *3s-love P 3s*

   a rullii   a **te'a**$_i$ el mo ungil a rengul
   made-3s   *who L go good   heart-3s*

   Who$_i$ did the news that Ngiraklang loves her$_i$ make ____$_i$ happy?

For reasons external to the anaphora issue, it is difficult to elicit well-formed versions of these sentences in which the antecedent is in operator position, leaving a variable in A position. And clearly, it is not necessary for the antecedent to precede the pronoun in these examples. Note also that the slight preference for names to precede their pronouns, which we observed in the monoclausal examples, is not exhibited in these sentences. This suggests that the precedence effect is limited to the clause immediately containing the pronoun.

All indications are that further research will not reveal a weak crossover effect in the multiclausal structures, although at this point the analysis is incomplete. I return now to the general discussion of the properties of variables in anaphoric constructions.

4.4. Impact; Summary

It is clear how these facts reflect on the theories mentioned earlier. On the one hand, the Leftness Condition appears to be validated, since the

206 CHAPTER SIX

configuration it rules out does not arise: Palauan being VOS, extraction of an object does not leave a variable to the right of its pronoun in these sentences. On the other hand, the facts are a problem for the accounts which focus on multiple variable binding by a single quantifier: not only does one quantifier bind multiple variables, but also the variables are nonparallel (one is lexical and one is null).

The c-command analysis considers WCO in terms of the A positions involved, on the assumption that not only the quantifier itself but also its variable must c-command the pronoun in order for A′ binding of the pronoun to be well-formed. Focussing on the A positions then, what we have seen is that in Palauan a variable is a better binder for a pronoun than is a quantified NP. The variable *can* antecede a pronoun to its left, though a QP or a WH-P cannot; this issue of precedence is general and goes well beyond WCO configurations (recall, for example, the contrast of examples (46b) and (46d)). In nontopicalized structures, coindexing between quantifier and pronoun is impossible, while coindexing between variable and pronoun (cf. WCO examples (37)) is unproblematic. This finding conflicts with the general view that the distribution of empty categories is more restricted than that of overt phrases.[19] But it also poses a grave problem for the c-command analysis of WCO.

This analysis assumes that a pronoun can be construed as a bound variable only by being coindexed with a c-commanding 'true' variable. I repeat (24) here:

(24)   If a pronoun P and a variable V are bound by the same quantifier, then V must c-command P.

In WCO structures, presumably the pronoun fails to be so bound.

Stowell (1987) and Stowell & Lasnik (1987) hold that the c-command account in (24) reflects the LF condition that underlies WCO. But we have by now seen many violations of (24). (24) not only does not determine the grammaticality of (37) and related examples, but, perhaps more important, it is also unable to account for the difference between these Palauan structures and their English counterparts. (Stowell 1987 argues, furthermore, that weak crossover is a special case of strong crossover, a point to be taken up below.)

One is forced to the conclusion, on the basis of the Palauan data (and data from other languages presented in Georgopoulos 1991b) that the presumably prohibited non-c-commanding relation between variable and pronoun is grammatical. I conclude that multiple variable binding is not ruled out on principle, and that well-formed A′ binding of variables and pronouns at LF depends on c-command by the quantifier but *does not require c-command of a pronoun by a variable*, i.e. (24) is not a necessary condition.

CROSSOVER CONSTRUCTIONS   207

4.4.1. *WCO as SCO?*

Stowell (1987) introduces an interesting analysis in which weak cross-over is reduced to a special case of strong crossover (SCO), via an extension of the device of slash indexing (Haïk 1984, Safir 1984). He suggests that a slash index may be given to any phrase containing a bound variable. Then the subject in a WCO configuration would have not only its own index but also that of the bound position it contains, and the latter index would c-command the index of the trace, violating strong crossover (Stowell's examples):

(50) a. *who$_i$ does his$_i$ boss dislike t_i

b. *who$_i$ does [[his$_i$ boss]$_{k/i}$ dislike t_i]

To see why this reduction cannot work, consider again the discussion of Sportiche's (1985) analysis of strong crossover constructions. There I argued that only a c-command account was appropriate to account for the presence of strong crossover in Palauan, which has both subject resumptive pronouns and object *pro*. It is easy to see how this discussion bears on Stowell's proposal to reduce WCO to SCO: Palauan has strong crossover but not weak crossover. SCO can only be analyzed in terms of c-command. The two effects therefore have different accounts. It is likely that SCO is 'universal', in the sense that all languages have it, while WCO evidently is not.

4.5. *Parasitic Gaps?*

When the antecedent is in operator position, coindexing between two A positions is grammatical in Palauan, even when this A´ binding structure is the configuration that is expected to give rise to weak crossover effects. The unexpected grammaticality of these structures is suggestive of the case of 'scrambling' in Japanese, described in Hoji (1985). Hoji shows that the leftward movement of NPs (scrambling) can create weak crossover configurations that are nevertheless grammatical. (Japanese does have weak crossover effects in other structures.) In order to account for this grammaticality, Hoji proposes that the empty pronoun over which the scrambled NP moves is actually a parasitic gap.[20] He points out that this empty category occurs in a position inaccessible to movement and appears to be licensed by the movement of the scrambled NP. Parasitic gap structures are more acceptable than weak crossover structures, so if Hoji's theory is correct, the sentences in question would be expected to be grammatical.

Consider the paradigm repeated in (51):

208   CHAPTER SIX

(51) a. ngte'a$_i$ a longull   er ngii$_i$ [a rengelekel *pro$_i$*]
       who   IR-3-respect P 3s   children-3s
       Who$_i$ do his$_i$ students respect t_i? (=(40b))

    b. a Ngiraklang$_i$ a longull   er ngii$_i$ [a rengelekel *pro$_i$*]
              IR-3-respect P 3s   students-3s
       His$_i$ students respect Ngiraklang$_i$. (=(48d))

    c. [a rebek el 'ad]$_i$ a loltoir   er tir$_i$ [a rederir   *pro$_i$*]
       every L person   IR-3-love P 3p   mother-3p
       Their$_i$ mother loves everyone$_i$. (=(47c))

The first NP in each sentence is an A$'$ binder: it is a WH phrase in
(51a), a topic in (51b), and a quantified phrase in (51c). The extraction
site in these cases is occupied by an overt pronoun. Though weak crossover configurations, the sentences in (51) are grammatical.

The hypothesis is now that the coindexing of the specifier in (51) is
parasitic on the coindexing between the resumptive pronoun and the A$'$
antecedent. It is true that when the object binder is in its D-structure
position, the grammaticality of the construction is marginal. Compare
(51) and (52), in which the antecedent is in situ at S-structure:

(52) a.   ?temengull *er a* te'a$_i$ [a rengelekel *pro$_i$*]
          3p-respect P   who   *students-3s*
          Who$_i$ do his$_i$ students respect t_i?

    b.   ??temengull er a **Ngiraklang**$_i$ [a rengelekel *pro$_i$*]
         3p-respect P   *students-3s*
         (His$_i$ students respect Ngiraklang$_i$)

    c.   ??toltoir er a **rebek el 'ad**$_i$ [a rederir   *pro$_i$*]
         3p-love P   every L person   *mother-3p*
         (Their$_i$ mother loves everyone$_i$)

Since (52a and c) and (51a and c) have the same structure at LF, the
grammaticality of structures like (51) is so far unexplained. Could the
specifier in (51) in fact be parasitic?

If the facts of (51) and (52) can be accounted for in the way Hoji
suggests for Japanese, the problem would be solved rather simply. It
does not seem that this analysis is available, however, for a number of
reasons. One is that nearly any NP position can independently be a
legitimate extraction site in Palauan. There is no sense in which these
variables in weak crossover structures can be regarded as 'parasitic' or
otherwise inaccessible to binding (see the discussion in Chapter Four).

CROSSOVER CONSTRUCTIONS 209

A more serious obstacle to the parasitic gap analysis for Palauan is the fact that the constraint that forces the antecedent of a pronoun to be in an A′ position extends beyond weak crossover structures to structures in which the antecedent is a subject. In these cases, when the subject c-commands the pronoun from its base position, it cannot be coindexed with that pronoun:

(53) a. ?ngmengull er [a rengelekel *pro$_i$*] a te'ang$_i$
  3s-respect P   students-3s   who

   Who$_i$ respects his$_i$ students?

 b.*ngmengull er [a rengelekel *pro$_i$*] a Ngiraklang$_i$
  3s-respect P   students-3s

   (Ngiraklang$_i$ respects his$_i$ students.)

 c.*toltoir er [a rederir   *pro$_i$*] a rebek el 'ad$_i$
  3p-love P   mother-3p   every L person

   (Everyone$_i$ loves their$_i$ mother.)

The examples in (53) are not weak crossover contexts. Coindexing should be unproblematic here, since the antecedent c-commands the pronoun. Yet the pattern of grammaticality in (53) is about the same as in (51). The sentences in (53) are grammatical when the subject is topicalized, as in (54):

(54) a. ngte'a$_i$ a mengull er [a rengelekel *pro$_i$*] ——$_i$
  who   R-respect P   students-3s

   Who$_i$ respects his$_i$ students?

 b. a Ngiraklang$_i$ a mengull er [a rengelekel *pro$_i$*] ——$_i$
          R-respect P   students-3s

   Ngiraklang$_i$ respects his$_i$ students.

 c. a rebek el 'ad$_i$ a oltoir er [a rederir   *pro$_i$*] ——$_i$
  every L person   R-love P   mother-3p

   Everyone$_i$ loves their$_i$ mother.

The contrasts of (53) and (54) show that the parasitic gap hypothesis for sentences like (51) cannot be maintained. This hypothesis rests on the structural similarity of weak crossover and parasitic gap structures: both involve non-c-commanding coindexed A positions. The difference is that weak crossover structures contain a pronoun and a trace, while parasitic gap structures contain two gaps, one licensed by the other. The reinterpretation proposed by Hoji involves, essentially, a switch in the identity of the pronoun. (53) and (54) do not have the structure necessary to this analysis, at any level. Since the same constraint must be at work in all the

210   CHAPTER SIX

examples in (51) through (54), the weak crossover issue (and therefore the parasitic gap analysis) is irrelevant.

A third difficulty in applying Hoji's approach to the Palauan case lies in the fact that Palauan grammar distinguishes variables from pronouns in a way that can be seen morphologically. As we know, both variables and pronouns in Palauan can be either null or lexical. Therefore it is not by their form that these two elements are distinguished, but rather by other properties. Variables trigger WH agreement, while other pronouns do not. This can be seen in (45b) and (43b), repeated here (the *resumptive* pronoun is in boldface):

(55) a. a rebek el 'ad   a longull   er **tir**   [a retonari   *er tir]*
       every L person   IR-3-respect P them   neighbors P them
       Their$_i$ neighbors respect everyone$_i$

   b. a rebek el 'ad   a oltoir   er [a rederir   *pro]* **pro**
      every L person   R-love   P   mother-3p
      Everyone$_i$ loves their$_i$ mother

In (55a) the pronoun specifier (**tir**) is overt, and in (55b) it is null; both are anaphoric to the quantified topic, but the mood morphology of the verb depends on the Case of the extraction site of the topic, not the Case of the (NP containing the) pronoun. In (55a) the extraction site is assigned a non-Nominative Case; therefore the verb is irrealis. The specifier in (55a) is within the Nominative NP, however, so if it were the variable it would trigger realis agreement. Conversely, in (55b) the resumptive pronoun is Nominative, and the verb is realis; the pronoun in the object NP has no effect on verb morphology. If (55) represented a parasitic gap structure, however, the parasitic element would be construed as a variable, just as it is in other parasitic gap structures in Palauan (see Chapter Four). It should therefore have an effect on WH agreement. Since it does not (and *cannot*, without altering the interpretation of these sentences), the facts of (55) must count as another obstacle to the parasitic gap analysis.

The foregoing argument suggests that the non-extraction-site pronoun in WCO structures is not a variable (since it does not trigger WH agreement). This may be considered indirect support for my rejection of (17), and for the featural analysis suggested in this chapter. By (17), both A positions are variables. But only the A position that shares its θ-role with the A′ binder (the extraction site) acts like a variable for WH agreement.

4.6. *The Conditions on Anaphora*

Let us sum up our findings to this point. Weak crossover constructions involving WH quantifiers, logical quantifiers, and other A′ binders in

CROSSOVER CONSTRUCTIONS   211

Palauan have exhibited practically the mirror-image of what is predicted of these constructions. The cases that are predicted to be bad, those in which an operator is coindexed with both a variable and a pronoun, are perfectly good. And the cases in which (the potential) A′ binder is in situ are bad. So far we have seen no evidence of weak crossover, but the facts call for some explanation.

As an initial hypothesis, we suggested that Palauan requires both c-command and linear precedence of the antecedent at S-structure. Precedence alone is not sufficient to allow coindexing. In the examples repeated below, the quantified phrase precedes the pronoun, but co-indexing is marginal or impossible:

(56) a. ??temengull   er a **te'a** [a rengelekel *pro*]
　　　　 R-3p-respect P   who   students-3s

　　　　 (Who$_i$ do his$_i$ children respect t_i?)

　　 b. *temengull er a **rebek el 'ad**   [a retonari   er tir]
　　　　 3p-respect P   every L person   neighbors P   3p

　　　　 (Their$_i$ neighbors respect everyone$_i$.)

　　 c. *toltoir   er a **rebek el 'ad**   [a rederir   *pro*]
　　　　 R-3p-love P   every L person   mother-3p

　　　　 (Their$_i$ mother loves everyone$_i$.)

　　 d. ??temengull   er a **Ngiraklang** [a retonari   er ngii]
　　　　 R-3p-respect P   neighbors P   3s

　　　　 (His$_i$ neighbors respect Ngiraklang$_i$.)

Nor is c-command alone sufficient to permit anaphora between these positions. The grammaticality is roughly the same in the reverse con-figuration, where the quantified phrase or name is the subject:[21]

(57) a. ?ngmengull er [a rengelekel *pro$_i$*] a **te'ang**$_i$
　　　　 3s-respect P   students-3s   who

　　　　 Who$_i$ respects his$_i$ students?

　　 b. *ngmengull er [a rengelekel *pro$_i$*] a **Ngiraklang**$_i$
　　　　 3s-respect P   students-3s

　　　　 (Ngiraklang$_i$ respects his$_i$ students.)

　　 c. *toltoir   er [a rederir   *pro$_i$*] a **rebek el 'ad**$_i$
　　　　 3p-love P   mother-3p   every L person

　　　　 (Everyone$_i$ loves their$_i$ mother.)

212   CHAPTER SIX

The sentences in (58), with a subject topic, have unblemished grammaticality:

(58) a.   **ngte'a**$_i$ a   mengull   er   [a   rengelekel   *pro*$_i$]   ____$_i$
          who   *R-respect P*   *students-3s*

          Who$_i$ respects his$_i$ students?

    b.   a **Ngiraklang**$_i$ a   mengull   er   [a   rengelekel   *pro*$_i$]   ____$_i$
                               R-respect P   *students-3s*

          Ngiraklang$_i$ respects his$_i$ students.

    c.   a **rebek el 'ad**$_i$ a   oltoir   er   [a   rederir   *pro*$_i$]   ____$_i$
          every L person   *R-love P*   *mother-3p*

          Everyone$_i$ loves their$_i$ mother.

These examples strengthen the conclusion that both precedence and c-command constrain coindexing in the structures we have observed.

So far, all the examples we have considered involve coindexing between the subject and a position within VP. We should now consider whether both conditions on anaphora — precedence and c-command — also constrain coindexing more generally. That is, we need to know whether there is a general rule for all Palauan anaphora that refers to precedence as well as c-command. There is evidence from other structures in Palauan that precedence is neither necessary nor sufficient to account for the whole range of anaphora possibilities.

First, within VP, precedence is not a necessary condition to coindexing between complements. The examples in (59) and (60) illustrate this:

(59) a.   a Dirrabkau   a   milsa   a   urerel   a Ngiraklang
                            R-gave-3s   *work-3s*

          Dirrabkau gave Ngiraklang$_i$ his$_i$ job.

    b.   a Dirrabkau   a   milsa   a   Ngiraklang   a   urerel
                            R-gave-3s   *work-3s*

          Dirrabkau gave Ngiraklang$_i$ his$_i$ job.

(60) a.   ngliliang   a   ngalek   er   a   bet   er   ngii   a Latii
          R-3s-put   *child   P   bed   P   3s*

          Latii put the child$_i$ in her$_i$ bed.

    b.   ngliliang   er   a   bet   er   ngii   a   ngalek   a Latii
          R-3s-put   P   bed   P   3s   child

          Latii put the child$_i$ in her$_i$ bed.

The verb **msa** 'give', exhibited in (59), subcategorizes two NP complements; (59) shows that coreference is permitted between these NPs, in

CROSSOVER CONSTRUCTIONS 213

whichever order they occur. Similarly, **loiang** 'put', exhibited in (60), subcategorizes an NP complement and a PP complement. NPs in these positions may corefer, regardless of their relative order. By the usual assumptions, these two positions c-command each other, and both are governed by V.

In contrast, in sentences with VSO order, precedence is not sufficient for coreference. In the examples in (61) and (62), sentences with VSO order are contrasted with their VOS counterparts. VSO order is very restricted in Palauan but is permitted under certain conditions, usually when no ambiguity of grammatical function (on the basis of animacy and so on) is possible between subject and object. As we saw above, the subject cannot be coindexed with a pronoun in the VP unless it has been topicalized; this is shown in the VOS sentences in (61a) and (62a). In the (b) sentences, the subject *precedes* the pronoun, but coreference is still not possible:

(61) a. ngrirellii   [a bet er ngii] a Dan
      R-3s-made-3s   *bed P 3s*

     Dan_i made $\text{his}_{j/*i}$ bed.

    b. ngrirellii   a Dan [a bet er ngii]
      R-3s-made-3s   *bed P 3s*

     Dan_i made $\text{his}_{j/*i}$ bed.

(62) a. ngulterau [a mlil   *pro*] a Merii
      R-3s-sold   *car-3s*

     Merii_i sold $\text{her}_{j/*i}$ car.

    b. ngulterau a Merii [a mlil   *pro*]
      R-3s-sold   *car-3s*

     Merii_i sold $\text{her}_{j/*i}$ car.

Even when VSO order is grammatical, the subject cannot antecede the pronoun. I will not attempt an analysis of VSO sentences in Palauan here; I will simply assume that the conditions on coindexing between subject and object are not satisfied in the configuration of VSO sentences.

In sum, examination of a wider range of facts shows that precedence of an antecedent is neither necessary nor sufficient to account for all cases of coindexing between an NP, definite or indefinite, and a pronoun. Between external subject and an argument within VP, however, both precedence and c-command appear to be crucial to coindexing.

214   CHAPTER SIX

4.7. *Anaphora between Subject and Object*

One way of analyzing the necessity of topicalizing the antecedent in cases of anaphora between the positions of subject and complement is in terms of the external and internal arguments of the verb. It appears that a variable in IP is able to serve as antecedent for a pronoun in VP, even when a name or a quantified NP cannot. If this is the case, it is an unusual and interesting finding, since, as mentioned earlier, it is usually assumed that variables have more restricted coindexing properties than names.[22]

Assuming this hypothesis about variables, consider again (39b)/(40b) and (48a, c), repeated in (63) and (64):

(63) a. ??temengull   er a te'a [a rengelekel *pro*]
         R-3p-respect P   who   children-3s

         Who$_i$ do her$_i$ children respect t_i?

     b. ngte'a a longull   er ngii [a rengelekel *pro*]
         who   IR-3-respect P her   children-3s

         Who$_i$ do her$_i$ children respect t_i?

(64) a. ??temengull er a Ngiraklang [a retonari   er ngii]
         3p-respect P   neighbors P him

         (His$_i$ neighbors respect Ngiraklang$_i$.)

     b. a Ngiraklang$_i$ a longull   er ngii$_i$ [a retonari   er ngii]
                           IR-respect P him   neighbors P him

         His$_i$ neighbors respect Ngiraklang$_i$.

(63a) and (64a) contrast with (63b) and (64b) in that in the latter the variable can be an A position antecedent of the pronoun. The apparently greater freedom of a variable to antecede a pronoun is also observed in structures in which the variable c-commands the pronoun. Subjects in the examples below alternately follow and precede pronominal specifiers. In the (a) sentences the subject is in argument position, in the (b) sentences a variable occupies this position:

(65) a.*temilengede'du' el kirel [a urerir   *pro*] a Sabino
        3p-talk   L about   work-3p

       me a Moses
       and

       (*Sabino and Moses* were talking about *their* work.)

CROSSOVER CONSTRUCTIONS   215

(65) b. a Sabino me   a Moses a milengede'edu' el kirel
         and   *talk*   *L about*

    [a urerir   *pro*] ____
      work-3p

    Sabino and Moses were talking about *their* work.

(66) a. *nguridii [a til   *pro*] a Naomi
     3s-lost   bag-3s

    (*Naomi* lost *her* bag.)

   b. a Naomi a uridii [a til   *pro*] ____
          lost   bag-3s

    Naomi lost *her* bag.

When the subject in these sentences is in A position, it cannot control
the reference of the pronoun. When the subject is replaced by a variable,
however, the variable *can* antecede the pronoun. In other words, a
pronoun can be coindexed with a variable that follows it, but not with a
name in the same position.

In the examples we have considered so far, the variable does not
necessarily c-command the pronoun, so even the c-command account of
weak crossover is too strong to allow for the Palauan facts: in Palauan, a
pronoun is able to be anteceded by a variable that does not c-command
it. Recall that this analysis holds only for anaphoric relations between
external and internal arguments of the verb. Palauan evidently imposes
special conditions on the relation between these positions, conditions
that do not hold elsewhere.

The optimal way of looking at the condition underlying these effects
may be, after all, in terms of the S-structure position of the antecedent,
rather than its variable. So far I have discussed directionality only in
terms of head government. But there may be a directional component to
antecedent government as well, if (some) antecedents must precede. Of
course, the strict directionality of canonical government should be distinguished from the notion of linear *precedence*. In a SOV language, for
example, directionality is presumably from right to left, while precedence
always refers to a left to right relation; if antecedents must precede, in
the SOV grammar, this is not canonical government. But the view of
binding articulated, e.g., by Stowell & Lasnik (1987), that "it is now
widely assumed that the precedence relation is irrelevant to . . . quantifi-
cational phenomena in general" is coming more and more into question.
I have already referred to Barss & Lasnik's (1986) proposal, based on
phenomena within the VP of double-object constructions, that precedence be included in the definition of bound anaphora domains. I have
presented evidence suggesting that precedence is necessary to bound

216   CHAPTER SIX

anaphora in another range of constructions. Barss & Lasnik's proposed definition of *domain*, which includes both c-command and precedence,

(67)   Y is in the domain of X iff X c-commands Y
        and X precedes Y.

seems a good start to the statement of the A′ binding condition that would apply to Palauan as well.

Before the exact status and applicability of a definition like this can be known, a wider range of languages and constructions showing precedence effects must be analyzed. It is important to note, however, that the definition makes the role of precedence explicit even for S-before-O languages, for which this role is usually automatic and is therefore usually not stated. Inclusion of a precedence statement for bound anaphora might also facilitate the account of *why* languages with Comp on the right have no WH movement, and are limited to scrambling to Spec(I) (e.g. Japanese).[23,24]

5. A GOVERNMENT-THEORETIC ACCOUNT OF WEAK CROSSOVER

Ungrammatical WCO structures typically illustrate the subject-object asymmetries that have revealed so much about the nature of government: in these structures the (bound) pronoun is typically in the subject, and the variable is in the complement; when the variable is (in) the subject and the pronoun (in) the complement, there is no crossover effect. This type of asymmetry suggests an ECP account.

Some recent formulations of the ECP impose directionality of head-government (i.e. canonical government à la Kayne), and in addition have replaced the earlier disjunction of the ECP with a conjunction: traces must be both head-governed *and* antecedent governed (Jaeggli 1982, 1985; Rizzi 1987; Stowell 1985; Aoun et al. 1987). In arguing for the Connectedness Condition (described in Chapter Four), this paper supports a conjunctive ECP, with the explicit condition on head government that it be canonical. Such an ECP, interacting with the position of the specifier, allows the grammar to account directly and automatically for the distribution of WCO effcts I have discussed.

In essence, the proposal is this: a specifier is set parametrically to be either initial or final in the phrase, and is thereby governed either canonically or contra-canonically; the WCO effect results from the failure of a specifier pronoun, construed as a variable, to be governed canonically. This proposal captures what we have observed so far: in a uniformly right-governing VOS language, all variables, pronominal or otherwise, are canonically governed, extraction is free, and WCO does

CROSSOVER CONSTRUCTIONS 217

not arise. Specifiers in a language like English, in contrast, are not in a canonically governed position, and English has WCO and related effects.

The connection between canonical government and WCO seems inescapable. Constructions that show the WCO effect involve a position that is not governed in the proper direction. No other account can distinguish between English on the one hand and Palauan on the other in a way that *predicts* this distribution of WCO effects. I will argue further that weak crossover is not an independent phenomenon, that structures that have been claimed to exhibit the weak crossover effect actually fall into more than one class, and that it is the core cases of weak crossover that result from failure of proper government.

The facts of this chapter will thus provide support for a directional approach to the Empty Category Principle. Although directionality analyses have been offered for a variety of phenomena, such analyses have sometimes lacked strong empirical support, and the recent literature has contained retreats from such explanations (see, e.g., Rizzi 1990). This paper supports directionality in a particular case, in showing a contrast in the extractability of subjects that depends on the direction in which they are governed.

It is interesting to note that the earliest account of WCO, Chomsky's leftness condition, is really based on the position of subjects relative to objects, and in that sense is a precursor of the ECP account proposed here. However, setting the specifier parameter is necessarily *prior* to application of the connectedness condition (if all positions were canonically governed, there would be no left-branch effect, etc.). In fact, the position of the subject, relative to complements, must be determined prior to application of *many* government-based principles. Specification of the subject position is much more than a descriptive fact.

Of course, generalization of the ECP to overt pronouns needs motivation of its own; such motivation is crucial to my analysis. I argue in the next section that a principle like the ECP should, and in fact already does, apply to all bound positions, null or overt. The result of these arguments will be not only to firmly ground the claim that WCO is a government-theoretic effect, but also to add fuel to the controversy over how the grammar ought to distinguish null and overt categories.

We turn now to arguments that bound pronouns are subject to the ECP.

5.1. *Resumptive Pronouns Subject to the ECP*

In this section I will first consider the theory-internal reasons why the coverage of the ECP should include both null and overt resumptive pronouns, then turn to some empirical support for this extension.

218   CHAPTER SIX

5.1.1. *Resumptive Pronouns as Syntactic Variables: Theory*

Here, I would like to present a view of the ECP that refers to syntactic rather than phonological properties of NPs. As basically a recoverability condition on referentially empty quantifier-bound categories, the ECP 'sees' only syntactically defined variables. Only from this viewpoint can the ECP be stated at a sufficient level of abstraction to cover all languages, from English to fully resumptive-pronoun type languages like Palauan.

First, we focus on the overtness of the variable. Consider the syntactic properties of NPs involved in WCO. There is the 'extraction-site' variable, or WH-trace, which is often defined as follows (Chomsky 1981 and much other literature):

(17) α is a variable if α is in an A position and is locally A'
        bound.

Another characterization of variable is found in the typology of NPs in Chomsky 1982 (p. 84, reworded):

(69)   A locally A' bound category is [−pronominal, −anaphor].

(17) is a strictly configurational definition, while (69) refers to "the internal constitution" (Chomsky 1981) or internal properties of the variable. The features mentioned in (69) define a type of NP, which may be contextually or intrinsically defined. Whether contextual or intrinsic, the *level* at which these features become visible to the syntax is crucial, as we will see below. Both R-expressions (referring expressions like names) and variables have the feature values [−pronominal, −anaphor], so the difference between an R-expression and a variable is that the variable has no (independent) reference and depends on its binder for its denotation.

As Koopman and Sportiche (1982) have pointed out, definition (17) also holds for the coindexed pronoun in WCO, since it too is in an A position and is locally A' bound. This makes the pronoun resumptive. By virtue of being A' bound, the pronoun has the syntactic feature values [−pronominal, −anaphor], that is, it also conforms to (69). Being a bound variable, the resumptive pronoun lacks the possibility of referentiality it would have as a pronoun. Like a trace, the pronoun depends on its binder for its denotation. I have already argued (section 3.1) that (69), if taken to define an element by its syntactic feature values, uniquely identifies a variable, while (17), referring essentially to the position of the binder, does not.

Another important property of the resumptive pronoun in a WCO configuration is that it has no A binder: this is by definition, if it is A' bound, and also follows from the fact that in WCO configurations there

CROSSOVER CONSTRUCTIONS 219

is no c-command relation between the two A positions. I have already discussed the failure of the c-command account of WCO: it is evidently not an additional requirement on the binding of pronouns that they be coindexed with a c-commanding variable in order to have a bound interpretation. The pronoun can be bound directly by its operator, without the mediation of a c-commanding trace.

What the description in the foregoing paragraphs amounts to, intuitively, is that resumptive pronouns are subject to the same recoverability requirements as traces: both lack referential features and neither can find its denotation in terms of any A position; both must have a local A′ antecedent, which is in a nonthematic position.

Summing up to this point, we have the following results:

(70) i. Variables are [−pronominal, −anaphor].

   ii. Variables are null or overt.

   iii. Variables, null or overt, are directly bound by the A′ antecedent.

Given these three points, the problem is actually to *restrict* the ECP to just those categories that actually are phonologically empty (as opposed to, e.g., syntactically [−pronominal]). The ECP has no actual mechanism to discern a category that is without phonemes.[25] So the word 'empty' in its name is merely a label; the *extension* of this word must be determined. From its application in the grammar, this principle appears to constrain elements that are [−pronominal, −anaphor], have no intrinsic reference, and are construed as variables.[26] These elements can be null or overt in phonological terms, but the distinction may be syntactically inert. The WCO resumptive pronouns conform to this definition.

Put another way, does the 'nonpronominal' stipulated in some definitions of the ECP mean 'nonlexical' or [−pronominal]? In the larger context of GB theory, it is clearly the latter.[27] The [±lexical] feature does not uniquely distinguish pronouns from variables. On the one hand, there are [+pronominal] nonlexical categories (PRO and *pro*) that are exempt from ECP jurisdiction because their reference can be recovered *without* antecedent binding (and because of the [+pronominal] feature). On the other hand, there are lexical categories that are [−pronominal]: resumptive pronouns, as well as reflexives and so on. The ECP constrains the [−pronominal] (and in the cases at hand, [−anaphor]) elements, in regulating A′ dependencies modeled on quantifier-variable binding in logic: an A′ binder provides the range of values that can be assigned to an A′ bound position, that position not having any constant value of its own. Functionally, the ECP is a recoverability condition; in A′ binding, it connects an element having the minus value for both syntactic features with its antecedent.

220   CHAPTER SIX

Thus the force of my argument that "the ECP applies to resumptive pronouns" is that the ECP applies to [−pronominal] (and [−anaphor]) categories. This is essentially the standard view of the ECP, typified by statements like "a nonpronominal empty category must be properly governed". The ECP simply applies to variables. I regard the criterial feature values as consequent on the formation of the A′ chain, which in Palauan (but not in English) is at S-structure. (These values are either part of the output of chain binding or necessary to the well-formedness of structures on which the chain algorithm acts as a filter.)

It is in fact not even necessary to assume that what we are informally calling 'resumptive pronouns' are ever [+pronominal] in Palauan. These A positions may be viewed as unspecified for these features in D-structure and become specified as [−pronominal] through chain binding at S-structure. In this view no value switching is required from one level of representation to another.

5.1.2. *Resumptive Pronouns as Syntactic Variables: Fact*

Empirical support for this analysis comes from the facts of resumptive pronouns in other structures in Palauan. The main arguments that resumptive pronouns in this language are A′ bound at S-structure have been presented in Chapter Four. These arguments are based on coordination and parasitic gap structures, locality facts, and other tests of syntactic variables. I also argued in Chapter Four that *all* A′ bound A positions are resumptive pronouns, even when the antecedent is within the local CP. For purposes of this chapter I will give examples chosen for their relevance to the ECP account of WCO.

It has been established in a number of arguments that Palauan is a VOS language, in which all argument positions are canonically governed. It has also already been established, with abundant data, that nearly any A position can anchor an A′ chain at S-structure. Consider now the binding of specifiers in particular. The specifier of N in English is unextractable, and extraction of the specifier of I is limited. But in Palauan, since all NP positions are in canonical government configuration,[28] positions like specifier of N and specifier of I can contain variables under conditions not possible in English. The fact that Spec(N) and Spec(I) can be A′ bound, i.e. [−pronominal] categories, shows that these positions satisfy the ECP. These positions are empty in (71):

(71) a. ngte'a$_i$ a 'omulsa [$_{NP}$ a delal   ____$_i$] *pro*
     who   *2-saw*   *mother-3s*

Whose did you see mother?

(Lit. Who did you see 's mother?)

CROSSOVER CONSTRUCTIONS   221

(71) b. a Merii$_i$ a kltukl [el kmo ngoltoir er a Moses [____$_i$]]
        clear   Comp   3s-love   P

Merii (it's) clear that ____ loves Moses.

Recall that positions marked with a preposition must be overt. These include the specifiers of some nouns (borrowings and optionally possessed nouns). Compare (71a) with the examples below:

(72) a. ngte'a$_i$ a longuiu [a buk **er ngii**$_i$] tirkei el ngalek
        who   3-read   book P her   those L child

Whose book are those kids reading?

(Lit. Who$_i$ are those kids reading her$_i$ book?)

     b. a Carol$_i$ a k'iliuii [a buk **er ngii**$_i$] *pro*
        1s-read   book P her

I read Carol's book.

These sentences correspond to the sentences in (71). As in all other cases we have looked at in Palauan, the lexical resumptive pronoun is equivalent to the gaps that occur in other positions. The lexical pronoun is canonically governed (ultimately by the head N, from which it receives a θ-role) and locally (and grammatically) A′ bound.

Such a pronoun appears even in simple clauses. Recall the arguments in section 2.5 of Chapter Four on the theory of resumptive pronouns (see also section 3.1 of this chapter): there I showed that a resumptive pronoun in subject position could be locally A′ bound. These bound pronouns do not observe Principle B of the binding theory. This is further evidence of their [−pronominal] nature. One prediction of my analysis is therefore that pronouns A′ bound at S-structure should not trigger Principle B effects (if in subject position). I repeat (54a) here, which illustrates this:

(54) a. ngte'a$_i$ [a mengull   er [a rengelekel *pro*$_i$] *pro*$_i$]
        who   R-respect P   students-3s

Who$_i$ ____$_i$ respects his$_i$ students?

A [+pronominal] category must be free in the matrix (simple) clause (cf. **Who$_i$ does he$_i$ respect Mary?, *Who$_i$ does Mary respect him$_i$?*). So the subject of (54a) cannot be [+pronominal]. Of course, if the bound position is a resumptive pronoun, it is [−pronominal]. Certainly an empty resumptive pronoun in any language is an A′ bound, nonpronominal, empty category, which is exactly what a trace is. These are the

222   CHAPTER SIX

categories to which it is stipulated that the ECP applies. The gaps in (71) (and (54a)) and the overt pronouns in (72) have equivalent distribution, however, so must ultimately be treated alike.

I assume that the *[P ____] effect reflects a fact about P's recoverability properties: the language has *one* preposition; it is nonthematic, does not assign Case, and does not carry agreement morphology (contrast V and N). The fact that it does not license an empty category is a reflection of the condition on *pro*, not a condition on variables. P's restricted properties therefore do not implicate the Connectedness Condition directly.

Perhaps the most unusual and the strongest evidence for S-structure A' binding, in the WCO configuration as elsewhere, is WH agreement. I will only recall its essential properties here: it applies equally to structures with A' bound gaps and to those with overt A' bound pronouns, being indifferent to the phonological form of the bound position. It has both morphological and interpretive effects, and so has been argued to apply at S-structure. The A' binding of which it is a reflection has been analyzed in terms of the Connectedness Condition, applying to chains at S-structure.

Considering all the foregoing arguments about binding, there is no motivation for a syntactic distinction between the empty variables in (71) and the overt ones in (72). And when these variables cooccur in the same structure, as they do in WCO configurations, they are indistinguishable to the ECP, which sees them only as variables on a par with traces. Resumptive pronouns in English and many other languages, of course, do not have these properties at S-structure, but are read as (free) pronouns at that level (Chomsky 1982).

This discussion can perhaps shed some light on the issues of homogeneity and multiple variable binding. As already noted, Safir (1984) suggested a relaxation of Koopman & Sportiche's (1982) bijection analysis to the effect that multiple variable binding is allowed so long as all variables bound by the same quantifier are [α lexical]. Since Safir takes *pro* to be lexical, however, the lexicality distinction is weakened. But the homogeneity approach would work if the variables were parallel, or homogeneous in their *syntactic* feature composition. Palauan illustrates this, since both overt and null variables are defined in terms of the features [−pronominal, −anaphor], and grammatically cooccur in A' binding structures (at S-structure). (Resumptive pronouns in English, again, would not be homogeneous with traces in these features, since, in English, RPs are bound by a late LF rule of predication.)

In sum, in a uniformly right-governing language, specifiers satisfy the ECP just as other positions do, so no WCO effect is observed as long as other conditions are satisfied.[29] The distribution of core WCO effects thus follows *directly* from an ECP requiring canonical government.

CROSSOVER CONSTRUCTIONS 223

5.2. *The Specifier Parameter*

5.2.1. *The Parameter*

We have now seen how setting the position of the specifier, interacting with the ECP, accounts for the core cases of WCO. At this point it is appropriate to gather together the properties of the proposed parameter, to see if they are at least descriptively harmonious with current assumptions:

(73)   *Properties of the proposed specifier parameter*:

   a. A single setting has wide-ranging effects throughout the grammar (e.g. government and extraction phenomena of various kinds).

   b. The parameter accounts for surface (typological) variation among languages (e.g. S-initial vs. V-initial languages; SVO languages).

   c. The parameter gives theoretical substance to distinctions previously made on the observational level (e.g. accounts for position of subject)

   d. The parameter can be argued to have a default setting (see below).

   e. The parameter is category-neutral (sets specifier of *XP*).

   f. The parameter is independent (see below).

As parameter theory matures, these descriptive statements will be weighted.

We now turn to the question of the form in which the specifier parameter should be stated. First, assume the head-complement parameter can be stated in terms of schemata showing the two settings available, e.g.:

(74)   *The Head Parameter*

$$X' = X \quad YP \text{ or}$$
$$X' = YP \quad X$$

We could depict the specifier parameter similarly:

(75)   *The Specifier Parameter*

$$XP = X' \quad YP \text{ or}$$
$$XP = YP \quad X'$$

224 CHAPTER SIX

This statement is simpler than one that also mentions the position of the head and its complement. But is it necessary to mention the order within X'? It seems not. The setting of the head parameter (order within X') defines canonical government. The specifier parameter can then be set with reference only to the relative position of X' and YP; the specifier is canonically governed if it is governed in the direction determined for the head-complement parameter, otherwise not. (No extrinsic ordering relation between the two is necessary.) I will assume, therefore, a statement of the parameter along the lines of (75). The settings of the two parameters (74) and (75) are independent.[30]

The two word order parameters taken together yield the following four grammars; 'uniform' and 'split' refer informally to the presence or absence of canonical government over all A positions:

(76)
	I				II		
	uniform				*split*		
(VOS)	XP	= X'	YP	(OVS)	XP	= X'	YP
	X'	= X	ZP		X'	= ZP	X
(SOV)	XP	= YP	X'	(SVO)	XP	= YP	X'
	X'	= ZP	X		X'	= X	ZP

The consequences for government that are manifested in the four grammars in (76) follow from the settings with no further explicit statement.

OVS languages are of course very rare, and an SVO language is prone to more constraints on surface rearrangements than, say, a VOS language. What of VSO and OSV langauges? Perhaps there are none. VSO grammars have been convincingly argued to be generated from underlying SVO order by V-fronting (e.g. Sproat 1985; Chung & McCloskey 1987),[31] or by movement of S from basic VOS order (Chung, to appear). OSV languages, like OVS, either do not occur or are extremely rare (see Derbyshire & Pullum 1986). Such languages in any case could not be generated by one of the grammars in (76). If the approach to ordering taken here is correct, VSO and OSV languages (i.e. those 'without a VP') are eliminated in principle, or are radically different from other types and would require special phrase structure principles.

5.2.2. *Default Values?*

It has been suggested (Hyams 1986 and others) that parameters have default (Hyams' term is "initial") settings. A default setting would be the unmarked one for a particular parameter, and it is reasonable to expect that markedness applies to all parameters this way.

In the case of the headedness parameter, it is likely that the default

CROSSOVER CONSTRUCTIONS 225

setting is VO. Many government phenomena prefer left-to-right ordering, for example, verb/infl movements, WH movements, clitic movements, and topicalization and subjectivization. Antecedents are rarely on the right, and such movements are much reduced for OV languages.

If VO is default, then the default for the specifier parameter should be XP = X' YP, the two default settings yielding a VOS grammar. All selected positions are canonically governed (from the left) in such a grammar, making it, in terms of these two parameters alone, the most likely to occur. But VOS languages are by no means common. We have seen that even the presumably unmarked VOS grammar of Palauan has a preference for being NP-initial. (This preference actually goes beyond binding, and speakers often produce SVO and other NP-V-NP (topicalized) sentences.) This suggests that topicalizing processes may be historically responsible for changes from VOS to, say, SVO. Though this general approach suggests ways of predicting historical change, much more diachronic work must be done before connections between synchronic parameters and historical change can be firmly established.

Furthermore, in a grammar in which the head of XP and the head of X' uniformly have the same orientation (SOV or VOS grammar), direction of government of the specifier can be predicted from the setting for canonical government without recourse to further evidence. Such a grammar is simpler than a grammar in which specifier position is *not* predictable on this basis, i.e. in which further evidence is needed or further grammatical operations are referred to (SVO or OVS grammar).[32] Thus the former type is to be preferred by acquisition theory, and may instantiate the default or initial settings for word order (modulo OV/VO choice).

6. EXTENSIONS; CONCLUSIONS

6.1. *Extraction Site Bound Separately From Other Positions*

One apparent problem that remains is in determining the nature of the difference between an extraction-site variable and the other A' bound position in WCO structures. The coindexing of both to the antecedent is read via chain formation. If both are bound at S-structure, both are variables at that level. This would result in two A' chains terminating at the same A' binder, giving that binder two θ-roles. Though this does not, strictly speaking, violate the Theta Criterion (which refers only to A positions), it would seem to create an incoherent interpretive situation. Furthermore, WH agreement refers only to the extraction site (and the position of the antecedent at S-structure). Third, the discussion of the examples in (55) showed that in Palauan A' binding structures there is

226 CHAPTER SIX

only one variable. (77a and b) below are similar; only (77a) has the configuration of a weak crossover structure:

(77) a. ngte'a$_i$ a loltoir   er ngii$_i$ [a delal   *pro*$_i$]
        who   *IR-3-love P 3s*   *mother-3s*

     Who$_i$ does her$_i$ mother love _____$_i$?

    b. ngte'a$_i$ a oltoir   er ngii$_i$ [a delal   *pro*$_i$]
         who   *R-love P 3s*   *mother-3s*

     Who$_i$se mother loves her$_i$?

     (Who$_i$ _____$_i$ mother loves her$_i$?)

The interpretation of (77a) is such that the object pronoun **ngii** is taken as the variable, while the interpretation of (77b) is such that the *pro* specifier of the subject is taken as the variable.[33] The surface difference between these two sentences is in the verb morphology. Since the object pronoun is the variable in (77a), the verb is irrealis, and since the variable is contained in the subject in (77b), the verb form is realis. I assume (see above and Chapter Four) that WH agreement is contingent upon the prior existence of the A' binding chain, so that the identity of the variable is established before WH agreement applies. The difference in WH agreement in these two sentences is readily explainable in terms of the position occupied by the (single) variable in each case, but would be difficult to account for otherwise. In fact, if WH agreement were sensitive to the non-extraction-site pronoun, the interpretation of the two expressions could be reversed!

These considerations argue that the pronoun in weak crossover (and other coindexed positions in examples above) is not chain-bound until LF, where the ECP applies. If this is correct, our earlier conclusion that the A' chain at S-structure contains only two elements, variable and antecedent, can be maintained. In view of the facts presented in Chapter Four, there is no doubt that WH agreement applies at S-structure and not later. The assumption that LF binding of the pronoun in weak crossover is at LF is consistent with all of the foregoing.

I conclude, then, that weak crossover configurations involve two A' chains and binding at both S-structure and LF. This is consistent with our general approach, in which extraction-site pronouns in Palauan are bound at S-structure. It is also consistent with the parameter for binding of resumptive pronouns suggested earlier, that a language may designate the level at which pronouns are bound. Here, pronouns with different properties are bound at different levels. So a position bound at LF may naturally differ from an S-structure-bound position (e.g. the former does not trigger WH agreement; it is not an S-structure variable, and so on). By the output of LF, all A positions coindexed with an A' binder are bound.

Though assignment of the θ-role (and Case) of the WCO pronoun to the A' binder is still awkward, at this point it violates no principle of grammar. I will leave that issue here. WH agreement itself applies only to a single θ-role/chain. Though many structures may have multiple variables from the point of view of the Connectedness Condition, only one variable is visible to WH agreement. This seems to be an irreducible fact about this unusual agreement rule, and suggests that there is more to the issue of *intrinsic* definition of 'variable' than previously assumed.

To sum up, I have argued that the variable-binding approach to weak crossover is flawed. If this approach is dispensed with, then we have recourse to approaches that focus on the contexts which license coindexing of a pronoun with a variable and with an A' antecedent. These contexts appear to vary cross-linguistically, with the result that weak crossover turns out not to be universal. I have also argued that the distinction between variables and pronouns is crucial to the analysis of a range of anaphoric constructions, and that this distinction cannot be based either on the overtness of the variable or pronoun, or on the hierarchical definition of variable commonly appealed to. Rather, we must view the element 'variable' at a more abstract level, as having the syntactic features that are a necessary concomitant of A' chain binding.

The findings of this chapter, then, are like those of the previous chapters: that what on the surface appear to be striking differences between Palauan and better known languages can be reduced to the effects of familiar theoretical concepts, clothed in new guises.

NOTES

[1] In EST, these anaphoric relations are referred to both as "coreference" and as "coindexing". Since quantified phrases and WH phrases do not refer to any object, they and their variables of course do not *co*-refer in any real sense. This point is taken up in Lasnik (1976), Reinhart (1979), Bach and Partee (1980), Reinhart (1983), Haïk (1984) and elsewhere.

[2] Langacker (1969) proposes the two primacy relations PRECEDE and COMMAND to account for pronominalization. To *precede* is to be to the left of. *Command* is defined as follows: A node A commands a node B if (1) neither A nor B dominates the other and (2) the S node that most immediately dominates A also dominates B. In Langacker's analysis, a pronoun may not both precede and command its antecedent.

[3] One of the first arguments for LF as a distinct level of representation (see Chomsky 1977) was based on weak crossover with quantified phrases.

[4] Reinhart illustrates c-command domains with this tree:

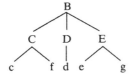

228   CHAPTER SIX

The tree includes the following domains:

> c c-commands f and vice versa; e c-commnds g and vice versa;
> C, D, and E c-command the entire domain dominated by B; d also
> c-commands the domain dominated by B, since D does not branch;
> e and f, for example, are c-commanded by d.

[5] As it is stated, the rule in (7) would eliminate a number of grammatical sentence types, including copular sentences with pronominal subjects (like *I am the president*). See Bach and Partee (1980), Evans (1980).

[6] In the crossover analysis in Higginbotham (1980b), Leftness appears in the Reindexing Rule which allows the index of a pronoun (optionally) to be changed to the index of an empty category to its left. Higginbotham (1980b) is written in the 'On Binding' framework. Higginbotham (1980a) ultimately rejects this rule, however, in favor of c-command.

[7] Koopman and Sportiche (1982) analyze strong crossover in terms of bijection and Principle B of the Binding theory.

[8] R-expressions *can* have a local binder in Comp, however. Principle C, like Reinhart's rule, applies only to coindexing between A positions. (But see Higginbotham 1983, for an alternative analysis).

[9] In Chomsky (1982), the bijection principle is retained to assign parasitic gap structures "their marginal status at LF" (p. 38). The relation of ATB to the bijection analysis of crossover is not discussed (see Chomsky's note 31). I include parasitic gap structures in the list of multiple variable binding despite current accounts that relate a parasitic gap to its own operator.

[10] Hoji refers also to Higginbotham's (1983) notions of "linking rule" and "antecedent-of". This allows Hoji to define a non-c-commanding variable as an (indirect) antecedent, and the weak crossover effect as in (i):

> i.   A variable cannot be the antecedent of a pronoun that it does not c-command.

[11] Recall that pronominal subjects are always phonetically null in Palauan.

[12] The matrix verb is not affected by WH agreement in (29), since it is not within the S-structure domain of the WH operator.

[13] While a variable may be an empty category in languages with syntactic WH movement, I suggest in this and other work that nonovertness is not criterial of syntactic variables in universal grammar.

[14] This argument runs counter to Brody (1984) and Safir (1984). However, the argument (and those in section 5) also show the contextual definition (17) not to work.

[15] L. Rizzi (personal communication) suggests that a combination of Safir's and my approaches could account for (40a): at S-structure, A' binding involves resumptive pronouns, so the subject here is *pro*; at LF, movement of the object WH phrase leaves a 'real' (nonpronominal) variable; the *pro* and variable together would then violate parallelism. See section 5, however, where I argue that A' bound pronouns are [−pronominal], like traces.

[16] The expression **a ta me a ta el senator** is phonetically [tamatal senator]. Another Palauan quantified expression, **dersta**, also translates as 'each' but also coindexes only plural pronouns.

[17] According to Reinhart (1983, p. 83), cases in which universal quantifiers "control the reference of plural pronouns . . . [are] cases of coreference rather than bound anaphora."

[18] The examples in (39) are better than (45a) (?? vs. *) apparently because WH phrases, but not other quantified NPs, can be interpreted in situ as having scope over the whole sentence.

CROSSOVER CONSTRUCTIONS 229

[19] This observation is due to S. Chung (personal communication).

[20] Engdahl (1983) makes a similar suggestion for English sentences in which a pronoun can be 'replaced' by a gap.

[21] (56d), in which the name is in object position, is slightly better than (57b), in which the name is the subject. This reflects a tendency for a name to more readily antecede a pronoun in the subject when it precedes the subject.

[22] Higginbotham (1983) interprets this contrast as due to the fact that names have intrinsic semantic content, while variables must be anaphoric to some other element. Higginbotham argues that variables should not be treated as names; Palauan provides support for his arguments.

[23] Saito & Hoji (1983) argue that scrambling *is* subject to WCO (which suggests that scrambling is an instance of Move α). But the facts are far from clear. First, many examples involve names, presumably not subject to WCO. Second, they are forced to stipulate a distinction between "true" quantifiers and "quasi" quantifiers. Third, the pronoun **kare** '3sg.' cannot be bound, so there are no WCO examples with **kare**. The form **zibun** 'self' occurs as a variable, but the examples with **zibun** that supposedly show the WCO effect have factive (**koto**) subjects, not the simple genitive ones. Can **zibun** otherwise be bound inside a **koto**-clause? What are the condtions allowing binding of **zibun** to a WHP or a QNP? At any rate, Saito & Hoji note that the WCO effect in Japanese is weaker than in English.

[24] Hoji's (1985) analysis of grammatical but WCO-like structures in Japanese as parasitic gap structures can be expressed with equal efficiency in terms of linearity, as described here.

[25] If the ECP applies only in LF, it is further limited in this arena, as it has no access to PF.

[26] The ECP also constrains [+anaphor] elements (NP-trace); the context of this book is limited to A' binding, however.

[27] Jaeggli (1985) gives another view of these issues. See also Chomsky (1981) (p. 330, (11)).

[28] Not all lexical heads license empty categories in Palauan; prepositions and adjectives do not (cf. the use of a resumptive pronoun after P). See below.

[29] This analysis predicts that a uniformly left-governing (SOV) language would also fail to have WCO effects and would allow the extraction of specifiers. However, other factors come into play. See the more detailed discussion in Georgopoulos (1991b), which also considers the 'residue' of this ECP account, much of it also due to connectedness.

[30] The question of the relation between (74) and (75) raises the question of Exhaustive Constant Partial Ordering (ECPO) in Generalized Phrase Structure Grammar (GPSG). Grammars having ECPO have the same linear order in each category; i.e. an SVO grammar does not have ECPO. ECPO is considered not to be a "linguistic universal" (Gazdar et al. 1985, p. 49). But if the presence or absence of ECPO is as presented here, i.e. derived from parametric settings, ECPO itself is derived within the core grammar of UG.

[31] Chung and McCloskey currently are working under the assumption that there are two types of VSO languages: ones that are SVO at S-structure (like Irish) and ones that are VOS at S-structure (like Chamorro) (personal communication). My claim would be that WCO should be seen in the Irish type but not in the Chamorro type. Chung informs me that spec(N) is not extractable in Chamorro, but, more generally, nothing can be extracted out of a Chamorro NP. Clearly, there are other factors involved.

[32] In an earlier version of this material I suggested that the 'split-government' grammars, SVO and OVS, were *marked* in contrast to the canonically governing grammars VOS and SOV. I no longer consider this contrast to be a case of markedness.

[33] See the discussion of extraction from NP in Chapter Three.

REFERENCES

Abney, Steven: 1986, 'Functional Elements and Licensing', unpublished ms., presented at the GLOW Colloquium, Gerona.

Anderson, Stephen R.: 1982, 'Where's Morphology?', *Linguistic Inquiry* **13**, 571–612.

Anderson, Stephen R.: 1984, 'Kwakwala Syntax and the Government-Binding Theory', in E.-D. Cook and Donna B. Gerdts (eds.), *Syntax and Semantics* **16**, Academic Press, New York.

Aoun, Joseph: 1985, *A Grammar of Anaphora*, Linguistic Inquiry Monograph 11, MIT Press, Cambridge, MA.

Aoun, Joseph, Norbert Hornstein and Dominique Sportiche: 1981, 'Some Aspects of Wide Scope Quantification', *Journal of Lingusitic Research* **1**, 69–95.

Aoun, Joseph, Norbert Hornstein, David Lightfoot and Amy Weinberg: 1987, 'Two Types of Locality', *Linguistic Inquiry* **18**, 537–577.

Aoun, Joseph and Y.-H. Audrey Li: 1989, 'Three Cases of Logical Relations: Relative Scope, Bound Pronouns and Anaphoric Relations', unpublished ms., presented at the Second Princeton Workshop on Comparative Grammar, April 1989.

Aoun, Joseph and Dominique Sportiche: 1983, 'On the Formal Theory of Government', *The Linguistic Review* **2**, 211–236.

Bach, Emmon and Barbara Partee: 1980, 'Anaphora and Semantic Structure', in Jody Kreiman and Almerindo E. Ojeda (eds.), *Papers from the Parasession on Pronouns and Anaphora*, CLS.

Baker, C. L.: 1968, *Indirect Questions in English*, University of Illinois Ph.D. dissertation.

Baker, C. L.: 1970, 'Notes on the Description of English Questions: The Role of an Abstract Question Morpheme', *Foundations of Language* **6**, 197–219.

Barss, Andrew: 1985, 'Chain Binding', paper delivered at WCCFL 4, UCLA.

Barss, Andrew and Howard Lasnik: 1986, 'A Note on Anaphora and Double Objects', *Linguistic Inquiry* **17**, 347–354.

Belletti, Adriana and Luigi Rizzi: 1981, 'The Syntax of *ne*', in *Theory of Markedness in Generative Grammar* (Proceedings of the 1979 GLOW Conference), Scuola Normale Superiore di Pisa.

Belletti, Adriana and Luigi Rizzi: 1988, 'Psych-Verbs and θ-Theory', *Natural Language and Linguistic Theory* **6**, 291–352.

Bender, Byron: 1971, 'Micronesian Languages', in T. Sebeok (ed.), *Current Trends in Linguistics 8: Linguistics in Oceania*, Mouton, The Hague.

Bender, Byron: 1984 (ed.), *Studies in Micronesian Linguistics*, Pacific Linguistics, Series C, No. 80, The Australian National University.

Borer, Hagit: 1984a, 'Restrictive Relative Clauses in Modern Hebrew', *Natural Language and Linguistic Theory* **2**, 219–260.

Borer, Hagit: 1984b, *Parametric Syntax: Case Studies in Semitic and Romance Languages*, Foris, Dordrecht.

Bresnan, Joan: 1970, 'On Complementizers: Toward a Syntactic Theory of Complement Types', *Foundations of Language* **6**, 297–321.

Bresnan, Joan and Jane Grimshaw: 1978, 'The Syntax of Free Relatives in English', *Linguistic Inquiry* **9**, 331–392.

Bresnan, Joan and Sam Mchombo: 1987, 'Topic, Pronoun, and Agreement in Chichewa', in M. Iida, S. Wechsler, and D. Zec (eds.), *Working Papers in Grammatical Theory and*

REFERENCES   231

Discourse Structure: Interactions of Morphology, Syntax, and Discourse, CSLI Lecture Notes 11, Stanford.

Brody, Michael: 1984, 'Contextual Definitions and the Role of Chains', *Linguistic Inquiry* **15**, 355—380.

Capell, A.: 1949, *A Grammar of the Language of Palau*, Coordinated Investigation of Micronesian Anthropology (CIMA) 1947—1949, Part 6b of the Final Report to the Pacific Science Board, National Research Council. (Mimeographed, retyped by Clayton Carlson.)

Carlson, Clayton: 1968, *Palauan Phonology*, M.A. thesis, University of Hawaii.

Carstens, Vicki: 1985, 'Proper Government in Yoruba', *Proceedings of WCCFL 4*, 58—70.

Chao, Wynn and Peter Sells: 1983, 'On the Interpretation of Resumptive Pronouns', in P. Sells and C. Jones (eds.), *Proceedings of NELS 13*, GLSA, Amherst.

Chomsky, Noam: 1964, 'Current Issues in Linguistic Theory', in J. A. Fodor and J. J. Katz (eds.), *The Structure of Language: Readings in the Philosophy of Language*, Prentice Hall, Englewood Cliffs.

Chomsky, Noam: 1965, *Aspects of the Theory of Syntax*, MIT Press, Cambridge, MA.

Chomsky, Noam: 1973, 'Conditions on Transformations', in S. R. Anderson and P. Kiparsky (eds.), *A Festschrift for Morris Halle*, Holt, Reinhart and Winston, New York.

Chomsky, Noam: 1977, 'Conditions on Rules of Grammar', in R. W. Cole (ed.), *Current Issues in Linguistic Theory*, Indiana University Press, Bloomington.

Chomsky, Noam: 1977, 'On Wh-Movement', in P. Culicover, T. Wasow, and A. Akmajian (eds.), *Formal Syntax*, Academic Press, New York.

Chomsky, Noam: 1981, *Lectures on Government and Binding*, Foris, Dordrecht.

Chomsky, Noam: 1982, *Some Concepts and Consequences of the Theory of Government and Binding*, Linguistic Inquiry Monograph 6, MIT Press, Cambridge, MA.

Chomsky, Noam: 1986a, *Knowledge of Language; Its Nature, Origins, and Use*, Praeger, New York.

Chomsky, Noam: 1986b, *Barriers*, MIT Press, Cambridge, MA.

Chomsky, Noam and Morris Halle: 1968, *The Sound Pattern of English*, Harper and Row, New York.

Chung, Sandra: 1982a, 'Unbounded Dependencies in Chamorro Grammar', *Linguistic Inquiry* **13**, 39—78.

Chung, Sandra: 1982b, 'On Extending the Null Subject Parameter to NPs', *Proceedings of WCCFL 1*, Stanford.

Chung, Sandra: 1984, 'Identifiability and Null Objects in Chamorro', *Proceedings of the Tenth Annual Meeting of the Berkeley Linguistics Society*, Berkeley.

Chung, Sandra: 1985, 'On the Notion "Null Anaphor" in Chamorro', unpublished manuscript, UCSD.

Chung, Sandra: 1991, 'Sentential Subjects and Proper Government in Chamorro', in C. Georgopoulos and R. Ishihara (eds.), *Interdisciplinary Approaches to Language: Essays in Honor of S.-Y. Kuroda*, Kluwer, Dordrecht.

Chung, Sandra: to appear, 'VPs and Verb Movement in Chamorro', *Natural Language and Linguistic Theory*.

Chung, Sandra and Carol Georgopoulos: 1988, 'Agreement with Gaps in Chamorro and Palauan', in M. Barlow and C. Ferguson (eds.), *Agreement in Natural Language: Approaches, Theories, and Descriptions*, CSLI, Stanford.

Chung, Sandra and James McCloskey: 1987, 'Government, Barriers and Small Clauses in Modern Irish', *Linguistic Inquiry* **18**, 173—237.

Cinque, Guglielmo: 1984, 'A´-bound pro vs. variable', ms., Università di Venezia.

Clark, Robin: 1983, 'Clitics as A´-binders', in W. Harbert (ed.), *Cornell Working Papers in Linguistics* 4.

Clements, George: 1985, 'Binding Domains in Kikuyu', *Studies in the Linguistic Sciences* **14**, pp.

232   REFERENCES

Comrie, Bernard: 1981, *Language Universals and Linguistic Typology*, University of Chicago Press, Chicago.

Contreras, Heles: 1984, 'A Note on Parasitic Gaps', *Linguistic Inquiry* 15, 698—701.

Dahl, Otto Christian: 1976, *Proto-Austronesian*, Scandinavian Institute of Asian Studies Monograph Series, No. 15. (Second revised edition.)

Dempwolff, Otto: 1934—38, *Vergleichende Lautlehre des austronesischen Wortsschatzes*, Berlin, Reimer.

Derbyshire, D. and G. Pullum, eds.: 1986, *Handbook of Amazonian Languages: Volume I*, Mouton de Gruyter, Berlin, New York, Amsterdam.

DeWolf, Charles: 1977, A Syntactic and Comparative Analysis of Palauan a', LSA Austronesian Symposium, August 1977.

Dyen, Isidore: 1965, 'A Lexicostatistical Classification of the Austronesian Languages', *International Journal of American Linguistics* Memoir 9.

Dyen, Isidore: 1971, 'Review of Patzold, Die Palau-sprache und ihre Stellung zu anderen indonesischen Sprachen', *Journal of the Polynesian Society* 80, 247—58.

Emonds, Joseph E.: 1976, *A Transformational Approach to English Syntax*, Academic Press, New York.

Engdahl, Elisabet: 1982, 'Constituent Questions, Topicalization, and Surface Structure Interpretation', in D. Flickinger, M. Macken, and N. Wiegand (eds.), *Proceedings of the First West Coast Conference on Formal Linguistics*, Stanford.

Engdahl, Elisabet: 1983, 'Parasitic Gaps', *Linguistics and Philosophy* 6, 5—34.

Engdahl, Elisabet: 1984, 'Parasitic Gaps, Resumptive Pronouns, and Subject Extractions', unpublished manuscript, University of Wisconsin at Madison.

Engdahl, Elisabet and Eva Ejerhed: 1982, *Readings on Unbounded Dependencies in Scandinavian Languages*, Umeå, Stockholm, Sweden.

Erteschik-Shir, Nomi: 1973, *On the Nature of Island Constraints*, unpublished Ph.D. dissertation, MIT.

Evans, Gareth: 1980, 'Pronouns', *Linguistic Inquiry* 11, 337—362.

Flora, Sister Jo-Ann: 1969, 'Analysis of the Segmental Phonemes of Palauan', *Languages and Linguistics* 4, 1—30.

Flora, Sister Jo-Ann: 1974, *Palauan Phonology and Morphology*, unpublished Ph.D. dissertation, UCSD.

Flora, Sister Jo-Ann: 1984, 'Schwa in Palauan', in Bender (ed.).

Fodor, Janet Dean: 1978, 'Parsing Strategies and Constraints on Transformations', *Linguistic Inquiry* 9, 427—474.

Gazdar, Gerald, Ewan Klein, Geoffrey Pullum and Ivan Sag: 1985, *Generalized Phrase Structure Grammar*, Harvard University Press, Cambridge, MA.

George, Leland: 1980, *Analogical Generalizations of Natural Language Syntax*, Unpublished Ph.D. dissertation, MIT.

Georgopoulos, Carol: 1984, 'Palauan as a VOS Language', presented at the Fourth International Conference of Austronesian Linguistics (FOCAL), Suva, Fiji. In *Proceedings of FOCAL*, The Australian National University.

Georgopoulos, Carol: 1985, 'Variables in Palauan Syntax', in *Natural Language and Linguistic Theory* 3, 59—94.

Georgopoulos, Carol: 1991a, 'On Psych Predicates', in C. Georgopoulos and R. Ishihara (eds.), *Interdisciplinary Approaches to Language: Essays in Honor of S.-Y. Kuroda*, Kluwer, Dordrecht.

Georgopoulos, Carol: 1991b, 'Canonical Government and the Specifier Parameter: An ECP Account of Weak Crossover', in *Natural Language and Linguistic Theory* 9, 1—46.

Goldsmith, John: 1981, 'The Structure of *wh*-Questions in Igbo', *Linguistic Analysis* 7, 367—393.

REFERENCES

Goodall, Grant: 1984, 'Across-the-Board Movement, the ECP, and the Bijection Principle', in *Proceedings of the Third West Coast Conference on Formal Linguistics*, Stanford.

Goodall, Grant: 1987, *Parallel Structures in Syntax*, Cambridge University Press, Cambridge.

Grimshaw, Jane: 1979, 'Complement Selection and the Lexicon', *Linguistic Inquiry* **10**, 279–326.

Groos, Anneke and Henk van Riemsdijk: 1981, 'Matching Effects in Free Relatives: A Parameter of Core Grammar', A. Belletti, L. Brandi, and L. Rizzi (eds.), *Theory of Markedness in Generative Grammar*, Scuola Normale Superiore di Pisa.

Haïk, Isabelle: 1984, 'Indirect Binding', *Linguistic Inquiry* **15**, 185–223.

Haïk, Isabelle: 1985, *The Syntax of Operators*, Ph.D. dissertation, MIT.

Hale, Kenneth, LaVerne Jeanne and Paula Pranka: 1991, 'On Suppletion, Selection, and Agreement', in C. Georgopoulos and R. Ishihara (eds.), *Interdisciplinary Approaches to Language: Essays in Honor of S.-Y. Kuroda*, Kluwer, Dordrecht.

Hankamer, Jorge: 1974, 'On WH-Indexing', in *NELS V*, Harvard.

Higginbotham, James: 1980a, 'Anaphora and GB: Some Preliminary Remarks', *NELS 13*, John T. Jensen (ed.), (Cahiers Linguistiques d'Ottawa).

Higginbotham, James: 1980b, 'Pronouns and Bound Variables', *Linguistic Inquiry* **11**, 679–707.

Higginbotham, James: 1983, 'Logical Form, Binding, and Nominals', *Linguistic Inquiry* **14**, 395–420.

Higgins, F. R.: 1973, 'The Pseudo-cleft Construction in English', Ph.D. dissertation, MIT. (New York: Garland, 1979.)

Hoji, Hajime: 1985, *Logical Form Constraints and Configurational Structures in Japanese*, Ph.D. dissertation, University of Washington.

Huang, C. T. James: 1982, *Logical Relations in Chinese and the Theory of Grammar*, unpublished Ph.D. dissertation, MIT.

Huang, C. T. James: 1984, 'On the Distribution and Reference of Empty Pronouns', *Linguistic Inquiry* **15**, 531–575.

Hyams, Nina: 1986, *Language Acquisition and the Theory of Parameters*, D. Reidel Publishing Co., Dordrecht.

Jackendoff, Ray: 1972, *Semantic Interpretation in Generative Grammar*, MIT Press, Cambridge, MA.

Jackendoff, Ray: 1977, *X' Syntax: A Study of Phrase Structure*, Linguistic Inquiry Monograph # 2, MIT Press, Cambridge, MA.

Jackendoff, Ray: 1987, 'The Status of Thematic Relations in Linguistic Theory', *Linguistic Inquiry* **18**, 369–411.

Jackson, Frederick H.: 1984, 'On the External Relationships of the Micronesian Languages', presented at the Fourth International Conference of Austronesian Linguistics (FOCAL), Suva, Fiji.

Jaeggli, Osvaldo: 1982, *Topics in Romance Syntax*, Foris, Dordrecht.

Jaeggli, Osvaldo: 1985, 'Subject Extraction and the Null Subject Parameter', *Proceedings of NELS 14*, Amherst, University of Massachusetts.

Jelinek, Eloise: 1984, 'Empty Categories, Case, and Configurationality', *Natural Language and Linguistic Theory* **2**, 39–76.

Josephs, Lewis S.: 1975, *Palauan Reference Grammar*, PALI Language Texts: Micronesia, The University Press of Hawaii, Honolulu.

Josephs, Lewis S.: 1984, 'Complementation in Palauan', in Bender (ed.).

Katz, J. J. and Paul M. Postal: 1964, *An Integrated Theory of Linguistic Descriptions*, Research Monograph No. 26, MIT Press, Cambridge, MA.

Kayne, Richard: 1981, 'ECP Extensions', *Linguistic Inquiry* **12**, 93–133.

234 REFERENCES

Kayne, Richard: 1983a, 'Connectedness', *Linguistic Inquiry* **14**, 223–249.

Kayne, Richard: 1983b, 'Chains, Categories External to S, and French Complex Inversion', *Natural Language and Linguistic Theory* **1**, 107–139.

Kayne, Richard and J.-Y. Pollock: 1978, 'Stylistic Inversion, Successive Cyclicity, and Move NP in French', *Linguistic Inquiry* **9**, 595–621.

Keenan, Edward: 1974, 'The Functional Principle: Generalizing the Notion "subject of"', *CLS 10*.

Keenan, Edward: 1978, 'The Syntax of Subject-Final Languages', in W. Lehmann (ed.), *Syntactic Typology*, University of Texas Press, Austin.

Keenan, Edward and Bernard, Comrie: 1977, 'Noun Phrase Accessibility and Universal Grammar', *Linguistic Inquiry* **8**, 63–100.

Koopman, Hilda: 1984, *The Syntax of Verbs: From Verb Movement Rules in the Kru Languages to Universal Grammar*, Foris, Dordrecht.

Koopman, Hilda and Dominique Sportiche: 1982, 'Variables and the Bijection Principle', *The Linguistic Review* **2**, 139–160.

Koster, Jan: 1978, *Locality Principles in Syntax*, Foris, Dordrecht.

Kuno, Susumo: 1985, 'Anaphora in Japanese', paper presented at the Japanese Syntax Workshop, La Jolla, March 1985.

Kuno, Susumo and Jane Robinson: 1972, 'Multiple WH Questions', *Linguistic Inquiry* **3**, 463–487.

Kuroda, S.-Y.: 1988, 'Whether We Agree or Not', *Linguisticae Investigationes* **12**, 1–47.

Langacker, Ronald W.: 1969, 'On Pronominalization and the Chain of Command', in D. A. Reibel and S. Schane (eds.), *Modern Studies in English*, Prentice Hall Englewood Cliffs.

Langacker, Ronald W.: 1974, 'The Question of Q', *Foundations of Language* **11**, 1–37.

Lasnik, Howard: 1976, 'Remarks on Coreference', *Linguistic Analysis* **2**, 1–22.

Lasnik, Howard and Mamoru Saito: 1984, 'On the Nature of Proper Government', *Linguistic Inquiry* **15**, 234–289.

Levin, Juliette and Diane Massam: 1985, 'Surface Ergativity: Case/Theta Relations Reexamined' in *NELS 14*, GLSA, Amherst.

Li Mei-du: 1985, *Reduction and Anaphoric Relations in Chinese*, Ph.D. dissertation, UCSD.

Lieber, Rochelle: 1980, *On the Organization of the Lexicon*, Ph.D. dissertation, MIT.

May, Robert: 1977, *The Grammar of Quantification*, Ph.D. dissertation, MIT.

McCloskey, James: 1979, *Transformational Syntax and Model Theoretic Semantics*, Reidel, Dordrecht.

McCloskey, James: 1983, 'On the Binding of Resumptive Pronouns in Modern Irish', GLOW, York, England.

McCloskey, James: 1989, 'Resumptive Pronouns, A′ Binding and Levels of Representation in Irish', to appear in R. Hendrick (ed.), *The Syntax of the Modern Celtic Languages, Syntax and Sematics Vol. 23*, Academic Press.

McCloskey, James and Kenneth Hale: 1984, 'On the Syntax of Person-Number Inflection in Modern Irish', *Natural Language and Linguistic Theory* **1**, 487–533.

McManus, Fr. Edwin G.: 1977, *Palauan-English Dictionary*, Lewis S. Josephs (ed.), with the assistance of Masa-aki Emesiochel, PALI Language Texts: Micronesia, The University Press of Hawaii, Honolulu.

Palau Orthography Committee: 1972, 'Palauan Orthography — A Final Report', xeroxed, PALI, University of Hawaii.

Pesetsky, David: 1982a, 'Complementizer-trace Phenomena and the NIC', *The Linguistic Review* **1**, 297–343.

Pesetsky, David: 1982b, *Paths and Categories*, unpublished Ph.D. dissertation, MIT.

Pinkham, Jessie and Jorge Hankamer: 1975, 'Deep and Shallow Clefts', *CLS 11*.

REFERENCES

235

Pollock, Jean-Yves: 1987, 'Verb Movement, UG, and the Structure of IP', *Linguistic Inquiry* **20**, 365–424.

Postal, Paul: 1971, *Crossover Phenomena*, Holt, Reinhart and Winston, New York.

Pullum, Geoffrey: 1981, 'Languages with object before subject: a comment and a catalogue', *Linguistics* **18**, 269–288.

Reinhart, Tanya: 1976, *The Syntactic Domain of Anaphora*, unpublished Ph.D. dissertation, MIT.

Reinhart, Tanya: 1979, 'Syntactic Domains for Semantic Rules', in Guenthner and Schmidt (eds.), *Formal Semantics and Pragmatics for Natural Languages*, Reidel, Dordrecht.

Reinhart, Tanya: 1981a, 'A Second COMP Position', in *Theory of Markedness in Generative Grammar* (Proceedings of the 1979 GLOW Conference), Scuola Normale Superiore di Pisa.

Reinhart, Tanya: 1981b, 'Definite NP Anaphora and C-Command Domains', *Linguistic Inquiry* **12**, 605–636.

Reinhart, Tanya: 1983, 'Coreference and Bound Anaphora: A Restatement of the Anaphora Questions', *Linguistics and Philosophy* **6**, 47–88.

Republic of Palau (Beluu era Belau): n.d., Publication produced by The Office of the President, the Olbiil Era Kelulau (Palau Legislature), the Belau National Museum, the Palau Visitors Authority, and the Language Office, Bureau of Education.

van Riemsdijk, Henk, and Edwin Williams: 1986, *Introduction to the Theory of Grammar*, MIT Press, Cambridge, MA.

Rizzi, Luigi: 1982a, *Issues in Italian Syntax*, Foris, Dordrecht.

Rizzi, Luigi: 1982b, 'On Chain Formation', Ms., Università della Calabria.

Rizzi, Luigi: 1986, 'Null Objects in Italian and the Theory of *pro*', *Linguistic Inquiry* **17**, 501–557.

Rizzi, Luigi: 1987, 'Relativized Minimality', Ms., Université de Genève.

Rizzi, Luigi: 1990, *Relativized Minimality*, MIT Press, Cambridge, MA.

Ross, John R.: 1967, *Constraints on Variables in Syntax*, unpublished Ph.D. dissertation, MIT. Distributed by the Indiana University Linguistics Club, Bloomington.

Rothstein, Susan: 1983, *The Syntactic Forms of Predication*, unpublished Ph.D. dissertation, MIT.

Rouveret, Alain and Jean-Roger Vergnaud: 1980, 'Specifying Reference to the Subject: French Causatives and Conditions on Representations', *Linguistic Inquiry* **11**, 97–202.

Rudin, Catherine: 1988, 'On Multiple Questions and Multiple WH Fronting', *Natural Language and Linguistic Theory* **6**, 445–501.

Russell, Bertrand: 1905, 'On Denoting', *Mind* **14**, 479–493.

Safir, Ken: 1982, *Syntactic Chains*, Cambridge University Press, Cambridge.

Safir, Ken: 1984, 'Multiple Variable Binding', *Linguistic Inquiry* **15**, 603–638.

Safir, Ken: 1986, 'Relative Clauses in a Theory of Binding and Levels', *Linguistic Inquiry* **17**, 663–689.

Sag, Ivan, Gerald Gazdar, Thomas Wasow, and Steven Weisler: 1985, 'Coordination and How to Distinguish Categories', *Natural Language and Linguistic Theory* **3**, 117–171.

Saito, Mamoru: 1984, *Some Asymmetries in Japanese and Their Theoretical Implications*, unpublished Ph.D. dissertation, MIT.

Saito, Mamoru and Hajime Hoji: 1983, 'Weak Crossover and Move Alpha in Japanese', *Natural Language and Linguistic Theory* **1**, 245–259.

Schwalbenberg, Brother Henry M.: 1984, *Micronesians on the Move*, Micronesian Seminar Memo #12. (Quoted in *Rengel Belau* (newspaper published in Koror, Palau), Volume 1, Number 20, June 1984.)

Sells, Peter: 1984, *Syntax and Semantics of Resumptive Pronouns*, unpublished Ph.D. dissertation, UMass.

236 REFERENCES

Sirk, U.: 1978, 'Problems of High-Level Subgrouping in Austronesian' in Wurm and Carrington (eds.), *SICAL Proceedings* Fascicle 1, Pacific Linguistics, The Australian National University.

Sportiche, Dominique: 1985, 'Remarks on Crossover', *Linguistic Inquiry* **16**, 460–469.

Sproat, Richard: 1985, 'Welsh Syntax and VSO Structure', *Natural Language and Linguistic Theory* **3**, 173–216.

Stowell, Timothy: 1981, *Origins of Phrase Structure*, unpublished Ph.D. dissertation, MIT.

Stowell, Timothy: 1985, 'Licensing Conditions on Null Operators', paper delivered at the Fourth West Coast Conference on Formal Linguistics (WCCFL), UCLA.

Stowell, Timothy: 1987, 'Adjuncts, Arguments, and Crossover', ms., UCLA.

Stowell, Timothy and H. Lasnik: 1987, 'Weakest Crossover', ms., UCLA and University of Connecticut.

Strawson, Peter F.: 1950, 'On Referring', *Mind* **59**, 320–344.

Stump, Gregory T.: 1984, 'Agreement vs. Incorporation in Breton', *Natural Language and Linguistic Theory* **2**, 289–348.

Taraldsen, K. Tarald: 1978a, 'The Scope of *Wh* Movement in Norwegian', *Linguistic Inquiry* **9**, 623–640.

Taraldsen, K. Tarald: 1978b, 'On NIC, vacuous application, and the *that*-t filter', unpublished ms., MIT.

Toman, Jindrich: 1981, 'Aspects of Multiple WH Movement in Polish and Czech', in R. May and D. Koster (eds.), *Levels of Syntactic Representation*, Foris, Dordrecht.

Torrego, Esther: 1984, 'On Inversion in Spanish and Some of Its Effects', *Linguistic Inquiry* **15**, 103–130.

Voegelin, Carl F. and Frances M. Voegelin: 1964, *Languages of the World: Indo-Pacific* Fascicle One, Anthropological Linguistics 6:4, Indiana University.

Walleser, Salvator: 1911, 'Grammatik der Palausprache', in *Mitteilungen des Seminars für Orientalische Sprachen* **14**, 121–213.

Walleser, Salvator: 1913, *Palau-Wörterbuch*, Mission Society, Hong Kong.

Wasow, Thomas: 1972, *Anaphoric Relations in English*, unpublished Ph.D. dissertation, MIT.

Waters, Richard C.: 1979, 'Topicalization and Passive in Palauan', unpublished manuscript, Harvard.

Whitman, John: 1985, 'A Unified Account of Zero Pronoun Phenomena', Japanese Syntax Workshop, UCSD.

Whitman, John: 1991, 'Argument Positions and Configurationality', in C. Georgopoulos and R. Ishihara (eds.), *Interdisciplinary Approaches to Language: Essays in Honor of S.-Y. Kuroda*, Kluwer, Dordrecht.

Williams, Edwin: 1978, 'Across-the-Board Rule Application', *Linguistic Inquiry* **9**, 31–43.

Williams, Edwin: 1983, 'Semantic vs. Syntactic Categories', *Linguistics and Philosophy* **6**, 423–446.

Williams, Edwin: 1984, 'Grammatical Relations', *Linguistic Inquiry* **15**, 639–673.

Wilson, Helen: 1972, 'The Phonology and Syntax of Palauan Verb Affixes', in *University of Hawaii Working Papers* 4:5.

Xu Liejiong and D. T. Langendoen: 1985, 'Topic Structures in Chinese', *Language* **61**, 1–27.

Zaenen, Annie: 1983, 'On Syntactic Binding', *Linguistic Inquiry* **14**, 469–504.

Zaenen, Annie, Elisabet Engdahl and Joan Maling: 1981, 'Resumptive Pronouns can be Syntactically Bound', *Linguistic Inquiry* **12**, 679–682.

Zubizarreta, Maria Luisa: 1982, *On the Relationship of the Lexicon to Syntax*, unpublished Ph.D. dissertation, MIT.

Zwicky, Arnold and Geoffrey Pullum: 1983, 'Cliticization vs. Inflection: English *n't*', *Language* **59**, 502–513.

APPENDIX

ORTHOGRAPHY

For the most part, I use the standard orthography that was recommended by the Palau Orthography Committee (1972). The exception is the case of the glottal stop, which I write with an apostrophe but which the orthography writes **ch**. **ng** represents the velar nasal in all cases. The complementizer/linker **el** is usually pronounced as final -**l** on the preceding word. I write it as an independent morpheme in every case.

The conjunction **me** is phonetically a syllabic **m**, and is pronounced as a single word with a following **a**. Since the conjunction is usually followed by an NP and NPs begin with **a**, the result is **ma**. This is the way Palauans perceive and usually write the conjunction, so from the Palauan point of view the standard orthography would be more transparent if it also wrote **ma**.

GLOSSES

The morpheme **a** is an NP marker, and is not glossed. Though I use hyphens to set off certain bound forms, most surface verb forms cannot be 'sliced' into morphemes. The imperfective marker, tense, and other morphemes are not set off, either. In other words, what remains when agreement morphemes are separated by hyphens from the stem is not necessarily a complete lexical unit of any description.

I use the following abbreviations:

Cl	cleft	p	plural	Ptc	particle
Im	imperfective	P	preposition	R	realis
IR	irrealis	Pf	perfective	s	singular
L	linker	Pst	past		

Words ending in back vowels in Palauan are felt to have an epenthetic final **ng**. This consonant disappears in normal rates of speech, and usually in writing. It is normally observed only clause-finally. Following the orthographic standard, I omit this **ng** except in final position. This may seem odd to Palauans who are accustomed to write this final segment. Some common words that have the final **ng** in careful speech are listed below:

mera	real, really	mo	go
ngera	what	msa	see
ta	one	'imo	one
teblo	two	oumera	believe
te'a	who		

INDEX OF NAMES

Abney, S. 20
Anderson, S. 49, 89, 99
Aoun, J. 7, 8, 12, 86, 126, 138, 152, 163, 166, 174, 177, 180, 216

Bach, E. 142, 227, 228
Baker, C. 142, 144, 147, 164, 167, 177
Barss, A. 66, 68, 132, 215, 216
Belletti, A. 9, 117, 128, 138
Bender, B. 21, 59, 60
Borer, H. 52, 124
Bresnan, J. 5, 61, 99, 131, 142, 143, 147, 178, 180
Brody, M. 16, 132, 228

Capell, A. 21, 22, 55, 59, 60
Carlson, C. 22, 60
Carstens, V. 132
Chomsky, N. 5, 6, 7, 8, 9, 10, 11, 12, 13, 14, 15, 16, 17, 20, 44, 47, 48, 49, 62, 66, 77, 79, 82, 83, 96, 99, 102, 103, 109, 111, 113, 125, 131, 132, 133, 137, 138, 143, 152, 163, 174, 176, 183, 184, 187, 188, 217, 222, 228, 229
Chung, S. 12, 61, 86, 89, 94, 99, 136, 139, 224, 229
Cinque, G. 20, 46, 123
Clark, R. 61
Clements, N. 136
Comrie 77
Contreras, H. 113

Dahl, O. 59, 76
Dempwolff, O. 21, 60
Derbyshire, D. 224
Dyen, I. 22, 59

Emesiochel, M. 22
Engdahl, E. 103, 109, 110, 111, 113, 124, 145, 229
Erteschik-Shir, N. 42
Evans, G. 228

Fodor, J. D. 96

Fodor, J. A. 143
Flora, Sr. E. 22, 59

George, L. 190
Georgopoulos, C. 12, 41, 54, 89, 94, 96, 139, 151, 175, 176, 177, 179, 180, 206, 229
Goldsmith, J. 124
Goodall, G. 138
Grimshaw, J. 9, 99, 131, 137, 147
Groos, A. 99

Haïk, I. 132, 207, 227
Hale, K. 45, 50, 52, 54
Hankamer, J. 99, 144, 145
Higginbotham, J. 187, 228, 229
Hoji, H. 45, 187, 188, 191, 207, 209, 228, 229
Hornstein, N. 152, 163, 166, 174, 177
Huang, J. 6, 20, 46, 77, 82, 103, 114, 117, 128, 131, 140, 164, 165, 166, 173, 174
Hyams, N. 224

Jackendoff, R. 5, 7, 47, 79
Jackson, F. 21
Jaeggli, O. 12, 44, 77, 216, 229
Jelinek, E. 61
Josephs, L. 22, 32–38, 55, 60, 75

Katz, J. 142, 143
Kayne, R. 12, 16, 48, 53, 110, 111, 117, 118, 119, 123, 127, 132, 136, 180, 181, 216
Keenen, E. 77
Koopman, H. 127, 188, 189, 190, 198, 218, 222, 228
Kuno, S. 143
Kuroda, S-Y. 20, 152, 177, 180

Langacker, R. 184, 227
Langendoen, T. 46, 136
Lasnik, H. 114, 140, 152, 164, 166, 175, 176, 177, 180, 187, 191, 206, 215, 227

239

INDEX OF NAMES

Levin, J. 94
Li, A. 126
Li, M. 46
Lieber, R. 52

Maling, J. 103
Massam, D. 94
May, R. 93, 181, 189
McCloskey, J. 45, 50, 52, 103, 124, 126, 131, 132, 136, 138, 224, 229
Mchombo, S. 61
McManus, Fr. E. 21, 22
Mester, A. 9

Partee, B. 227, 228
Pesetsky, D. 47, 96
Pinkham, J. 99
Pollock, J-Y. 20, 136
Postal, P. 142, 183
Pullum, G. 52, 56—58, 224

Reinhart, R. 136, 185, 186, 187, 189, 191, 195, 227, 228
van Riemsdijk, H. 10, 99
Rizzi, L. 6, 8, 12, 16, 47, 61, 82, 117, 128, 131, 132, 138, 180, 216, 217, 228
Robinson, J. 143
Ross, J. R. 3, 40, 107, 158
Rothstein, S. 49
Rouveret, A. 14
Rudin, C. 140, 178

Safir, K. 16, 126, 127, 132, 138, 190, 198, 207, 222, 228

Sag, I. 61
Saito, M. 8, 114, 140, 152, 164, 166, 175, 176, 177, 180, 187, 188, 191, 229
Sells, P. 99, 125, 126
Sportiche, D. 7, 8, 126, 152, 163, 166, 174, 177, 180, 188, 189, 190, 196, 197, 198, 207, 218, 222, 228
Sproat, R. 224
Stowell, T. 9, 12, 94, 111, 113, 187, 191, 206, 207, 215, 216

Tallermann, M. 124
Taraldsen, T. 44
Toman, J. 140
Torrego, E. 136

Vergnaud, J-R. 14
Voegelin, C. and Voegelin, F. 21

Walleser, Bishop 21
Wasow, R. 183
Waters, R. 38—40, 71
Whitman, J. 46, 47, 61
Williams, E. 9, 10, 73, 74, 99, 107, 109, 137, 138
Wilson, H. 22, 35, 59, 60

Xu, L. 46, 136

Zaenen, A. 95, 103
Zubizarreta, M-L. 52
Zwicky, A. 52, 56—58

INDEX OF SUBJECTS

a 31, 33, 66
  marks all NPs 32
  marks nominalized clauses 32
  marks relativizations 75
A vs. A′ position 14
A′ movement, landing site 8
A′ binding 14, 101
  coordination evidence at SS for 107 ff.
  of resumptive pronouns at SS 102 ff.
  WH agreement evidence for 104 ff.
adjuncts 114
  and parasitic gaps 114ff.
  distinct from arguments 117
  optional resumptive pronoun 129
  optional WH agreement trigger 129
adverbs 54
  as raising predicates 55
  take agreement 55
agreement marking
  affix vs. clitic **51—59**
  clitic doubling 53
  on both Aux and V 56
  Romance clitics 61
± anaphor 12
  contextual definition 13

base generation 5
  for resumptive pronouns 79
  due to lack of island effects 82
  vs. movement **101**
barrier 9
base generation 15
  move α relation 15
  trace 16
Bijection Principle 127
  see also *weak crossover*
binding theory 13, 14
bounding theory 9
Bulgarian 140

Canonical Government Configuration (CGC) 118, 127
Case 9
  and WH agreement 84 ff.
  filter 14

of CP 94
  theory 14
Categorial component 9
c-command conditions on anaphora 185—187
  and [+pro] categories 195
  see also *weak crossover*
CED 117
chain 11
  alternative to movement 16
  and resumptive pronouns 133 ff.
  A′ chain formation **130 ff.**
  defined 131
  representational 131
  two A′ chains in WCO 226
  underlies WH agreement 134
Chamorro 21, 61, 96
Chinese 140, 174, 180
clefts 66 ff.
clitic hypothesis for agreement 51 ff.
clause structure in Austronesian 76
Comp-indexing 174
Comp-trace effect 48
complementation 42—43
  'bridge verb' complementizer 42, 129
  relative clause complementizer 42
Connectedness Condition 118 ff., 138, 180
  account of weak crossover 216—222
  see also *weak crossover*
  application to resumptive pronouns 120—124
Coordinate Structure Constraint 107
  across-the-board exceptions 108 ff.
  not like other island constraints 110, 138
coordination 49—50
  counterexample to bijection 190
  of resumptive pronouns and gaps 107 ff.
  with *pro* 49—50
copying rules, chopping rules 4
Core Grammar 6

ECPO 229
embedded questions **141 ff.**

241

INDEX OF SUBJECTS

connectedness theory and Q theory 181
distinguished from free relatives 147 ff.
extraction from 80
filters 164, 166
multiple interrogation 168 ff.
narrow WH scope 142, 151, 153
   of all WH under +WH verb 170 ff., 175
Q morpheme theory 142, 177
WH complementizer rule 143
WH in situ in embeddings 152 ff.
   'effectively in situ' 170, 178
±WH subcategorization 143 ff., 146, 166, 168 ff.
wide WH scope 143, 144
empty categories 11
NP trace 11
pro 11, 13
PRO 11
WH trace 11
Empty Category Principle (ECP) 12, 79, 128
accounts of embedded WH scope 173 ff.
account of weak crossover **216—222**
   see also *weak crossover*
null vs. overt features not relevant 218 ff.
resumptive pronouns subject to 217 ff., 220
'ergative' as unaccusative 60
EST 5
extraction from NP 71

functional categories 20

gap, evidence for 1
government 7, 8, 215
Government-Binding Theory 3, 6
GPSG, finite VP 95
relevance of WH agreement 95
relevance of identity of WH gap and *pro* 99

interpretive rule 15
alternative for Move α 15
irrealis mood morphology 26—27, 60, 62, 85ff., 180
island constraints 4, **80—84**
extraction from ebmbedded question 80, 81

extraction from relative clause 80
extraction from sentential subject 80
gap or resumptive pronoun 81

Japanese 140, 143, 145, 167, 216, 229

Leftness Condition 184, 186, 187, 205, 217, 228
lexicon 9
LFG, relevance of WH agreement 95
licensing 8
locality condition in Palauan 18, **135 ff.**
dissociated from movement 137
similar effects in other languages 136
WH agreement as reflex of 136
Logical Form (LF) 9, 15
LF movement 184, 185, 186, 189, 193, 199

Micronesian languages
nonnuclear 21
nuclear 21
Move α 9, 101
m-command 7

null arguments **43—51**
distribution of agreement 44
objects 43
Palauan as *pro*-drop 44, 59
possessors 43
same status as overt 50
subjects 43

Palau 21
Palauan 21
NP structure 31
   head-initial 31
   possessor marking 31, 53
   relative clause 31
objects, definite 24
   indefinite 24
   pronominal 30
orthography 23, 237
phonemes 23, 59
verb morphology **24—28**
   imperfective aspect 24
   imperfective marker (IM) 24, 60
   object agreement suffix 24
   passive 35—40
   perfective aspect 24
   subject agreement 26
   'syntactic' mood 28, 84 ff.
   verb marker (VM) 24, 60

INDEX OF SUBJECTS

243

VP structure 28
  head-initial 29
  object marking and aspect 29
  prepositional direct object 29
  prepositional oblique object 29
parallelism 126—127
  and homogeneity 222
  see also *weak crossover*
parasitic gaps 110 ff., 228
  connectedness condition account 110,
    117 ff.
  mix of overt and null variables 112
  not alternative to WCO 207—210
  operator movement account 111
  other ECP accounts 117
  resumptive pronouns in 111—112
  WH agreement and 210
passive 35—40
  properties of 37, 38
Phonetic Form (PF) 9
Polish 140, 180
precede-and-command relations 184,
    227
precedence 202
  distinguished from government 215
  domain for anaphora 216
  in non-WCO binding structures 209,
    212, 213
  subsumes WCO effect 202, 203
predication 17, 49
  rule for resumptive pronoun 17, 102
    ff.
preposition 29, 60
  does not licence EC 52, 222
  requires resumptive pronoun 63, 98
Principle C and strong crossover 187,
    194
  Sportiche's account 196
Principles and Parameters 6
pro arguments 29 ff.
  same distribution as WH gap 78
pro-drop parameter 13, 44
  and government theory 47
  identification hypothesis fails 45—48,
    61, 123
  'long' movement of subject 47—48,
    51
  role of selectional information 47
  structural existence of *pro* 48—51
  topic-variable hypothesis fails 46
Projection Principle 10, 48, 49, 53
  Extended 10
± pronominal 12, 125, 194

anaphora rule disallows [+pro] 195
contextual definition 13, 196
pronominal variable 123
all variables in Palauan 194
pronouns 30
  as topics 54, 72
  complementarity of overt and null 30
  independent 30, 54, 99
Proper Government 12, 77
pseudoclefts 66 ff.
  predicational, specificational 73, 74

quantifier-variable interpretation 5

realis mood morphology 26, 27, 60, 62,
    84 ff.
relative clauses 63 ff., 75
  extraction from 80, 128
  free relatives **64 ff.**, 73, 78, 147 ff.
  gap or resumptive pronoun 63
resumptive pronouns 3, 4, 16, 17, 62
  and ECP 220 ff.
  and Principle B 221
  and processing 138
  and strong crossover 195—197
  as [-pronominal] at SS 126, 195, 219
  as subjects 220
  as syntactic variables **104 ff., 123 ff.,**
    219
  complementarity with gaps 62 ff., 77
  distinguished from WH traces 102
  identification hypothesis fails 76 ff.
  in coordination 109 ff.
  level of binding parameter 125, 222
  LF analysis of 83
  productivity of 79, 103, 124
  same distribution as overt pronouns
    79 ff.
Rumanian 140

sentential subjects
  extraction from 80, 128
  extraposition 82
  properly governed 128
S-structure 9
  coindexing at 15
specifier 8
  of C, universally on left 178, 179
Specifier Parameter 179, 216, **223—225**
  and acquisition 225
  default value 224 ff.
  role in distribution of WCO 216—
    222

INDEX OF SUBJECTS

SOV grammar 229
uniform vs. split grammars 224
VOS grammar 224
strong crossover 183, 184, 185
  contrasted with absence of WCO 207
  Principle C account 187 ff., 191
  resumptive pronouns and Pr. C 193
  WH agreement and Principle C 192
Subjacency Condition 5, 8, 15, 82, 83, 173
  as condition on movement 82, 99, 123, 128
  at LF 173, 175
  base generation distinct 101 ff.
  parametrizing nodes for 82
subjacency effects, lack of 62
Superiority Condition 180
Swedish, subject resumptive pronoun 109
syntactic variable 3

Theta Criterion 10, 11, 53
  position 14
  roles 9
topicalization 38, 39, **71 ff.**, 74, 158, 199, 202, 203
trace 3, 5, 9, 15
Turkish 144, 167

unbounded dependencies 2, 14
Universal Grammar 6

variable 14
  as antecedent to pronoun 206, 214
  as nonpronoun 185
  contextual definition 188, 196
  D-structure pronominals 83
  extraction site vs. WCO pronoun 225 ff.
  intrinsic definition 197, **218**, 222, 227
  null and overt 83, 195, 219, 222, 228
  subject to anaphora rule 185
VSO 40, 60, 224, 229

weak crossover 183, 184, 185, 186, **197—210, 216—222**
  as case of strong crossover 207
  biclausal structures in 204 ff.
  bijection account 188—190, 198
  c-command accounts 191, 198
  ECP account 216-222

homogeneity of feature values 222
other multiple variable binding 189
none in Palauan 198 ff.
Palauan has SCO 207
Parallelism Constraint 190, 198
parasitic gap alternative 207—210, 229
precedence 203, 204, 209, 211
resumptive pronouns and 189—190
WCO configuration is grammatical 206
Western Austronesian family 21
WH Agreement 14, **84—97, 104—107**
  abstract Case is trigger 85
  Case of containing XP 90
  evidence for S-structure binding 104 ff., 222
  lack of scope position 104 ff., 178
  long-distance binding 90 ff.
  morphological effects 87
  multiple variables, local binder 96 ff.
  resumptive pronoun trigger 93 ff.
  semantic mood and 89 ff.
  specifier-head coindexing in 134
  statement of 95, 105
  subjects vs. nonsubjects 85 ff.
WH gap
  same distribution as *pro* 44
WH movement 5, 75
  associated parameters 140
  in LF **162 ff.**, 175
  filters in embedded questions 164, 166
  maintaining narrow scope 163 ff.
WH questions **69 ff.**
  designated scope position 141, 150, 176, **178**
  gap or resumptive pronoun 70
  nesting and crossing allowed 96 ff.
  Q morpheme theory 142, 177
  scope interpretation 141, 155
  scope position not taken as SS 104, 142, 149, 151, 154, 155, 166
  specifier-head coindexing in CP 152, 166, 178
  WH phrase follows C 149 ff., 180
  WH phrase in intermediate position 91 ff.
  WH phrase in situ 69, 152, 199
  preposed 69 ff.
word order **32—42**
  SVO analysis 32—38

INDEX OF SUBJECTS

VOS analysis **38—42**, 39, 216, 224
in embedded clauses 41
of Western Austronesian languages 41

X′ theory 7

yes/no question 156 ff.
agreement and embedded questions 156, 161
presupposition, vs. WH question 159

Studies in Natural Language and Linguistic Theory

Managing Editors

Joan Maling, *Brandeis University*
James McCloskey, *University of California, Santa Cruz*
Ian Roberts, *University of Wales, Bangor*

Publications

1. L. Burzio: *Italian Syntax*. A Government-binding Approach. 1986.
   ISBN Hb 90-277-2014-2; Pb 90-277-2015-0
2. W.D. Davies: *Choctaw Verb Agreement and Universal Grammar*. 1986.
   ISBN Hb 90-277-2065-7; Pb 90-277-2142-4
3. K. É. Kiss: *Configurationality in Hungarian*. 1987.
   ISBN Hb 90-277-1907-1; Pb 90-277-2456-3
4. D. Pulleyblank: *Tone in Lexical Phonology*. 1986.
   ISBN Hb 90-277-2123-8; Pb 90-277-2124-6
5. L. Hellan and K. K. Christensen: *Topics in Scandinavian Syntax*. 1986.
   ISBN Hb 90-277-2166-1; Pb 90-277-2167-X
6. K. P. Mohanan: *The Theory of Lexical Phonology*. 1986.
   ISBN Hb 90-277-2226-9; Pb 90-277-2227-7
7. J. L. Aissen: *Tzotzil Clause Structure*. 1987.
   ISBN Hb 90-277-2365-6; Pb 90-277-2441-5
8. T. Gunji: *Japanese Phrase Structure Grammar*. A Unification-based Approach. 1987.   ISBN 1-55608-020-4
9. W. U. Wurzel: *Inflectional Morphology and Naturalness*. 1989
   ISBN Hb 1-55608-025-5; Pb 1-55608-026-3
10. C. Neidle: *The Role of Case in Russian Syntax*. 1988 ISBN 1-55608-042-5
11. C. Lefebvre and P. Muysken: *Mixed Categories*. Nominalizations in Quechua. 1988.   ISBN Hb 1-55608-050-6; Pb 1-55608-051-4
12. K. Michelson: *A Comparative Study of Lake-Iroquoian Accent*. 1988
    ISBN 1-55608-054-9
13. K. Zagona: *Verb Phrase Syntax*. A Parametric Study of English and Spanish. 1988   ISBN Hb 1-55608-064-6; Pb 1-55608-065-4
14. R. Hendrick: *Anaphora in Celtic and Universal Grammar*. 1988
    ISBN 1-55608-066-2
15. O. Jaeggli and K.J. Safir (eds.): *The Null Subject Parameter*. 1989
    ISBN Hb 1-55608-086-7; Pb 1-55608-087-5
16. H. Lasnik: *Essays on Anaphora*. 1989
    ISBN Hb 1-55608-090-5; Pb 1-55608-091-3
17. S. Steele: *Agreement and Anti-Agreement*. A Syntax of Luiseño. 1990
    ISBN 0-7923-0260-5
18. E. Pearce: *Parameters in Old French Syntax*. Infinitival Complements. 1990   ISBN Hb 0-7923-0432-2; Pb 0-7923-0433-0

Studies in Natural Language and Linguistic Theory

19. Y.A. Li: *Order and Constituency in Mandarin Chinese.* 1990
ISBN 0-7923-0500-0
20. H. Lasnik: *Essays on Restrictiveness and Learnability.* 1990
ISBN 0-7923-0628-7; Pb 0-7923-0629-5
21. M.J. Speas: *Phrase Structure in Natural Language.* 1990
ISBN 0-7923-0755-0; Pb 0-7923-0866-2
22. H. Haider and K. Netter (eds.): *Representation and Derivation in the Theory of Grammar.* 1991
ISBN 0-7923-1150-7
23. J. Simpson: *Warlpiri Morpho-Syntax.* A Lexicalist Approach. 1991
ISBN 0-7923-1292-9
24. C. Georgopoulos: *Syntactic Variables.* Resumptive Pronouns and A' Binding in Palauan. 1991
ISBN 0-7923-1293-7
25. K. Leffel and D. Bouchard (eds.): *Views on Phrase Structure.* 1991 (in prep.)
ISBN 0-7923-1295-3
26. C. Tellier: *Licensing Theory and French Parasitic Gaps.* 1991
ISBN 0-7923-1311-9; Pb 0-7923-1323-2
27. S.-Y. Kuroda: *Japanese Syntax and Semantics.* Collected Papers. 1992 (in prep.)
ISBN 0-7923-1390-9; Pb 0-7923-1391-7

Kluwer Academic Publishers – Dordrecht / Boston / London